If You Like This Wine You'll Probably Like

A Simple, Intuitive Guide to Discovering New Wines Through the Flavours You Already Love

Chris Sutherland

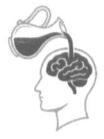

Decanting Veritas Ltd.

Copyright © 2025 by Chris Sutherland

All rights reserved.

No part of this publication may be reproduced, distributed, or transmitted in any form or by any means, including photocopying, recording, or other electronic or mechanical methods, without the prior written permission of the publisher, except as permitted by U.S. copyright law. For permission requests, contact [include publisher/author contact info].

The story, all names, characters, and incidents portrayed in this production are fictitious. No identification with actual persons (living or deceased), places, buildings, and products is intended or should be inferred.

Book Cover by Jamie Keenan

1st edition 2025

Dedication

Émilie,

On our first date, you told me that wine felt like a world with a high barrier to entry. It is full of language and pretence that made it seem like a closed door. This book exists because that moment stayed with me. You inspired me to help open that door for others, to help replace intimidation with curiosity and confidence. You remain the rare kind of wine that lingers long after the last sip, reminding me why I began this journey at all.

-chris

Foreword by Vince Anter

Host and Founder of V is for Vino

I've dedicated most of my adult life to wine education, even though it was never my intended path. I began my career in hospitality, like many others, with frustration and a catch-22: I needed wine knowledge to get a serving job, and I needed the serving job to gain wine knowledge. I tried to research wine on my own, but the information I needed to start my career was gatekept, disorganized, inconsistent, and scattered. Wine classes were prohibitively expensive and geared almost exclusively toward professionals. That is fine if you want to work in wine, but far less accommodating for people who, like me, learn through story, emotion, and enjoyment.

So I set out to create a resource, a wine TV show called V is for Vino, built around the kind of learning experience I wish I had when I first got into wine. Something approachable, clear, and able to solve the problems I ran into as a beginner. I am happy to say this book does the same.

One of the challenges we all face at the start of our wine journey is simply knowing what we like. Or more specifically, being able to *describe* what we like. Most of us already have wines we prefer; we just do not know why. Before we have technical language and a mental Rolodex built from years of tasting, it is hard to find wines that match our palate. So what do most people do? They keep drinking the same wines. I cannot think of a bigger tragedy. I say this constantly: the world of wine is too wonderful to limit yourself to the same dozen bottles your whole life.

I'm happy to say, this book is now your new Rolodex, so you'll never fall into that trap. It fast-tracks the knowledge you would gain from years of study, hundreds of bottles, and countless tasting rooms. It puts in your hands the kind of instant recall that some sommeliers seem to have. It helps you pick something new, exciting, different, and yet familiar, and exactly what you were looking for.

If you are new to wine, this book will inspire you. Chris uses emotional, relatable language that gets you excited about exploring. If you are studying wine more formally, reading this cover to cover will give you a deeper understanding of the wine world as a whole. And if you are a seasoned professional, this is a reference you will use again and again.

I have seen people compare wines to other wines in blogs or in sections of books, but I have never seen an entire book dedicated to the topic. It is such a simple and helpful idea, and honestly, something I have Googled many times. Questions like "wines similar to Napa Cabernet" have so many practical uses. Building a wine list. Finding a better value bottle. Exploring new grapes. Narrowing down a wine during a blind tasting. This book puts all that information in one place.

So dive into this book with confidence, knowing that wherever you are in your wine journey, there is something here for you. I have been in the industry a long time, and there is plenty in here for me, too. Jump headfirst into the topic I have dedicated my life to. A topic I love, not because it is challenging or stuffy, but because it is exploratory, eye-opening, and emotional. Just like this book.

Vince Anter

Host and Founder of V *is for Vino*

Acknowledgments

Mum, thank you for your unwavering support, your curiosity, and for being ideal representatives of my intended audience.

Andrew and Jeremy, we've literally been through the fire together and you have been wonderful companions in travel and in wine. I look forward to many more decades of shared discoveries and stories.

Andy, thank you for being simultaneously curious about my wine obsessions and mildly exasperated by my refusal to stop talking about them. Your patience has not gone unnoticed.

My cat, ThatOne, deserves recognition for insisting that I step away from the keyboard at regular intervals to provide both company and treats.

Adam and Jo, Hannah, Lorraine and Roddy, Dave and Sam, and Erin and Mo, your thoughtful questions helped confirm that this book might genuinely be useful.

Phil, Shiobhan, Emily, and the rest of the team at La Jupe in Helensburgh, your warm hospitality, excellent wine list, and shared enthusiasm for wine have kept me motivated throughout this project.

Jonny, my Level 3 classmate and consistently good egg, thank you for tolerating my dad jokes and encouraging me to take risks.

Pieter, Chris, and Abbie, my wine instructors, thank you for nurturing my love of learning. I appreciate your instruction immensely and blame you only slightly for where this has led.

And of course, Émilie, whose casual remark set this entire journey in motion. I sincerely hope you enjoy this book.

Introduction

Wine can feel beautiful and bewildering at the same time. Labels speak in unfamiliar languages. Wine lists read like puzzles. And even when a glass tastes wonderful, it can be hard to explain *why*, or to know what else you might enjoy next.

This book exists to make wine feel simple, intuitive, and entirely yours. Its purpose is not to turn you into an expert. It is to show you the one skill that changes everything: understanding your own taste. Once you know how a wine *feels*, its brightness[1], its weight[2], its texture[3], its shape[4], you can find dozens of other wines you'll love, even if their names are unfamiliar. When we refer to a wine's "structure," it is the way it feels in your mouth: its acidity, weight, texture, tannin, and balance.

That is the heart of this book:

If you like this wine… you'll like these wines and here's why.

No jargon. No memorisation. No long lists to study. Just clear, narrative guidance that connects each wine to others that share its structure, its personality, and the sensations you enjoy.

Wine becomes easy when you stop chasing perfection and start following pleasure. This book gives you exactly what you need to do that, confidence, clarity, and a map you can use for the rest of your life. Everything after that is simply curiosity, and the joy of discovering one delicious new connection at a time.

Welcome. Let's open the door.

IF YOU LIKE THIS WINE YOU'LL PROBABLY LIKE

1. Brightness: The sensory impression of a wine's acidity and energy, often perceived as freshness or lift on the palate.

2. Weight: The sense of how heavy or light a wine feels in the mouth, influenced by alcohol, body and texture.

3. Texture: The tactile impression of a wine on the palate, such as smooth, crisp, creamy, or grippy.

4. Shape: The overall structural progression of a wine across the palate, including how it enters, expands and finishes.

Contents

1. How Wine Becomes Wine — 1
2. Finding Your Wine Family — 5
3. Using Feelings to Taste Wine — 7
4. The Spectrum of Wine Styles — 11
5. Aromatic Whites — 15
   New Zealand Sauvignon Blanc
   Sancerre
   Albariño
   Viognier
   Pinot Grigio (Fuller Styles)
   Pinot Gris
6. Rosé Wines — 42
   Provence Rosé
   Tavel Rosé
   White Zinfandel
   Spanish Rosado
   Rosé of Pinot Noir
   Rosé of Sangiovese
   Loire Rosé (French Cabernet Franc-Based)
   Rosé of Syrah or GSM Rosé
   New World Rosé (South Africa, Australia, USA)
7. Crisp & Light Bodied Whites — 79

    Chablis
    Unoaked Chardonnay
    Muscadet (Melon de Bourgogne)
    Vinho Verde
    Soave
    Riesling (Dry Styles)
    Txakoli
    Grüner Veltliner
    Picpoul de Pinet
    Verdicchio
    Pinot Grigio (Lean Styles)

8. Rich & Full Bodied Whites   127
    Oaked Chardonnay
    Chenin Blanc
    White Rhône Blends
    White Rioja
    Alsace Pinot Gris (Rich Expression)

9. Sparkling Wines   150
    Champagne
    Crémant
    Traditional Method Sparkling
    Prosecco
    Cava
    Sparkling Rosé

10. Sweet Wines   180
    Moscato d'Asti
    Ice Wine
    Sauternes
    Tokaji Aszú
    Late-Harvest Riesling

      Recioto della Valpolicella

11. Fortified Wines   207
      Port
      Sherry
      Madeira
      Rutherglen Muscat
      Vin Doux Naturel
      Marsala

12. Fruity & Juicy Reds   234
      Merlot
      Pinot Noir (Fruit Driven)
      Valpolicella Classico
      Zinfandel
      Gamay
      Beaujolais

13. Structured & Full Bodied Reds   261
      Bordeaux (Red)
      Cabernet Sauvignon
      Syrah or Shiraz
      Valpolicella Ripasso
      Malbec
      Rioja Crianza
      Châteauneuf-du-Pape
      Amarone della Valpolicella

14. Earthy & Savoury Old-World Reds   299
      Chianti (Sangiovese)
      Tempranillo
      Pinot Noir (Savoury Burgundy-Inspired Expressions)
      Barolo
      Brunello di Montalcino

	Pinotage	
15.	Grape Families & Clones	328
16.	How Wine Is Made: From Grape to Glass	332
	Organic, Biodynamic & Natural Wines	
	How Wine Ages	
17.	Sulphites: Myths or Facts	345
18.	Wine Components	349
19.	The Future of Wine	374
20.	Practical Wisdom	378
21.	References	407
22.	Glossary	410
23.	Author's Note	430
24.	About the Author	432

Chapter 1

How Wine Becomes Wine

A friendly orientation to what influences the way wine tastes

Before we begin exploring wine by feeling and familiarity, it helps to have a small sense of what shapes a wine long before you taste it. This is not technical knowledge and you do not need to study it. It is simply a friendly orientation, the kind that makes the rest of the journey feel steadier underfoot. With that in mind, let us take a moment to look at how wine becomes wine, and how those early influences translate into the flavours and sensations you will notice in the glass.

Wine starts with climate, because climate sits at the foundation of how a wine will feel on the palate. Cool climate regions such as New Zealand, coastal Chile, England, parts of Germany and much of Burgundy produce wines that taste bright, refreshing and crisp. These wines often show flavours like citrus, green apple and fresh herbs because the grapes ripen slowly and hold onto their natural acidity. In contrast, warm climate regions such as California, Australia, South Africa and southern Italy produce wines that taste fuller, rounder and riper. You may notice stone fruit, tropical fruit, darker berries and a softer, more generous feel on the palate. There are also moderate climates in between these two ends of the spectrum, such as Bordeaux, northern Spain and parts of northern Italy, where wines can feel balanced and versatile. You do not need to draw a map in your mind, but having a sense of the major climate styles helps you recognise why wines differ in brightness, richness or weight.

The vineyard carries the character of its growing season. A cool or rainy year can make a wine taste sharper or more restrained, while a warm, dry year often makes it taste softer and more fruit forward. This is what vintage variation really means. It is not a test or a concept you need to study. It simply helps you understand why the same wine can taste slightly different from one year to the next.

Fermentation is where the juice becomes wine, and the choices made here influence taste more than people often realise. A cool, steady fermentation tends to preserve delicate fruit flavours such as lemon, lime, pear or fresh flowers. A warmer fermentation draws deeper flavours such as peach, apricot or baked fruit. You do not need identify these processes when tasting to enjoy the wine. You will simply find that some wines taste light and brisk while others taste fuller and richer, and fermentation sits quietly behind that difference.

Another important influence is the amount of time the juice spends with the grape skins. Red wines remain in contact with their skins, which is what gives them their colour and the grip or firmness you sometimes feel. Most white wines are separated from their skins early, which is why they taste clearer and more streamlined. Orange or amber wines, made from white grapes left on their skins for a period of time, develop deeper colours and flavours that can feel slightly nutty, savoury or tea like. Even a brief understanding of this makes these styles far less surprising when you encounter them.

After fermentation, the vessel in which a wine rests can change how it tastes. Stainless steel keeps flavours sharp and precise, giving you wines that taste clean and refreshing. Oak barrels soften the wine and add warmth, which can create flavours that feel rounder, broader or lightly spiced. Clay and concrete create a gentle weight without obvious flavour influence. These vessels do not need to be identified in the glass. They simply explain why some wines taste tight and bright while others feel smoother or more expansive.

Time also shapes flavour. Young wines often taste vivid and fruit driven. As they age, fruit becomes subtler, textures soften and earthier, more savoury notes begin to appear. An older wine can feel quieter, more layered and more reflective. This is not better or worse, only different, and it explains why two bottles of the same wine can offer different experiences across years.

There is one more influence worth mentioning before we move on, and that is the grape variety itself. Grapes do shape the flavour of a wine, but not in the fixed or predictable way many people imagine. A grape is more like a starting point, a set of natural tendencies rather than a finished identity. Chardonnay, for example, can taste bright, lean and citrus driven in a cool climate, yet feel soft, ripe and gently creamy in a warm one. Pinot Noir can taste earthy and restrained in Burgundy, yet juicy and fruit driven in parts of California or New Zealand. The grape provides a kind of outline, but everything else fills in the details.

Once you understand climate, winemaking choices and time, you begin to see why the same grape can behave so differently across regions and styles. The variety influences the wine, but it does not decide its personality on its own. This is why relying solely on grape names can be misleading. They tell you something, but never the whole story. What matters more is the shape and sensation of the wine in your mouth, and the balance of brightness, weight and texture that makes it feel familiar or not. Grapes are part of the picture, not the picture itself.

All of these influences affect the sensations you will come to recognise: the crispness of acidity, the warmth of alcohol, the firmness of tannin, the softness created by fruit ripeness, the texture that carries everything across your palate. These sensations translate directly into taste. Bright wines taste refreshing. S$oft wines taste gentle. Full wines taste rich or mouth filling. Textural wines taste structured or complex. You already know these feelings from everyday food and drink. This note simply gives you the practical grounding that connects them to wine.

If you wish to explore any of these ideas further, the later sections in the book offer more detail in a friendly, accessible way. For now, let this orientation sit beside you as context. The chapters ahead are built around taste, feeling and recognition, and this small piece of grounding should help you make sense of those connections with confidence.

Chapter 2
Finding Your Wine Family
Understanding wine by recognising how it feels

Everyone has a wine family, a small cluster of wines that feel instantly right the moment they touch your palate. You may not know the names yet. You may not know the grapes or regions. But your senses already recognise the patterns: the way these wines move, the way they brighten or soften, the way they settle into your mood.

Your wine family is not determined by expertise, but by instinct.

Some people naturally gravitate toward wines that feel bright and crisp, the kind that taste like citrus, cold air, and clean water over stone. Others prefer wines that feel soft and smooth, or rich and textural, or deep and earthy. Some are drawn to exuberant fruit and others to savoury complexity. These preferences aren't random. They're reflections of your palate's architecture, your sensitivity to acidity, tannin, alcohol, sweetness, and texture.

Finding your wine family is not about memorising bottles. It's about paying attention to the sensations that make you feel at home.

If you love wines that feel *fresh, zesty, and light*, your family sits near the bright end of the spectrum. Sauvignon Blanc, Vinho Verde, Muscadet, and Txakoli will all feel like familiar faces at the same gathering.

If you love wines that feel *aromatic, floral, or gently fruity*, you'll find kinship in Albariño, Pinot Gris, Viognier, and expressive rosés, wines that carry fragrance as part of their personality.

If you love wines that feel *rich and textured*, you'll recognise yourself in oaked Chardonnay, Chenin Blanc, White Rhône blends, and Champagne aged on lees, wines that wrap the palate rather than race across it.

If you prefer *juicy, fruit-forward reds* with soft tannins, your family includes Gamay, fruit-driven Pinot Noir, Valpolicella Classico, and Merlot, wines that feel easy, warm, and openhearted.

If you gravitate toward *structured reds* with power and depth, Cabernet Sauvignon, Syrah, Malbec, and GSM blends will feel like familiar territory, wines with presence, gravity, and the ability to ground a meal or a moment.

And if you love *earthy, savoury, Old-World reds*, you will find your home among Sangiovese, Tempranillo, Nebbiolo, and Burgundy-style Pinot Noir, wines that feel like soil, herbs, stone, and memory.

You may even have more than one family, or a primary family and a set of cousins. Wine families are not boundaries; they are starting points. Once you know where you belong, you can step outward, to wines that differ just enough to surprise you without leaving you lost.

This is why these chapters are organised the way they are. When you turn the page to your first wine, the one that feels like *you*, you'll find not just a story about that wine, but a map to every wine that shares its shape, its tone, its emotional rhythm.

Finding your wine family is not a test. It is a recognition, a moment of clarity when you realise that the world of wine is not vast and confusing, but familiar and full of connections waiting for you.

And once you find your family, the entire spectrum becomes navigable. You'll know where you are and where you'd like to go next.

Chapter 3

Using Feelings to Taste Wine

Noticing the styles your palate naturally returns to

Tasting wine is not about technique. It is about noticing. Anyone can do it, and most people already do, without realising it. When you take a sip of cold water on a hot day, you instinctively feel its freshness. When you sip coffee, you sense its bitterness, its warmth, its weight. Wine works the same way. The only difference is that wine gives you more to notice.

The goal isn't to identify every aroma. It's simply to understand how a wine *moves*, how it feels in your mouth, how it rises or settles, how it lingers or fades. When you focus on sensation instead of vocabulary, wine becomes a language you already speak.

Take a sip. Don't analyse it. Just pay attention to the moment it touches your tongue. Does it feel bright or soft? Light or full? Smooth or firm? These sensations reveal more about your preferences than any list of flavours ever could. Aroma matters too, but only after you've noticed the structure, the shape of the wine, the way it behaves.

Acidity creates lift and brightness. Tannin creates structure and grip. Alcohol warms. Sugar softens. Texture carries everything across the palate. You don't need to memorise these terms; you'll feel them as soon as you stop forcing yourself to "taste" wine and simply let the wine show you how it moves.

The final step is noticing what happens after you swallow. Some wines disappear quickly; others linger with a faint echo of fruit, spice, or earth. That quiet aftertaste is the wine's way of telling you its mood. Some are cheerful. Some are contemplative. Some are bold. Some are delicate.

This is tasting, not hunting for notes, not proving expertise, but paying attention to sensation.

Once you understand how a wine feels, you can find dozens of others that feel the same. That is the key to discovering new favourites, and the reason this book is organised the way it is. You don't need to learn every grape. You just need to learn *your palate*.

Taste slowly. Notice simply. Trust what you enjoy.

The rest will follow naturally.

Wine and Emotion

Wine is often described in technical terms, acidity, tannin, varietals, vintages, but the real reason people fall in love with wine has very little to do with vocabulary. It has to do with *feeling*.

Every wine carries an emotional signature. Some wines feel bright and uplifting, the way a clear morning feels. Others feel calm and grounding, like a slow afternoon. Some wines invite conversation; others invite quiet. Some feel playful, some serious, some comforting, some romantic. These responses are instinctive. They happen before words.

You don't need training to know whether a wine feels right for the moment you're in. You've already had this experience in other parts of life: choosing tea or coffee based on mood, picking a playlist that matches your energy, reaching for your favourite foods not because you analysed them, but because they fit how you feel.

Wine works the same way. It isn't just a flavour. It's a mood:

- Sauvignon Blanc feels like sunlight and fresh air.

- Malbec feels like warmth and dusk.

- Rosé feels like a breeze between two warm hours.

- A glass of Champagne feels like the moment someone opens a door and everyone smiles.

Once you begin to recognise wines emotionally, not just technically, your confidence grows. The question shifts from *"Is this the right wine?"* to *"Does this feel like the wine I want right now?"* And suddenly the entire world of wine becomes welcoming, flexible, intuitive.

Emotion is the secret map.

If you follow it, you will find the wines that suit you, not by memorising grapes, but by sensing the mood they create. Once you understand both how a wine *feels* and how it makes *you* feel, everything else becomes simple.

You know what you like.

And this book will help you find more wines that share that feeling.

Why This Matters

Most people learn wine the hard way, by memorising grapes, regions, and terms they forget as quickly as they learn them. But wine becomes simple the moment you understand one idea:

Wines taste the way they do because of their structure, their brightness, their weight, their texture, their balance. Wines with similar structure feel similar to drink. This means you don't need to learn *every* wine. You only need to learn the *type* of wine you enjoy.

And once you know that you can predict what else you'll love with surprising accuracy:

- A crisp, citrus-driven Sauvignon Blanc shares its shape with Txakoli, Vinho Verde, and other bright, light-bodied whites.

- A soft, plush Merlot shares its comfort with Malbec and Zinfandel.

- A savoury, earthy Pinot Noir has more in common with Nebbiolo and Sangiovese than with many heavier reds.

- A creamy, oaked Chardonnay feels closer to certain Champagnes and White Rhône blends than to unoaked versions of itself.

These connections are the real path to enjoy wine, not the labels or the grape names, but the way each wine *behaves* on the palate.

Once you start navigating by structure and sensation rather than rules and jargon, the world of wine opens effortlessly. You'll recognise your "wine family," the group of wines that feel like home. And from there, it's easy to explore wines just outside that comfort zone, similar enough to feel familiar, different enough to feel exciting.

This book is built on that map.

Every wine chapter shows you not just what the wine is, but what it *feels* like, and the wines that echo or contrast with that feeling.

Because if you understand the shape of one wine, you suddenly understand *dozens*.

That's why this section matters: once you see the pattern, you'll never need a wine guide again. You'll have your own internal compass, and it will always lead you somewhere delicious.

Chapter 4

The Spectrum of Wine Styles

A map of textures and energies that connects every wine you encounter

Wine doesn't exist as a list of grapes or a catalogue of regions. It exists on a *spectrum*, a continuous line of textures, weights, energies[1], and moods. Once you see that spectrum, everything becomes easier. You stop memorising categories and start recognising sensations.

Think of wine not as hundreds of disconnected bottles, but as a gradient. On one end sit the brightest, most refreshing wines; on the other, the deepest and most powerful; and between them lie dozens of subtle transitions.

Just like light moving from dawn to dusk, wine moves gradually from *bright* to *bold*, from *crisp* to *rich*, from *aromatic* to *earthy*. And every wine you taste belongs somewhere on that map.

Bright & Crisp

This is the realm of cool air and clear light: wines that feel lively and energetic. They taste like citrus, herbs, fresh fruit, and clean water over stone. Their acidity wakes the palate. Their textures feel sleek. This end of the spectrum includes wines like Sauvignon Blanc, Vinho Verde, Muscadet, Txakoli, and crisp rosés. They are wines of movement and lift.

Aromatic & Expressive

As the spectrum warms, the wines gain perfume and colour. These wines feel like spring, scented with flowers, white apricot, tropical fruit, or herbs, usually in a dry style. They are vibrant without being sharp, expressive without being heavy. Think Albariño, Viognier, floral Rieslings, and many New World whites.

Rich & Textural

Move a little further and wines become broader, rounder, and more layered. These are wines shaped by warmth, by oak, by lees contact, by ripeness. They feel fuller, creamier, or more enveloping They feel fuller, creamier, or more enveloping, even when fully dry. Oaked Chardonnay, Chenin Blanc, White Rhône blends, richer Alsace whites, they all live here. These are wines that feel like late afternoon: warm but still illuminated.

Rosé: The Bridge

Rosé sits naturally at the centre of the spectrum, neither fully white nor red, carrying the brightness of white wine and the gentle fruit of light reds. Some rosés are crisp and pale; others are deeper, fuller, almost red in disguise. Rosé is the hinge between two worlds.

Juicy & Fruit-Forward Reds

Here the spectrum transitions into red. These wines are light to medium bodied, driven by red fruit, soft tannins, and easy charm. They feel fresh and friendly: Pinot Noir, Gamay, Merlot, Zinfandel in its softer forms. They are wines of openness, best suited to conversation and ease.

Structured & Full-Bodied Reds

Crossing the midpoint deepens everything: colour, texture, flavour, and tannin structure. These reds carry weight, tannin, spice, and a darker fruit profile. Cabernet Sauvignon, Syrah or Shiraz, Malbec, GSM[2] blends, these are wines that stand up to rich food and long evenings. They feel like dusk: bold, confident, lingering.

Earthy & Savoury Reds

At the far end of the spectrum lie the wines shaped most strongly by place: Nebbiolo, Sangiovese, Tempranillo, earth-driven Pinot Noir. These wines feel rooted, shaped by place, herbs, soil, and savoury tones that reflect cooler climates or traditional styles. They show herbs, earth, leather, dried flowers, flavours that whisper of soil and time rather than fruit. They are wines that feel contemplative, wines made for slow meals and thoughtful moments.

Sweet & Fortified: The Vertical Dimension

Across all categories runs a second axis: sweetness and richness. Moscato d'Asti and Ice Wine sit near the bright end but rise in intensity. Sauternes, Tokaji, and Late-Harvest Riesling climb higher still, combining acidity with concentrated sweetness. Fortified wines, Port, Sherry, Madeira, Rutherglen Muscat, inhabit a world of warmth, depth, and complexity that feels almost vertical, like the chorus beneath the melody.

Why it matters

Once you understand this spectrum, you can place any wine you taste and predict what else you'll enjoy. The names no longer matter. The sensation does.

Wine stops being complicated and becomes familiar. You see that Sauvignon Blanc and Vinho Verde belong near each other, just as Malbec and Zinfandel share warmth, just as Barolo and earthy Pinot Noir share restraint.

The spectrum reveals the emotional architecture of wine. It shows you where you are, and where you want to go next.

1. Energies: The sense of movement or liveliness a wine expresses through acidity or aromatic lift.

2. GSM is industry shorthand for Grenache Syrah Mourvèdre blends. This is your typical backbone of Chateau Neuf du Pape and similar styles.

Chapter 5
Aromatic Whites
Expressive wines that lead with perfume and clarity

New Zealand Sauvignon Blanc

It does not ease its way into the glass. It arrives with a clarity that feels almost electric. New Zealand Sauvignon Blanc has a way of sweeping the senses clean, like stepping into bright coastal air after being indoors too long. Aromas rise immediately, lime zest, passionfruit, gooseberry, fresh-cut grass, sometimes a green herbal[1] streak like crushed tomato leaf or jalapeño. Nothing here is shy. The wine feels vertical, bright, full of motion. Even before you sip it, you know exactly what kind of experience you're about to have.

Part of its appeal is how emotionally transparent it is. There's no puzzle to solve, no quiet layers asking for contemplation. New Zealand Sauvignon Blanc gives itself away, all of it, in a single breath. But that doesn't make it simple. The freshness, the intensity, the coastal lift: these are sensations that register before your mind has time to name them. There are wines that invite thought. This is a wine that charges forward with feeling.

Why People Love It

People love New Zealand Sauvignon Blanc because it is immediate. It's bright without being sharp, bold without being heavy. The acidity is high enough to feel cleansing, like citrus squeezed over fresh seafood, but it carries the fruit rather than stripping it away. The flavours are vivid, even exuberant: tropical without sweetness, herbal without bitterness, citrusy without austerity.

There is something emotionally energising about it. It feels like the first warm day after winter, or a cold swim in summer, refreshing, awakening, pleasantly shocking. It pairs well with spontaneity: last-minute dinners, outdoor meals, casual moments. This wine doesn't demand quiet rooms or slow evenings; it thrives in motion.

How This Wine Feels

This is a dry, light- to medium-bodied wine carried by vivid, high acidity. From the first sip, that brightness snaps awake on the palate, a clean[2], mouthwatering jolt that invites another taste almost immediately. Its movement across the tongue is brisk rather than weighty, giving the wine a sleek, finely drawn texture shaped more by tension than by mass.

Much of its presence arrives through scent. A swirl sends up the grassy, citrus, and tropical notes, and as you swallow, those aromas seem to rise again, echoing the flavours in a gentle after pulse rather than a long finish. The fruit sits taut against the acidity, stretched into a line of freshness that carries the wine forward. As the flavours gradually quiet, the lifted sensation remains—like a cool breeze passing over the palate long after the wine is gone.

If You Like This Wine... You May Also Like

Awatere Valley Sauvignon Blanc (New Zealand)

Awatere Valley brings a cooler, finer expression of New Zealand's signature style. The fruit leans towards lime, green apple and subtle passion fruit, while the herbal notes are more restrained, carried on a breeze of sea salt and gentle minerality. The acidity feels taut and bright, giving the wine a quieter intensity. For drinkers who enjoy the clarity and lift of New Zealand Sauvignon Blanc but want a slightly more refined and ocean influenced interpretation, Awatere Valley offers a beautifully polished alternative.

Sancerre (France)

You'll recognise the same Sauvignon Blanc vibrancy, but Sancerre trades exuberance for refinement. The acidity is similarly high, yet the fruit is cooler-toned, lemon, white peach, elderflower, and the texture has a quiet mineral line running through it. The difference is restraint: where New Zealand shouts, Sancerre speaks in a confident whisper. It has wonderful elegance for those who want freshness but with more composure.

Touraine Sauvignon Blanc (France)

Touraine offers the same bright acidity and green, citrus-driven lift, but with softer aromatics and more approachable pricing. The difference is scale: less tropical intensity, more orchard-fruit clarity. If you like the freshness of New Zealand Sauvignon Blanc but want something gentler and more versatile with food, Touraine is a natural fit.

Chilean Coastal Sauvignon Blanc (Leyda, Casablanca)

These wines share the same crisp acid profile and herbal-citrus energy, thanks to cool Pacific influences. But they differ by leaning toward lime, sea spray, and subtle green pepper rather than bold passionfruit. It brings coastal purity, familiar structure, quieter flavours, ideal for those who prefer brightness with a touch more subtlety.

South African Sauvignon Blanc (Elgin, Constantia)

South Africa sits between New Zealand's exuberance and Sancerre's restraint. Expect high acidity, citrus, and herbs, with a savoury edge, sometimes a little flint, sometimes a little salt. Compared with New Zealand, it's less tropical and more textural. If you enjoy the brightness of NZ Sauvignon Blanc but want added complexity, these wines open the door.

Verdejo (Rueda Spain)

The kinship lies in the citrus snap and herbal lift, but Verdejo swaps tropical notes for fennel, peach skin, and a soft almond-like finish. The texture can be slightly rounder, the aromatics more floral. If you're drawn to Sauvignon Blanc's freshness but want something with a Mediterranean twist, this is a perfect next step.

Stretch Wines

Dry Riesling (Germany, Austria, Australia)

You'll find the same high acidity and piercing brightness, but Riesling trades green herbs for lime, white peach, and slate. It's less tropical, more mineral[3] and is tauter and more focused than Sauvignon Blanc, but with a different aromatic spectrum.

Grüner Veltliner (Austria)

Structurally similar in acidity and weight, Grüner adds white pepper, herbs, and a savoury, slightly earthy complexity. It's less explosive than NZ Sauvignon Blanc but more culinary, a wine of rhythm rather than punch. If you want freshness with subtlety and food versatility, Grüner is a rewarding stretch.

Txakoli (Basque Country Spain)

High acidity is the shared thread, but Txakoli brings a touch of spritz[4] and a salty Atlantic edge. It's leaner, sharper, more bracing, like NZ Sauvignon Blanc distilled into its mineral core showing exhilarating austerity for those who love tension.

Myths or Misunderstandings

One common misconception is that all Sauvignon Blanc tastes like New Zealand. In truth, this style is a particular expression of climate, light, and coastal winds. Sauvignon Blanc can be mineral, herbal, floral, or smoky depending on where it grows. New Zealand's version is iconic, but it is one voice among many. Another myth: that the intense aromatics mean the wine is sweet. Nearly all New Zealand Sauvignon Blanc is bone dry; the fruitiness comes from aromatic compounds, not sugar.

Closing Reflection

New Zealand Sauvignon Blanc is a reminder that wine can be joyful without being simple. It's a burst of freshness that needs no explanation, a wine that energises rather than soothes. It speaks in bright, confident flavours, but beneath the immediacy lies a sense of place, wind, sea, cool nights, long sunlight, translated directly into the glass.

It teaches us that intensity can be refreshing, that clarity can be delightful, and that sometimes the purest pleasure comes from wines that feel alive.

Sancerre

There is a quiet confidence to Sancerre, a kind of clarity that doesn't need to announce itself. Pour a glass and the aromas rise gently, nothing explosive, nothing shouting for attention. Citrus peel, white peach, a whisper of elderflower, and a faint mineral edge, like the cool scent of limestone after rain. Where New Zealand Sauvignon Blanc bursts forward, Sancerre seems to stand still and let you come closer. It is a wine built not on volume, but on precision.

Part of the pleasure is its sense of ease. Sancerre never feels hurried. Its flavours gather slowly on the palate; the way light deepens in a room as the sun moves across the floor. The acidity is bright but not sharp; the fruit is crisp but not aggressive; the herbal tones are subtle enough to feel like memory rather than scent. To drink Sancerre is to experience Sauvignon Blanc without the rush, the same structure, the same brightness, but expressed with restraint and grace.

Why People Love It

People love Sancerre because it feels balanced in a way that requires no explanation. The acidity is refreshing yet refined, carrying lemon, white peach, and delicate floral notes. There is always a sense of lift, but never a sense of push. Everything about the wine feels in proportion, fruit, minerality, texture, and length.

Emotionally, Sancerre appeals to people who want brightness without boldness. It's Sauvignon Blanc for moments of calm: long lunches, quiet evenings, food-focused gatherings. It doesn't insist on itself. Instead, it offers a kind of understated elegance, the pleasure of a wine that reveals itself gradually rather than all at once.

How This Wine Feels

Sancerre is dry, light to medium in body, and driven by vivid, palate-sharpening acidity. The first sip feels clean and focused, a narrow line of citrus running steadily from the front of the tongue to the finish. The texture stays smooth and almost silky, supported by the quiet firmness of Loire minerality, which creates an inner tension rather than outward weight.

The aromas are gentle but precise. A swirl lifts subtle green and citrus notes, and once the wine has passed, those same scents seem to rise again in a soft after-impression of elderflower, lemon zest and chalk. It is not a wine that relies on concentration. Its pleasure comes from detail and pacing, the way each taste reveals something small but exact. The finish lingers in a delicate way, more persistent than powerful, like the faint outline of something finely made.

If You Like This Wine... You May Also Like

Pouilly-Fumé (France)

You'll recognise the same elegant structure and mineral clarity, but Pouilly-Fumé often adds a subtle smokiness, a flinty edge shaped by its silex soils. Compared with Sancerre, it feels slightly more savoury and textured. Savour its nuance as a wine that keeps the calm precision of Sancerre yet adds an intriguing, atmospheric note.

Touraine Sauvignon Blanc (France)

Touraine mirrors the fresh acidity of Sancerre and the citrus–herbal spectrum, but with softer aromatics and a bit more roundness. It differs by offering more immediate fruit and less pronounced minerality. If you enjoy Sancerre but want something friendlier in price and slightly more open in style, Touraine is a natural extension.

Menetou-Salon (France)

This neighbour to Sancerre shares its limestone soils and its refined acidity, but the wines often feel gentler, a touch softer, a touch fruitier. The difference is subtlety rather than contrast. Familiarity with a hint of warmth as Sancerre's close cousin; easy to love and easy to trust.

South African Sauvignon Blanc (Elgin, Constantia)

The kinship lies in clarity: high acidity, citrus, and herbal lift. But South Africa adds a whisper of savoury depth, sometimes flinty, sometimes slightly smoky, giving the wine a bit more texture. If you love Sancerre's brightness but want a slightly richer or more layered version, these regions offer a graceful step outward.

Italian Sauvignon (Friuli, Alto Adige Italy)

You'll feel the same crisp acidity and clean structure, but Italian Sauvignon tends to tilt toward white peach, fresh herbs, and a touch of alpine coolness. Compared to Sancerre, it's warmer in fruit and slightly more aromatic. Lose yourself in freshness with a Mediterranean accent: familiar structure, brighter flavours.

Stretch Wines

Dry Riesling (Germany, Austria, Australia)

Riesling shares Sancerre's high acidity and linearity[5], but swaps citrus-peach elegance for lime, stone, and slate. It's more piercing, more mineral-focused, and often more aromatic. If you enjoy structure and freshness but want sharper definition and a touch more tension, Riesling is an exhilarating next step.

Vermentino (Corsica France, Sardinia Italy)

You'll recognise the citrus brightness and herbal lift, but Vermentino leans toward Mediterranean flavours: lemon peel, rosemary, salinity. It differs by being slightly rounder and more textured than Sancerre. It brings brightness with a warm-climate soul, crisp, but with sunlit edges.

Albariño (Spain)

The connection is acidity and freshness, but Albariño adds peach, apricot skin, and a soft floral perfume. It's more aromatic and slightly more succulent. If you want to move from Sancerre into something more expressive without losing that clean backbone, Albariño offers exactly that balance.

Myths or Misunderstandings

One common assumption is that Sancerre is simply "French Sauvignon Blanc." While true in the broadest sense, it overlooks how much terroir shapes the wine. The soils, limestone, flint, marl, narrow the grape's exuberance into something sleeker, more mineral, more composed. Another misconception is that Sancerre must be expensive to be good. Stylistic consistency across producers makes it one of the most reliably elegant white wines in the world, even at mid-level prices.

Closing Reflection

Sancerre shows that Sauvignon Blanc can be lyrical instead of loud. It offers brightness without brashness, flavour without force, elegance without effort. It reminds you that some wines are confident enough to remain understated, that clarity can be quiet, and quiet things can leave the deepest impression.

In its calm structure and mineral shine, Sancerre teaches that restraint is not the opposite of expression, but another form of it. And for the drinker who values grace over intensity, it may be the purest expression of Sauvignon Blanc in the world.

Albariño

There is a brightness to Albariño that feels like a coastal breeze, cool, saline[6], and touched with the scent of fruit just beginning to ripen. In the glass, it opens with a delicate perfume: white peach, nectarine skin, a hint of lime, and a faint floral lift like orange blossom drifting from a distance. Yet beneath the charm is something firmer, more grounded, a quiet minerality, a whisper of sea spray, a sense of place shaped by the Atlantic itself.

Albariño's beauty is its dual nature. It feels both soft and crisp, both aromatic and structured. The fruit glows with gentle sweetness, but the wine remains dry, bright, and refreshing. It is a wine that carries the memory of wind and water, from Galicia's cool green landscapes, where vines cradle clusters of golden grapes just above the ocean's reach. To drink Albariño is to taste sunlight filtered through mist, the comfort of ripeness held within the frame of acidity.

Why People Love It

People love Albariño because it offers pleasure without heaviness. It is expressive but not loud, aromatic enough to intrigue, yet subtle enough to remain elegant. The flavours are familiar and comforting: peach, melon, citrus, and soft floral notes. The acidity is lively, giving the wine lift and shape, but never so sharp that it feels severe.

Albariño is also deeply versatile. It suits seafood as naturally as a tide meeting the shore, yet it can brighten salads, pastas, and simple vegetable dishes with the same ease. Emotionally, it appeals to those who want a wine that feels joyful but composed, a wine that makes a warm day feel cooler, a meal feel more vibrant, or an evening feel more open.

How This Wine Feels

Albariño is dry, medium in body, and guided by crisp, refreshing acidity. The first sip feels like a cool wave crossing the palate, bright enough to wake it up but gentle in its movement. The fruit tastes precise and succulent, carried forward by the acidity rather than sitting heavily on the tongue.

The texture is one of the quietly memorable traits of this grape. Albariño often feels slightly silky, even rounded, because it holds more aromatic and textural compounds than many other light white varieties. A simple swirl releases peach, citrus and floral notes, and once the wine moves off the palate, those scents seem to rise again, creating a soft return of flavour rather than a sudden disappearance.

The finish often leaves a faint impression of salt. It is not literal salinity, but a sensation borrowed from the region's ocean influence, a gentle savoury touch that invites another taste.

If You Like This Wine... You May Also Like

Vinho Verde (Portugal)

You'll recognise the same citrus-bright freshness and easy drinkability. But Vinho Verde is lighter, sometimes with a faint spritz, and leans toward lime rather than peach. It showcases simplicity and refreshment as a breezier and more effortless cousin to Albariño.

Soave (Italy)

Soave shares Albariño's clean lines and gentle orchard fruit, but its flavours tend toward white peach, almond, and soft herbal tones. It's less aromatic and slightly more mineral. If you appreciate Albariño's balance of fruit and freshness, Soave gives you that in an even more understated form.

Chenin Blanc (South Africa or Loire Valley France)

The kinship lies in texture: dry styles of Chenin share Albariño's combination of fruit, brightness, and a softly rounded mid-palate. Chenin differs by showing more apple, quince, and honeyed[7] subtlety. Submerse yourself in depth with a wine that feels familiar in structure but more layered.

Pinot Gris (Alsace France or Oregon)

You'll find similar peach and melon notes, but Pinot Gris brings richer texture and a more opulent palate. It's less citrus-driven and more spicy, ripe, and lush[8]. If Albariño's fruit appeals to you but you're curious about a fuller, rounder aromatic white, this is the next step.

Gavi (Cortese Italy)

Crisp acidity and citrus-peach flavours align it with Albariño, but Gavi is leaner and slightly more floral, with a clearer mineral thread. If you enjoy Albariño's freshness but want a gentler aromatic footprint, Gavi offers a refined alternative.

Stretch Wines

Gewürztraminer (Alsace France)

You'll share the love of aromatic fruitiness, but Gewürztraminer is far more expressive, Turkish delight, lychee, rose, spice. The acidity is softer, the perfume louder. The payoff is sensuality: a wine that pushes you toward a more exotic, opulent aromatic experience.

Viognier (USA, Australia, France)

Structurally similar in being aromatic and full-fruited, Viognier diverges with apricots, honeysuckle, and warm floral notes. It's richer and lower in acidity. If you're ready for aromatic white wine with more weight and perfume, Viognier stretches Albariño's style in a delightful direction.

Dry Riesling (France, Austria, Germany, USA)

The connection is acidity and brightness; the difference is tension. Riesling is sharper, more linear, and more mineral than Albariño, trading peach for lime and slate. It has robust intensity: a lightning-strike clarity for drinkers who love freshness and want more precision.

Myths or Misunderstandings

A common misconception is that Albariño is sweet because of its peachy, floral aroma. In truth, most Albariño is bone dry. The fruity impression comes from aromatic compounds that suggest ripeness without sugar. Another misunderstanding is that Albariño is simple. While it is easy to drink, the best examples, especially from older vines in Rías Baixas, show remarkable minerality and depth, revealing complexity beneath their approachable charm.

Closing Reflection

Albariño offers a kind of generosity that doesn't feel indulgent, fruit that feels ripe without sweetness, brightness that feels refreshing rather than demanding. It is a wine shaped by the Atlantic winds and cool green landscapes of Galicia, carrying a sense of place in every sip.

More than anything, Albariño teaches that aromatic whites need not be loud to be expressive. They can glow instead of blaze, charm instead of push, refresh instead of shock. In its quiet radiance, Albariño captures the feeling of a coastal afternoon, sunlight, breeze, and the unhurried comfort of being exactly where you want to be.

Viognier

Viognier enters the glass with a kind of quiet glamour, not loud, but unmistakably sensual. Its aromas bloom slowly, like warm air drifting through an open window: ripe apricots, peach nectar, honeysuckle, soft jasmine, and sometimes a hint of musk or exotic spice. It's a fragrance that feels almost tactile. Before you even taste it, the wine seems to press gently against the edges of the glass, rich and perfumed, promising something lush.

What makes Viognier so distinctive is the way it balances perfume with presence. Aromatic wines often feel light, but Viognier is different: the aromatics float while the wine itself moves with a slow, silken weight across the palate. It's a wine that feels warm, generous, unhurried, a style that seems to glow from within. Whether grown on the steep granitic slopes of Condrieu or in the sunlit hills of California and Australia, Viognier speaks in a soft, golden voice.

Why People Love It

People love Viognier because it feels indulgent without being sweet. It offers the richness of stone fruit, the perfume of florals, and the texture of something almost creamy, all in a dry wine. The acidity tends to be mellow, creating a sense of smoothness and ease. It is a wine that wraps rather than cuts, one that complements moments of comfort: warm evenings, soft lighting, relaxed meals.

Emotionally, Viognier appeals to those who want generosity in their glass. It is aromatic but not sharp, full-bodied but not heavy, luxurious but not difficult. It feels like the white-wine equivalent of a silk scarf, elegant, flowing, and pleasing to touch.

How This Wine Feels

Viognier is dry, full-bodied, with gentle, low acidity. The first sip feels plush and almost velvety, with ripe apricot, peach and sometimes mango unfolding slowly across the palate. Where wines like Sauvignon Blanc or Albariño lean on acidity for structure, Viognier's balance comes from weight, aroma and texture, creating a sense of fullness rather than tension.

A light swirl lifts floral and stone-fruit notes with ease. Once the wine moves off the palate, those same scents seem to rise again, bringing honeysuckle, gentle spice and a faintly oily[9] richness that defines the variety's mouthfeel. The finish holds on for a long time, not through sharpness but through the persistence of fruit and perfume. It often feels like a warm imprint on the tongue, soft and steady rather than bright.

If You Like This Wine... You May Also Like

Condrieu (Northern Rhône France)

This is Viognier's birthplace and its most iconic form. You'll recognise the same apricot and floral perfume, but Condrieu intensifies everything: richer texture, deeper stone-fruit concentration, and a more pronounced mineral seam from granite soils. Revel in the grandeur of the fullest and most expressive version of Viognier the world offers.

Fiano (Campania Italy)

Fiano brings a different kind of richness to the glass. The fruit leans towards citrus, pear and gentle honeyed notes, supported by a smooth texture that feels both substantial and poised. There is often a quiet thread of smoke or warm stone beneath the fruit, adding depth without weight. For drinkers drawn to Viognier's fullness and perfume who would like to experience a style with greater freshness and a more subtly layered character, Fiano provides a beautifully balanced alternative.

Marsanne or Roussanne (White Rhône Blends France)

These blends share Viognier's weight and warm-fruited generosity, but they differ in tone. Marsanne brings almond, honey, and soft pear; Roussanne adds herbs, wax, and texture. Compared with Viognier, they're less perfumed but often more structured. The payoff is complexity, a savoury, layered evolution of the richness you love.

Gewürztraminer (Alsace France)

The kinship lies in potent aromatics, but Gewürztraminer is more exotic, lychee, rosewater, ginger, spice. It's more flamboyant, less peachy, and often lower in acidity. If Viognier's perfume seduces you, Gewürztraminer offers a more dramatic, aromatic feast.

Torrontés (Argentina)

Torrontés echoes Viognier's floral lift but with more citrus, white flowers, and a touch of green spice. It is lighter and more linear, with higher acidity and a drier, more refreshing profile. If you enjoy Viognier's aromatics but want something airier and more vibrant, Torrontés is a natural bridge.

Pinot Gris (Alsace or Oregon)

You will find a similar ripeness of stone fruit and gentle richness, but Pinot Gris leans toward pear, quince, and soft spice. It's less floral, more textural. Enjoy a quieter yet more grounded aromatic experience, familiar in feel yet different in flavour.

Stretch Wines

Oaked Chardonnay (USA, S. Africa, Australia, France, Chile)

You'll recognise the same roundness and mid-palate weight, but Chardonnay brings acidity and structure that Viognier lacks. With oak, it shows toast, vanilla, and savoury depth. It shows a distinct sophistication with fullness that also has edges and lift.

Sémillon (Australia or Bordeaux France)

Sémillon shares Viognier's smooth texture, but the flavours are more lemon, wax, and lanolin than peach and apricot. The acidity can be firmer, especially in Hunter Valley styles. If you're intrigued by texture and want something more subtle, Sémillon stretches your palate into savoury territory.

Chenin Blanc

Richer expressions of Chenin can feel textural and honeyed like Viognier, but they carry more acidity and complexity. Compared to Viognier, Chenin is more agile and layered. It is a wine that combines warmth and tension as a fascinating contrast to Viognier's plushness.

Myths or Misunderstandings

Many people assume Viognier is sweet because it smells sweet. The ripe fruit and heady florals create a strong sensory illusion, but most Viognier is fully dry. Another misconception is that Viognier must be heavy. In truth, its richness comes from low acidity and high aromatics, not from sugar or oak. The wine's generosity is natural to the grape, not a stylistic addition.

Closing Reflection

Viognier reminds us that aromatics can be soft rather than sharp, that richness can exist without sweetness, and that texture can be as expressive as acidity. It is a wine that feels warm, inviting, quietly seductive, a golden hour captured in a glass.

It teaches us to slow down, to savour ripeness and perfume, to trust wines that unfold gently rather than strike quickly. For anyone drawn to sensuality in wine, to the touch, the glow, the fragrance of it, Viognier offers one of the most rewarding experiences in the world of aromatics.

Pinot Grigio (Fuller Styles)

Pinot Grigio enters quietly, a pale, shimmering wine that feels like cool light across a white tablecloth. Its aromas rise gently rather than dramatically: lemon zest, green apple, white flowers, sometimes the faintest hint of pear. Nothing pushes. Nothing insists. Pinot Grigio's charm lies in this softness, this easy translucence. It feels effortless, familiar, immediately approachable, the kind of wine many people reach for without needing to think at all.

Fuller expressions of Pinot Grigio are most often found in warmer parts of northern Italy and in regions such as Friuli and certain pockets of Veneto, where the grapes can ripen more deeply. These wines feel broader and more expressive, gathering soft orchard fruit, hints of spice and a rounder, more textural mouthfeel. The warmth of the vineyards brings weight and gentle richness, allowing the wine to unfold slowly rather than rush across the palate. If a Pinot Grigio feels generous, smooth and quietly layered, it usually comes from places where the sun lingers long enough to give the grape a fuller voice.

But that very fullness is its strength. A good Pinot Grigio doesn't try to impress; it tries to refresh. The best examples carry a clarity that feels like crisp linen or cold mountain water, simple in shape, but clean and bright in a way that satisfies instantly. Behind the quiet flavours is a subtle aromatic lift that makes the wine feel lively: a little citrus oil, a little blossom, a suggestion of herbs on a breeze. It never feels heavy. It never feels sharp. It simply glides.

Why People Love It

People love Pinot Grigio because it fits into life without effort. It's the wine you can pour for anyone, at any moment, with any simple meal, and it just works. Its flavours are gentle and welcoming. Its acidity is refreshing but not aggressive. Its alcohol balances without warmth or weight.

Emotionally, Pinot Grigio speaks to drinkers who want clarity without intensity, those who prefer calm refreshment over complexity. It's perfect for warm afternoons, light lunches, salads, shellfish, or moments when wine should enhance the day rather than take it over. It never demands attention, yet its best expressions reward it quietly.

How This Wine Feels

Pinot Grigio is dry, light in body, and carried by crisp, medium to high acidity. The first sip moves quickly across the palate, fresh and clean, with citrus peel, green apple and pear skin giving it a bright, streamlined feel. It is not built to linger; its pleasure lies in the way it refreshes and clears the palate for the next taste.

Its delicacy makes texture especially important. Well-made Pinot Grigio feels sleek and polished, almost like cool river stone. A gentle swirl lifts faint floral and citrus notes, and once the wine leaves the palate, those same scents return in a soft after-impression of apple, lemon and a hint of almond or white blossom. The finish is short to moderate, and that simplicity is part of its appeal, a clean close that naturally leads to another sip.

If You Like This Wine... You May Also Like

Soave (Italy)

You'll recognise the same easy drinkability and citrus-orchard fruit clarity, but Soave adds gentle almond, soft herbs, and a clearer mineral line. Compared with Pinot Grigio, it's slightly rounder and more textured. It has familiarity with a touch more character, still refreshing, but more interesting.

Vinho Verde (Portugal)

Vinho Verde shares Pinot Grigio's light body and crisp acidity but adds a slight spritz and lime-driven zestiness. It's more playful, 'summerier.' If you enjoy Pinot Grigio's ability to refresh, Vinho Verde brings that sensation into sharper, brighter focus.

Albariño (Spain)

The kinship is refreshment, but Albariño adds peach skin, floral lift, and a touch of Atlantic salinity. It's more aromatic and slightly more textured. This is a wine that feels just as clean but with a bit more personality with a gentle expansion rather than a leap.

Dry Riesling (USA, Austria, Germany)

Dry Riesling mirrors Pinot Grigio's brightness but with higher acidity and more pronounced aromatics, lime, slate, green apple. It differs by offering tension rather than neutrality. It will surprise with you with its energy. It brings a sharper and more vibrant form of refreshment.

Pinot Bianco (Italy)

You'll find the same delicacy and lightness, but Pinot Bianco leans more toward pear, herbs, and mineral structure. It's less fruity, more subtle. If you like Pinot Grigio's calmness, Pinot Bianco gives you a refined, understated variation of the theme.

Stretch Wines

Grüner Veltliner (Austria)

Grüner shares Pinot Grigio's crispness but adds white pepper, herbs, and a savoury edge. It's more aromatic and more characterful. The payoff is discovery: a wine still refreshing, but with an intriguing culinary personality.

Muscadet (France)

The structure is similar, light body, crisp acidity, but Muscadet introduces intense minerality and saline sharpness. It feels leaner and more precise than Pinot Grigio. If you enjoy clean wines and want sharper definition, Muscadet is an ideal stretch.

Picpoul de Pinet (France)

Picpoul is like Pinot Grigio with sunlight, citrusy, zesty, fresh, but with more lemon-lime intensity. It differs by having a tangy, Mediterranean brightness. The result is a sprightlier, more vibrant expression of light-bodied refreshment.

Myths or Misunderstandings

Pinot Grigio suffers more from assumption than from fault. Many believe it is bland, but that reputation comes from industrial, overcropped examples that dominate supermarket shelves. In truth, well-made Pinot Grigio (especially from Alto Adige or Friuli) can be elegant, precise, and quietly expressive. Another misconception: that Pinot Grigio must be ice-cold.

While refreshment is part of its charm, serving it too cold mutes the aromatics and flattens the texture; a slight chill is enough.

Closing Reflection

Pinot Grigio shows that ease can be beautiful. It asks nothing complicated of the drinker; it offers clarity, freshness, and a sense of calm simplicity. It's a wine for relaxed moments, a companion rather than a focal point, and in that role it excels.

It teaches that not all wines need intensity to be pleasurable, that refreshment can be its own reward, and that a soft-spoken style can still leave a gentle, lasting impression. In a world full of bold, emphatic wines, Pinot Grigio reminds us of the beauty of quietness.

Pinot Gris

Pinot Gris carries its richness quietly. At first glance, it looks pale and modest, but the moment you bring the glass closer, the aroma deepens: ripe pear, baked apple, quince, soft spice, sometimes a trace of smoke or honey. There is a gentle warmth to it, a sense of ripeness that feels almost autumnal, like fruit gathered at the end of the season. Unlike Pinot Grigio, which skims lightly across the senses, Pinot Gris moves more slowly, with a grounded, textural presence. While Pinot Gris and Pinot Grigio are the same grape, they stylistically are so different that these names are used to denote the style of the wine to avoid confusion.

Part of its appeal is how effortlessly it bridges subtlety and depth. The aromatics are softer than Viognier and gentler than Gewürztraminer, but more expressive than most light whites. The palate is rounder, fuller, sometimes even luscious. A good Pinot Gris feels like a soft wool blanket or warm candlelight, comforting, enveloping, inviting without excess. It's a wine that asks you to settle into it, rather than rush past.

Why People Love It

People love Pinot Gris because it offers flavour without flamboyance. It's aromatic and ripe but never overwhelming. The fruit leans toward pear, apple, melon, and quince; the texture is smooth and lightly creamy; the acidity is gentle but supportive. It feels generous, but balanced, full of quiet detail rather than loud expression.

It appeals to drinkers who want something richer than Pinot Grigio but not as intense as Viognier or Gewürztraminer. Pinot Gris fits easily into meals built around roast chicken, creamy dishes, pork, mushrooms, or warmly spiced food. Emotionally, it satisfies those who want comfort and subtle complexity in the same glass, richness that doesn't demand attention, just rewards it.

How This Wine Feels

Pinot Gris can be dry or off-dry, medium minus to medium plus in body, with gentle acidity and a broad, layered texture. The first sip feels soft and rounded, fruit-forward without sweetness, rich without heaviness. The grape's natural concentration of phenolics and aromatic compounds creates a fuller mid-palate and a deeper, more expressive perfume than Pinot Grigio.

A swirl brings up warm fruit and subtle spice. Once the wine moves off the palate, those impressions gather again, carrying pear, quince, ginger and a faint honeyed warmth. The finish often has a touch of viscosity, more of a silky glide than a crisp close. Even the driest examples retain this sense of texture, shaped by fruit and mouthfeel rather than by acidity

If You Like This Wine… You May Also Like

Alsace Gewürztraminer (France)

You'll recognise the shared richness and aromatic charm, but Gewürztraminer takes the perfume further, rose, lychee, exotic spice. Compared with Pinot Gris, it's more flamboyant and lower in acidity. It is a bold, more expressive aromatic experience for those ready to explore the edges of perfume.

Oregon Pinot Gris (USA)

Technically the same grape and style, but worth distinguishing. Oregon Pinot Gris mirrors Alsace in texture and ripeness but often leans slightly crisper, with more citrus, pear, and mineral lift. If you love Pinot Gris but want a touch more freshness, Oregon offers a beautifully balanced variation.

Chenin Blanc (Loire France or South Africa)

You'll find a similar interplay of fruit and texture, but Chenin Blanc adds higher acidity and a more complex range of flavours, quince, apple, lanolin, honeycomb. Compared with Pinot Gris, it's more dynamic in its rich tension, yet still brings comfort and vibrancy.

White Rhône Blends (Marsanne or Roussanne France)

These wines share Pinot Gris's weight and warm-fruited generosity, but they replace pear and quince with almond, honey, herbs, and waxy texture. They differ by offering savoury depth rather than orchard fruit. They bring robust complexity with a deeper and more layered form of richness.

Alsace Riesling (Dry, France)

You'll recognise the same clarity of fruit, but Riesling sharpens everything, higher acidity, more tension, and more minerality. It's leaner and more linear than Pinot Gris, but with equally expressive aromatics. Admire the precision: this is a cleaner, cooler form of aromatic depth.

Stretch Wines

Viognier (France, Australia)

Viognier shares the soft texture and stone-fruit ripeness of Pinot Gris but brings fuller aromatics, apricot, honeysuckle, warmth. It feels heavier and more perfumed. If you enjoy the gentle richness of Pinot Gris but want more sensuality, Viognier stretches the style toward opulence.

Gewürztraminer (Alsace, France)

Though more aromatic and lower in acidity, Gewürztraminer offers the same textural weight and ripe-fruit generosity. It diverges through floral intensity and spice. The payoff is bolder flavour, a more dramatic aromatic version of the comfort you love in Pinot Gris.

White Pinot Noir (Blanc de Noirs, Oregon USA, New Zealand, France)

This still-white expression shares Pinot Gris's rounded texture but replaces orchard fruit with red-apple, gentle berry, and savoury notes. It's different in flavour but similar in feel. Indulge your curiosity and enjoy a wine that echoes the fullness of Pinot Gris in a completely unexpected register.

Myths or Misunderstandings

Pinot Gris is often misunderstood because of its association with Pinot Grigio. Many drinkers assume they are interchangeable, simply light, neutral white wines. The two are stylistic opposites: Pinot Grigio is crisp and clean; Pinot Gris can be rich, textural, and aromatic. Another myth is that all Pinot Gris is sweet. While some Alsace examples lean off-dry, many of the best are fully dry, with their sense of richness coming from fruit weight, not sugar.

Closing Reflection

Pinot Gris reminds us that richness can be gentle, that aromatics need not be flamboyant, and that texture can carry as much beauty as acidity. It offers warmth without weight, comfort without simplicity, and aromatic depth without excess. It's a wine that sits quietly between the extremes, neither lean nor opulent, neither sharp nor lush, and in that middle space, it finds its charm.

It teaches that subtlety can be luxuriant, that softness can be expressive, and that wines don't need sharp edges to leave a lasting impression. For those who value quiet complexity and warm flavours, Pinot Gris is one of the most rewarding whites in the aromatic world.

---

1. Herbal: A scent or taste suggesting fresh herbs or green plant character, often linked to varietal or climate.
2. Clean: A wine that shows clarity of flavour with no off aromas or distracting elements.
3. Mineral: A subtle stony or saline impression that evokes rocks, chalk, or wet stone.
4. Spritz: A light natural fizziness in young wines, often from retained carbon dioxide.
5. Linear: A wine that moves across the palate in a straight, focused line without widening or spreading.
6. Saline: A subtle salty impression found in wines from coastal or mineral soils.
7. A flavour or aroma suggesting honey, often found in richer white wines or those with some development.
8. Lush: A rich, generous flavour and texture profile often associated with ripe fruit.
9. Oily: A smooth, slightly viscous texture often found in warm climate whites or certain aromatic varieties.

Chapter 6
Rosé Wines

Wines that balance freshness with gentle fruit and clean movement

Provence Rosé

Provence Rosé feels like the colour of late afternoon sunlight, pale, warm, and softly luminous. Lift the glass, and the aromas rise in delicate threads: wild strawberries, pink grapefruit, white peach, rose petals, and the faintest brush of Mediterranean herbs. Nothing is loud. Nothing is sweet. The wine seems to glow with a cool, glimmering calm, as if it were made from light as much as from grapes.

Part of the magic of Provence Rosé is its sense of effortlessness. It doesn't push; it doesn't insist. It whispers. The flavours unfold slowly, citrus, melon, soft red fruit, all carried on a spine of freshness that feels like salt air drifting inland from the sea. Its pale colour is not just an aesthetic choice; it's a signal of its style: restrained fruit, crisp texture, and a dry, mineral-driven finish that tastes like warm stone touched by wind.

Provence is where rosé became not just a category, but an aspiration. The vineyards stretch toward the coast, framed by garrigue[1] shrubs, lavender, and olive groves, and the wines capture this landscape in their aromatics and textures. Drinking Provence Rosé feels like stepping briefly into its rhythm, languid lunches, sunlit terraces, quiet evenings, a kind of coastal serenity.

Why People Love It

People love Provence Rosé because it feels balanced and refined. It's refreshing without being sharp, fruity without being sweet, aromatic without being flamboyant. The flavours suggest strawberries and citrus, but softly, like a memory rather than a declaration. The wine seems to cool the palate gently, gliding across it with a smooth, almost silken texture.

Emotionally, Provence Rosé appeals to those who want elegance in their glass, effortless elegance. It fits into relaxed summer afternoons, rooftop dinners, seafood meals, and long conversations. It's the wine people choose when they want something that feels beautiful without trying hard to be beautiful.

How This Wine Feels

Provence Rosé is dry, light in body, and guided by gentle, refreshing acidity. The first sip feels bright without being sharp, a smooth wash of citrus and red fruit that moves evenly across the palate. Texture plays a central role. It is neither the crisp snap of a lean white nor the rounded weight of a fuller rosé. Instead, it glides with quiet ease.

A swirl releases delicate notes of strawberry, grapefruit, melon, rose petal and herbs. After the wine leaves the palate, a soft floral tone and a faint mineral impression return. The finish stays clean and calming, touched by a slight savoury edge from the grape skins and the garrigue influenced soils of Provence. It refreshes the mouth rather than coating it, leaving you ready for another sip.

If You Like This Wine... You May Also Like

Rosé of Pinot Noir (Global)

You'll recognise the same pale colour, soft red fruit, and clean, elegant frame. Pinot Noir rosés, though, tend to be a touch more floral and lighter in texture, with red cherry and pomegranate notes. This gives a more delicate, almost weightless interpretation of Provence's grace.

Loire Rosé (France, Cabernet Franc–based)

The connection is dryness and freshness. Loire rosés usually show more herbs, more minerality, and a slightly sharper profile, with cranberry and redcurrant at the core. Expect a brisk, refreshing alternative that keeps Provence's restraint while adding extra definition.

Rosado (Spain)

Rosado offers similar strawberry and citrus tones but with deeper colour and more pronounced fruit. It's a juicier, more upfront cousin of Provence Rosé. Think of it as moving toward fuller flavour while keeping the dry, clean finish.

White Zinfandel (USA)

White Zinfandel shares Provence's easy charm and red-fruit appeal but introduces gentle sweetness and softer acidity. It's rounder, simpler, and more playful. A friendly, fruit-forward option for drinkers who want a rosé that feels approachable and uncomplicated.

Sangiovese Rosé (Italy)

Sangiovese rosés bring cherry, strawberry, and a hint of spice, with slightly firmer acidity. They offer more red-fruit presence and a bit more structure. This creates a versatile, food-ready variation that keeps Provence's freshness while adding a sturdier backbone.

Stretch Wines

Tavel Rosé (France)

Tavel takes the idea of rosé and deepens it: darker colour, fuller body, savoury elements, and firm structure. It remains dry but shows far more power. For anyone who appreciates Provence's elegance and wants to explore rosé with depth, this is that next dimension.

Rosé of Syrah or GSM Blends (Global)

These rosés share the Mediterranean feel but layer in spice, darker fruit, and richer texture. They show more weight and warmth than Provence. Expect a style that remains dry yet feels broader and more expressive.

New World Dry Rosé (South Africa, Australia)

You'll find the same clean, dry framework, but often with brighter fruit with watermelon, strawberry, ripe cherry. These rosés feel sunnier and juicier, offering a more fruit-forward interpretation of Provence's easy elegance.

Myths or Misunderstandings

A common misconception is that Provence Rosé is simple because it's pale. In truth, its delicacy is intentional. The colour reflects a style of gentle pressing or brief skin contact, meant to highlight freshness and finesse, not intensity. Another myth is that Provence Rosé is a "summer wine." While refreshing in warm weather, its balance and subtlety make it exceptionally food-friendly year-round.

Closing Reflection

Provence Rosé shows that softness can be expressive. It doesn't need depth of colour or bold aromatics to make an impression. Instead, it offers harmony, small details in perfect balance. It feels like coastal air, like sunlight filtered through a curtain, like a calm afternoon made liquid.

It teaches us that elegance is not about intensity but about proportion. And for the drinker who values subtle beauty, Provence Rosé may be the most quietly captivating rosé in the world.

Tavel Rosé

Tavel Rosé arrives with more presence than any other rosé in the world. It pours deeper, a vivid pink or soft ruby rather than the pale blush of Provence. The aromas rise with a grounded warmth: ripe strawberry, redcurrant, raspberry, blood orange, rose petals, dried herbs, and a faint spice. This is not a whispering wine. It speaks in a clear, confident voice. Tavel has body, colour, and texture, all delivered without sweetness, while remaining unmistakably dry.

What sets Tavel apart is its structure. It feels like a rosé that remembers it is technically a wine made from red grapes, with all the depth and savoury nuance that implies. Yet the flavours stay bright and lifted, the acidity refreshing, the alcohol balanced. It strikes a rare chord between richness and freshness, fruit and minerality, delicacy and power. It is rosé with backbone.

Tavel is one of the Rhône Valley's treasures: a historic rosé appellation producing only rosé and treating the category with a seriousness few regions match. Drinking Tavel feels like experiencing the fullest expression of what rosé can be, not a light refreshment, but a complete, character-driven wine.

Why People Love It

People love Tavel because it delivers flavour, depth, and complexity while still offering the brightness of rosé. It's dry, savoury, and textural, with red fruit that feels ripe but never sugary. Tavel appeals to drinkers who want rosé to have substance, something to savour with food, something with layers and weight, something that holds your attention.

Emotionally, it speaks to those who appreciate richness but don't want heaviness; who enjoy red fruit but not tannin; who crave more presence in their rosé without tipping into sweetness or boldness. Tavel is rosé for people who love *wine* first, colour second.

How This Wine Feels

Tavel is dry, medium in body (sometimes edging toward medium plus), with fresh acidity and a rounded, almost velvety middle. The first sip delivers a vivid rush of strawberry, raspberry and redcurrant, followed by orange zest and gentle spice. Unlike lighter rosés, Tavel stays on the palate. It carries weight and breadth, with a faint savoury tone that reflects its brief skin contact and its Rhône varieties such as Grenache, Cinsault and Syrah.

A swirl deepens the aromas, bringing out floral notes and a touch of thyme or garrigue. After the wine leaves the palate, the red fruit and warm spice return in a quiet second impression, supported by a subtle mineral edge. The finish is dry and lingering rather than quick and crisp, the profile of a rosé that truly persists.

If You Like This Wine... You May Also Like

Rosado (Spain)

You'll notice the deeper colour, fuller body, and bolder fruit. Rosado is usually juicier and more overtly fruit-driven, while Tavel leans savoury and structured. This gives a bright, lively counterpoint to Tavel's more serious, grounded style.

Rosé of Grenache or GSM (Global)

GSM rosés carry the same Mediterranean imprint—ripe red fruit, herbs, spice—but vary in weight, some lighter, some richer. They feel like the same grape family translated into a gentler, more broadly styled expression.

Sangiovese Rosé (Italy)

The acidity and red-cherry lift sit close to Tavel's structural profile. Sangiovese rosés tend to be brisker and more linear. Expect a taut, food-friendly interpretation of fuller bodied rosé.

Loire Rosé (Cabernet Franc France)

You'll find the same dryness and herbal edge, but Loire rosés are cooler, more mineral, and centred on cranberry and redcurrant. It becomes a leaner, more refreshing take on Tavel's savoury character.

Provence Rosé (France)

This sits on the opposite end of the rosé spectrum: pale, delicate, airy. Provence offers lighter citrus-driven lift, less weight, and more finesse. A clear contrast—crisp, bright clarity after Tavel's depth.

Stretch Wines

Light Red Wines (Gamay or Pinot Noir from France, Oregon USA, New Zealand, Canada)

These wines echo Tavel's red-fruit brightness but in a deeper, drier register with added tannin. If you enjoy Tavel's interplay of fruit and savoury tones, light reds provide a natural progression into more structure.

White Rhône Blends (Marsanne or Roussanne, France)

Though white, these blends reflect Tavel's savoury weight and warm, textured mid-palate. They shift toward honeyed notes, herbs, and waxiness. This leads into full-bodied whites that share a similar sense of depth.

Sicilian Rosato (Nerello Mascalese Italy)

Salty, volcanic, mineral, and savoury, these Rosatos bring a smoky edge and a bit more austerity. They're leaner and more angular than Tavel yet equally serious. A complex expression shaped by volcanic soils and Mediterranean heat.

Myths or Misunderstandings

A persistent myth is that rosé is inherently light and simple, a wine meant only for casual, warm-weather drinking. Tavel destroys that misconception completely. It is one of the world's most structured, serious rosés, capable of pairing with rich foods and even ageing. Another myth is that deeper-coloured rosé is sweet. Tavel is the opposite: deeply coloured *and* bone dry.

Closing Reflection

Tavel Rosé stands as proof that rosé can be a full wine, complex, textured, savoury, and deeply satisfying. It has weight without heaviness, fruit without sweetness, elegance without delicacy. It captures the warmth of the Rhône Valley and the vibrancy of Mediterranean fruit, blending them into a style with both presence and poise.

Tavel teaches that colour is not destiny, that deeper rosé can be just as refined, and even more captivating, than the palest blush. For those who want rosé with soul, depth, and intention, Tavel offers one of the most compelling expressions in the world.

White Zinfandel

White Zinfandel feels like summer in a glass, soft, fruity, lightly sweet, and immediately welcoming. Its colour is unmistakable: a cheerful shade of cotton-candy pink or pale watermelon, bright enough to catch the eye and warm enough to feel instantly approachable. Lift the glass and the aromas rise gently: ripe strawberry, watermelon, raspberry sorbet, and a hint of citrus. It smells like ease, like something meant to be enjoyed without hesitation or thought.

Created almost by accident in California in the 1970s, White Zinfandel became one of the most iconic rosé styles in the world. Its appeal wasn't complexity or sophistication, it was comfort. It made wine feel friendly. It brought millions of new drinkers into the world of wine, people who might otherwise have felt intimidated by drier or more austere styles. It was, and remains, the most widely recognised sweet rosé on the planet.

Why People Love It

People love White Zinfandel because it is gentle. The flavours are ripe and playful, strawberry, melon, citrus candy, and the sweetness is soft rather than heavy. The acidity is modest, which makes the wine feel round and smooth. There's no sharpness, no bite, no tannin. It's a wine that meets the drinker where they are, not where tradition expects them to be.

Emotionally, it appeals to drinkers who want wine to feel pleasurable and easy. It suits relaxed gatherings, casual meals, warm afternoons, and moments when the mood calls for something light, fruity, and comforting. For many people, White Zinfandel was their first step into wine, a sweet, soft beginning from which curiosity could grow.

How This Wine Feels

White Zinfandel is off dry to semi sweet, light in body, and exceptionally smooth. The first sip brings ripe red fruit wrapped in gentle sweetness, with strawberry, watermelon and raspberry creating a soft, inviting opening. The acidity stays in the low to medium range, which gives the wine a rounded, plush feel rather than a crisp edge.

The texture is soft and almost silky, with sweetness that supports the fruit instead of overpowering it. A swirl lifts delicate, candy like aromas, light and playful. After the wine leaves the palate, those same berry and melon notes drift back in a gentle after impression that settles into a smooth, easy finish without dryness. It lingers just long enough to encourage another sip but never insists on being analysed.

If You Like This Wine… You May Also Like

Moscato d'Asti (Italy)

You'll recognise the gentle sweetness and playful fruit, but Moscato adds bubbles and floral lift—peach, orange blossom, honeysuckle. It delivers sweetness with sparkle, perfume, and a light, joyful touch.

Off-Dry Rosé (Global Styles)

These rosés keep the strawberry and cherry softness but add a little more acidity and balance. Sweetness is still present, just toned back, creating an easy, familiar style with a smoother finish.

Lambrusco Rosato (Italy)

Lambrusco Rosato brings sweet red fruit with a lively, frothy sparkle. Compared with White Zinfandel, it's bubblier, more vivid, and slightly tarter. It offers a more energetic, upbeat take on sweet rosé.

Rosé of Grenache (Fruit-Forward Styles)

Fruit-driven Grenache rosés show ripe strawberry and raspberry, finishing dry or slightly off-dry. They feel juicier and a touch more structured. This creates a smooth progression between sweeter rosé and fully dry styles.

Provence Rosé (France)

A contrast—but an essential one. Provence trades sweetness for delicate dryness, minerality, and a pale, airy profile. For fans of White Zinfandel curious about rosé at its driest and most elegant, this is the natural point of discovery.

Stretch Wines

Tavel Rosé (France)

A decisive step from sweet rosé into dry, structured territory. Tavel shows deeper colour, savoury notes, and medium body. Next to White Zinfandel, it feels almost like a light red shaped as rosé, bringing far more depth while keeping fruit at the core.

Rosado (Spain)

Rosado boosts red fruit, acidity, and colour, staying firmly dry. It's brighter, fuller, and more expressive than Provence rosé. For drinkers who want fruit without sweetness, Rosado provides a confident move in that direction.

Dry Riesling (Off-Dry or Kabinett)

These wines echo the playfulness and fruity charm of White Zinfandel but lift everything with higher acidity and more detail. Sweetness becomes balanced and crisp, offering a friendlier yet more nuanced style.

Myths or Misunderstandings

The most persistent myth is that White Zinfandel is the same as Zinfandel. While it's made from the same grape, White Zinfandel is fermented with minimal skin contact to create a light, pink, sweet style. Another misconception: that White Zinfandel lacks quality. In truth, its purpose is different, it's made to be approachable, fruity, and easy-drinking. Its role in wine culture is foundational, not derivative.

Closing Reflection

White Zinfandel is more than a style, it's an invitation. It introduced countless people to wine, offering sweetness and simplicity in a world that often equates seriousness with dryness. It reminds us that pleasure doesn't need to be complicated, and that wine can be friendly, comforting, and joyful.

For drinkers who love soft fruit, gentle sweetness, and ease, White Zinfandel offers one of the most welcoming experiences in the rosé world. And for those ready to explore further, it provides a bridge into the broader universe of dry rosé and beyond.

Spanish Rosado

Rosado from Spain enters the glass with more colour, more energy, and more fruit intensity than most of its pale pink cousins. Its hue ranges from vibrant coral to deep salmon, sometimes even strawberry-red, and the aromas rise vividly: ripe raspberry, cherry, redcurrant, watermelon, orange peel, and a lifted floral brightness. There is nothing shy about Rosado. It feels sun-warmed, expressive, and alive with flavour, the Mediterranean or continental Spanish climate captured in a burst of fruit.

Rosado is not a single style. In Navarra, Garnacha-based Rosado is juicy, bright, and refreshing. In Rioja, Tempranillo brings a more savoury profile, sometimes aged briefly in oak for added depth. In the Levante, wines can be bolder, more concentrated, more structured. But across regions, the common thread is personality: Rosado is rosé that tastes like ripe fruit on a sunny day, generous, flavourful, and full of life.

Why People Love It

People love Spanish Rosado because it offers flavour without heaviness. It's dry, refreshing, and full of red-fruit charm, but with more intensity than Provence Rosé and more brightness than many fuller Old-World rosés. The fruit feels juicy and immediate, the acidity lively, the finish crisp.

Emotionally, Rosado appeals to drinkers who want something joyful and expressive. It suits warm weather, casual meals, tapas, picnics, paella, and any moment where colour and freshness feel right. It's a wine that brings energy to the table, cheerful, bright, and unfussy.

How This Wine Feels

Rosado is dry, light to medium in body, and driven by medium plus acidity. The first sip bursts with red fruit (raspberry, cherry, strawberry, redcurrant) often brightened by a touch of citrus zest. Where pale rosés tend to glide softly, Rosado carries a bit more fruit weight and a slightly firmer feel.

The mid palate is smooth and juicy, sometimes touched by light spice or a gentle herbal thread. A swirl brings up fresh berry notes and citrus flower aromatics. After the wine leaves the palate, those flavours gather again in a soft return of cherry, redcurrant and a hint of savoury spice[2]. The finish stays refreshing and fruit forward, lingering just long enough to show its generosity before clearing the palate for the next sip.

If You Like This Wine... You May Also Like

Tavel Rosé (France)

Tavel shares Rosado's deeper colour and fuller flavour but brings more savoury tones and firmer structure. Rosado leans fruitier and more energetic; Tavel feels sturdier and more textured. It offers added depth and complexity while keeping red fruit at the centre.

Rosé of Grenache or GSM Rosé (Global)

These wines echo Rosado's ripe red fruit and Mediterranean warmth, though the level of ripeness and spice shifts with the blend. They deliver the same fruit-driven appeal, expressed through a broader, more international lens.

Sangiovese Rosé (Italy)

You'll notice the bright acidity and cherry-focused profile. Sangiovese Rosato tends to be leaner, more linear, and slightly more savoury than Rosado. This creates a taut, food-friendly take on cherry-and-strawberry rosé.

Rosé of Pinot Noir

Pinot Noir rosé keeps the refreshing dryness but shows lighter colour and more delicate flavours—strawberry, pomegranate, cherry skin. It's smoother, subtler, and more refined, offering a silkier, understated version of red-fruit rosé.

Provence Rosé (France)

The contrast is central to its charm. Provence Rosé is paler, more mineral, more citrus-driven, and more restrained. For fans of Rosado who want to explore a lighter, more elegant expression of dryness, this is the natural next step.

Stretch Wines

Light Red Wines (Gamay, young Tempranillo, Pinot Noir)

If you enjoy Rosado's brightness and red fruit but want greater depth, light reds provide an easy progression into red-wine territory. They share familiar flavours, adding tannin and a bit more structure.

Txakoli Rosado

A thrilling variation with high acidity, strong salinity, and a touch of spritz. It feels like Rosado reimagined with a cooler, coastal bite—leaner, tangier, and more electric.

Lambrusco Rosato

Sparkling, berry-driven, and ranging from slightly sweet to fully dry depending on style. Compared with still Rosado, it's bubblier and more playful, offering a festive twist on fruit-forward rosé.

Cerasuolo d'Abruzzo (Italy)

Cerasuolo d'Abruzzo sits between rosé and light red, carrying cherry bright fruit with a gentle herbal echo and a deeper colour that reflects its generous character. The palate feels fuller than many rosés yet remains brisk and refreshing, shaped by lively acidity and a steady mineral line. It is a wine that welcomes food but also shines on its own, offering both warmth and lift. For those who enjoy the vivid fruit of Spanish Rosado but want a style that steps softly towards red wine while keeping its clarity, Cerasuolo provides a beautifully balanced middle ground.

Myths or Misunderstandings

A common misconception is that deeper-coloured rosé must be sweet. Spanish Rosado proves the opposite: it is almost always fully dry, with the colour reflecting grape variety and brief skin contact, not sweetness. Another myth is that stronger colour means heavier body. Many Rosados remain crisp and refreshing despite their vibrant hue.

Closing Reflection

Rosado shows that rosé doesn't need to be pale to be refreshing, and that fruitiness does not require sweetness. It offers a joyful, generous, flavourful expression of rosé that feels warm and welcoming. It celebrates ripe fruit without heaviness, structure without austerity, and brightness without restraint.

For drinkers who love colour, charm, and expressive fruit, Rosado offers one of the most satisfying and approachable styles in the rosé world. It teaches that rosé can carry personality boldly, and that good wine can be both lively and dry, energetic yet balanced.

Rosé of Pinot Noir

Rosé of Pinot Noir feels like the gentlest expression of rosé, pale, precise, and quietly graceful. Bring the glass to your nose and the aromas rise delicately: wild strawberry, pomegranate seed, redcurrant, rose petal, and a soft hint of citrus. Nothing is exaggerated. Nothing is heavy. It feels like the memory of red fruit rather than the fruit itself, carried on cool air and light.

Pinot Noir is naturally thin-skinned and sensitive, which makes it ideal for producing rosé with clarity and finesse. A brief touch of skin contact is enough to tint the wine a delicate blush while preserving the grape's purity. This style of rosé is often associated with coastal climates, California's north coast, Oregon, New Zealand, Chile's southern valleys, places where Pinot Noir thrives under gentle sunlight and cool breezes. The resulting rosé feels linear, refreshing, and quietly expressive.

Why People Love It

People love Rosé of Pinot Noir because it offers elegance. The fruit is subtle and sophisticated: strawberry, cranberry, red cherry, and soft floral notes, without the ripe juiciness or richness found in deeper rosés. The acidity is refreshing but smooth, making the wine feel crisp without sharpness.

Emotionally, it appeals to drinkers who value restraint over intensity, grace over exuberance. It suits long lunches, light meals, thoughtful moments, or any situation where you want a rosé that feels refined and quietly beautiful. This is rosé that mirrors the delicacy of Pinot Noir itself, understated, charming, and poetic.

How This Wine Feels

Rosé of Pinot Noir is dry, light in body, and shaped by fine, polished acidity. The first sip tastes smooth and bright, with red berries, citrus peel and soft floral tones appearing in a gentle, even sweep. The wine moves lightly across the palate, leaving a clean, lifted sensation rather than any sense of weight.

The texture is silky, which is typical of Pinot Noir, and the finish is surprisingly long for such a delicate style, carried by acidity rather than fruit density. A slow swirl releases hints of rose, cherry blossom and redcurrant. Once the wine leaves the palate, those impressions rise again, creating a quiet return of floral and red fruit notes that linger in an elegant, understated way.

If You Like This Wine... You May Also Like

Provence Rosé (France)

You'll recognise the same pale colour and refined structure. Provence Rosé is equally delicate but leans toward citrus, melon, and herbal notes. It offers a slightly more mineral, finely etched take on Pinot Noir rosé's elegance.

Loire Rosé (Cabernet Franc)

The link is dryness and red-fruit freshness. Loire rosé tends to be brisker, with stronger herbal and mineral accents. It delivers a zestier, cooler style while maintaining similar delicacy.

Sangiovese Rosé (Italy)

Sangiovese rosé shares the cherry brightness but introduces firmer acidity and a touch more savouriness. It's livelier and a bit more structured than Pinot Noir rosé, giving a versatile, food-friendly twist on the pale, refreshing style.

Rosado (Spain)

A clear shift in character. Rosado shows deeper colour, juicier fruit, and more vivid flavours. For those who enjoy Pinot Noir rosé's gentle red fruit but want extra personality, Rosado supplies that added energy and richness.

Rosé of Grenache (Global)

Grenache rosés echo the strawberry notes of Pinot Noir but with riper fruit and softer acidity. They feel rounder, warmer, and more sun-soaked, offering a fuller, friendlier take on pale rosé.

Stretch Wines

Sancerre Rosé (Pinot Noir–based)

A graceful bridge between pale rosé and light red. Sancerre rosé is dry and subtle like Pinot Noir rosé but adds chalky minerality and a firmer frame. It presents the same grape through a more structured, terroir-driven lens.

Light Red Pinot Noir (slightly chilled)

If you enjoy the delicacy and red-fruit purity of Pinot Noir rosé, a chillable light red Pinot Noir is a natural next move. It adds depth and gentle tannin while preserving elegance and freshness.

Gamay (Beaujolais) Rosé or Red

Gamay's juicy red fruit and soft tannins make it an easy progression. As rosé, it's fruitier; as red, it remains light and supple. It offers a smooth transition into red wines that stay lively and approachable.

Myths or Misunderstandings

A common misconception is that pale rosé is always simple or watery. Rosé of Pinot Noir proves otherwise: delicacy is not the absence of character. Another misunderstanding is that pale rosé is inferior to deeper-coloured styles. In truth, colour reflects grape variety and winemaking choices, not quality or flavour.

Some people also assume Pinot Noir rosé must be sweet because of its soft fruit profile, most versions are bone dry, relying on acidity and subtle aromatics for balance.

Closing Reflection

Rosé of Pinot Noir shows that rosé can be as elegant as any white and as expressive as any light red. It delivers subtle fruit, fine acidity, and a texture that feels like silk drawn across the palate. It invites stillness, attention, and enjoyment without intensity.

This style teaches that rosé isn't just a warm-weather drink or a casual choice, it can be a wine of nuance, grace, and quiet beauty. For those who value delicacy and refinement, Rosé of Pinot Noir offers one of the most graceful experiences in the rosé world.

Rosé of Sangiovese

Rosé of Sangiovese feels like a breeze moving through a grove of cherry trees, bright, fragrant, and full of life. The colour is often a little deeper than Provence rosé, shifting from soft coral to pale sunset pink. Bring the glass to your nose and you sense cherry skin, wild strawberry, pomegranate, orange zest, and a subtle herbal edge that hints at Tuscan hillsides warmed by sun. It's rosé with Italian clarity: vibrant acidity, red-fruited brightness, and a savoury undertone that feels almost architectural.

Sangiovese, the grape behind Chianti and many of Italy's greatest reds, carries its natural character into rosé. Its high acidity gives the wine lift and definition; its cherry-driven flavours bring charm; its savoury backbone adds seriousness without weight. Rosé of Sangiovese sits comfortably between delicate and expressive, offering more structure than the palest rosés and more finesse than the richer ones.

Why People Love It

People love Rosé of Sangiovese because it balances joy with structure. The fruit is lively, cherry, strawberry, redcurrant, and the acidity is bright, giving the wine a refreshing, mouthwatering quality. Yet beneath the brightness lies a subtle savoury note: herbs, tomato leaf, or a faint echo of Tuscan earth. It's a rosé with personality, but still dry, crisp, and refreshing.

Emotionally, it appeals to drinkers who want rosé that goes beyond fruit and colour, a wine that feels purposeful. It shines with food: antipasti, grilled vegetables, charcuterie, seafood pastas, summer dishes, or even lighter pizzas. It's the perfect wine for long lunches, easy evenings, and meals where the wine should complement rather than dominate.

How This Wine Feels

Rosé of Sangiovese is dry, light to medium in body, and driven by high, zesty acidity. The first sip shows clear, bright flavours of cherry, strawberry, pink grapefruit and a touch of cranberry. The acidity moves straight through the palate and gives the wine a clean, linear profile.

The texture is sleek rather than soft. Sangiovese's natural structure appears lightly here, giving the wine more shape than many rosés without bringing bitterness or noticeable tannin. A swirl lifts fresh red fruit and gentle herbal notes. After the wine leaves the palate, those impressions rise again, adding hints of herbs, citrus peel and cherry skin that linger for a moment before settling into a crisp, refreshing finish.

If You Like This Wine... You May Also Like

Provence Rosé (France)

You'll recognise the dryness and soft red-fruit tones, but Provence is lighter, more citrus-driven, and more delicate overall. Rosé of Sangiovese has firmer lines and a more savoury edge. Provence offers a gentler, more ethereal expression of the structure you enjoy.

Côtes de Provence Sainte Victoire (France)

Sainte Victoire offers a more chiselled and mineral form of Provençal rosé. The fruit is delicate and finely drawn, the aromatics quiet and airy, and the palate shaped by a firm line of limestone freshness. The wine feels calm and precise with a lingering impression of citrus and pale red berries. For drinkers who love the elegance of Sangiovese rosé and wish to explore a style that deepens the minerality while softening the savoury edges, Sainte Victoire provides a serene and beautifully sculpted expression.

Rosado (Spain)

Rosado shares Sangiovese rosé's generosity of red fruit but usually comes with deeper colour and fuller, more vivid flavours. It leans toward vibrant juiciness rather than savoury nuance, giving a brighter, more expressive interpretation.

Loire Rosé (Cabernet Franc)

Loire rosés match the acidity and dryness but add a greener, herbal profile with redcurrant, cranberry, fresh cut herbs. They feel cooler, more linear, and more lifted, offering a crisp, refreshing alternative with similar precision.

Rosé of Grenache or GSM Rosé

Grenache rosés bring strawberry and cherry fruit wrapped in a softer, rounder body. They feel warmer and riper, offering an easy, sun-kissed take on red-fruit rosé.

Rosé of Pinot Noir (Global)

This style shares the elegance of Sangiovese rosé but with less structure and more delicacy. Strawberry, pomegranate, and floral notes take the lead. It's paler, lighter, and more graceful showing an especially soft, silky form of fruit-forward dryness.

Stretch Wines

Tavel Rosé (France)

Tavel carries the savoury backbone of Sangiovese rosé but heightens everything: deeper colour, fuller body, more structure. For those who appreciate the seriousness of Sangiovese rosé, Tavel offers an intensified, more commanding version.

Chinato or Light Italian Reds (Gamay, Frappato, Lambrusco)

These wines echo Sangiovese's cherry brightness but move into red or lightly sparkling formats. They add tannin or bubbles, creating a smooth step into red-wine territory while keeping freshness intact.

Dry Lambrusco Rosato (Italy)

Dry, fizzy, and cherry-bright, this style shares the red-fruit purity of Sangiovese rosé but adds lively bubbles and extra energy. It provides a playful, festive twist on savoury, food-friendly rosé.

Myths or Misunderstandings

Many people assume Sangiovese is too intense or tannic for rosé. In fact, its high acidity and medium body make it ideal for crisp, refreshing pink wine. Another misconception is that deeper rosé is always sweet or heavy. Rosé of Sangiovese is almost always bone dry, relying on acidity and savoury complexity rather than tannin or sweetness.

Some drinkers expect all rosé to be delicate. Rosé of Sangiovese proves that rosé can be both fresh and structured, lively yet serious.

Closing Reflection

Rosé of Sangiovese captures the essence of Italy's beloved red grape in a fresher, brighter form. It offers cherry-driven fruit, crisp acidity, and a savoury undertone that makes it both refreshing and food-friendly. It feels like the warmth of a Tuscan afternoon balanced by a cool breeze, grounded, expressive, and effortlessly versatile.

It teaches that rosé can carry the personality of a red grape without losing delicacy, and that complexity doesn't need to come at the expense of refreshment. For those who want rosé with intention and flavour, Rosé of Sangiovese is among the most satisfying expressions.

Loire Rosé (French Cabernet Franc–Based)

Loire Rosé feels like a cool breeze sweeping across a riverbank, crisp, herbal, and delicately red-fruited. Its colour ranges from pale salmon to a soft, translucent coral, and the aromas rise with quiet precision: redcurrant, cranberry, raspberry leaf, fresh herbs, and a faint floral touch. There's a freshness here that feels distinctly northerly, a sense of cool mornings and green landscapes reflected in the glass.

Made primarily from Cabernet Franc, sometimes with touches of Grolleau, Gamay, or Pinot Noir, Loire rosé carries the grape's signature herbaceous lift and bright acidity. It's a style shaped by climate: cooler temperatures preserve taut acidity and lean flavours, creating rosé that is dry, refreshing, and subtle. Where Mediterranean rosés offer sun and softness, Loire rosé brings shade and breeze, a cooler, cleaner expression of pink wine.

Why People Love It

People love Loire rosé because it offers clarity and tension. The fruit is delicate, redcurrant, cherry skin, cranberry, supported by herbal and mineral notes that add freshness without heaviness. The acidity feels vibrant and cleansing, giving each sip a sense of lift.

Emotionally, Loire rosé appeals to those who enjoy precision over fruitiness, restraint over sweetness, freshness over warmth. It pairs beautifully with light meals, spring vegetables, goat cheese, river fish, salads, and anything herb-driven. It's a wine for the moments when you want something refreshing and honest, crisp, dry, and simple in the best way.

How This Wine Feels

Loire rosé is dry, light in body, and shaped by brisk, lively acidity. The first sip brings bright red fruit such as cranberry, cherry and redcurrant, followed by the unmistakable herbal snap of Cabernet Franc. There is often a hint of green herbs, pepper or a gentle vegetal touch that comes across as clean rather than sharp.

The texture is sleek and light. There is no roundness or sweetness to cushion it, so the wine feels like a clear line drawn across the palate. A swirl lifts fresh aromatics that include crushed herbs, strawberry leaf and white flowers. After the wine leaves the palate, those scents rise again in a quiet echo of citrus peel and redcurrant. The finish is crisp, dry and refreshing, with a mineral clarity that lingers just long enough to spark the appetite.

If You Like This Wine… You May Also Like

Rosé of Pinot Noir

You'll recognise the pale colour, bright acidity, and red-berry delicacy. Pinot-based rosé is generally softer and more floral, while Loire rosé leans more herbal and linear. It offers a gentler, silkier alternative to Loire's crisp edge.

Sangiovese Rosé (Italy)

The connection is in the acidity and cherry-bright profile. Sangiovese rosé is a touch richer and more fruit-forward while remaining firmly dry. Expect a lively, cherry-laced expression that retains Loire's freshness but adds warmth and generosity.

Provence Rosé (France)

Provence shares Loire's dryness and delicacy but trades herbs for citrus, melon, and soft red fruit. Instead of herbal brightness, you get mineral softness and calm Mediterranean tones. It creates a smoother, more tranquil interpretation of the style.

Rosado (Spain)

Rosado keeps the red-fruit core but brings deeper colour, more juiciness, and greater impact. Loire rosé is leaner and more herbal in comparison. Rosado provides a fruitier, more expressive counterpoint.

Vinho Verde Rosé (Portugal)

Light, breezy, and faintly spritzy, Vinho Verde rosé captures the refreshing spirit of Loire but with softer fruit and a gentler structure. It offers an easy, casual, slightly sweeter-fruited approach to crisp rosé.

Stretch Wines

Tavel Rosé (France)

If Loire rosé evokes a cool morning, Tavel feels like late-afternoon warmth—deeper in colour, fuller in texture, and shifting from herbal crispness to savoury weight. It brings more dimension and a stronger sense of presence.

Etna Rosato (Sicily)

Etna Rosato brings a mountain freshness that feels both vivid and serene. Pale red fruit meets a subtle smoky undertone and a fine mineral presence shaped by volcanic soils. The palate is crisp and linear with a sense of altitude that keeps everything lifted. For drinkers who enjoy the clarity and herbal brightness of Loire rosé and wish to explore a style with more tension and a faint volcanic echo, Etna Rosato offers a captivating and quietly dramatic expression.

Light Red Wines (Chilled Gamay, Cabernet Franc, Pinot Noir)

These wines share Loire rosé's acidity, red-fruit profile, and mineral line, with tannin as the main point of departure. For those who enjoy Loire's energy but want to explore reds with similar lift, chilled light reds make an ideal progression.

Assyrtiko Rosé

Uncommon but compelling, these wines combine crisp acidity with volcanic, saline intensity. Compared with Loire rosé, they come across more powerful and more elemental. They offer a bold, adventurous reinterpretation of freshness.

Myths or Misunderstandings

A common misconception is that deeper rosé is sweeter and paler rosé is drier. Loire rosé disproves this completely: it is often very pale *and* one of the driest rosés available. Another myth is that all Loire rosé tastes the same. In truth, Cabernet Franc-based rosés from Chinon, Saumur, Anjou, and Touraine each offer subtle differences in herbaceousness, fruit intensity, and minerality.

Some drinkers assume the herbal notes indicate greenness or underripeness. Those fresh herbal tones are a signature trait of Cabernet Franc, part of its charm, not a flaw.

Closing Reflection

Loire rosé is crispness made elegant. It offers red fruit without heaviness, herbal lift without greenness, and minerality without austerity. It feels like cool water, like fresh air, like the quiet clarity of early summer.

For those drawn to wines that refresh with precision rather than fruitiness, Loire rosé offers one of the most honest and charming expressions in the rosé world. It shows that rosé can be subtle and serious, refreshing and refined, a wine that speaks softly but leaves a lasting impression.

Rosé of Syrah or GSM Rosé

Rosé made from Syrah or classic GSM blends (Grenache, Syrah, Mourvèdre) feels like the meeting point of sun and spice, fuller in colour, richer in texture, and more savoury than many other rosé styles. It pours a deeper shade of pink or pale ruby, and the aromas swirl with Mediterranean warmth: ripe strawberry, raspberry, watermelon rind, cherry, blood orange, rose petals, white pepper, dried thyme, and warm stone. There is a roundness to it, a sense of ripeness tempered by spice and herbs.

Syrah contributes structure, spice, and a darker-fruited edge. Grenache brings warmth, charm, and juicy red fruit. Mourvèdre adds savoury depth, earthiness, and subtle grip. Together, they create rosé with more dimension, a wine that feels both refreshing *and* substantial, capable of pairing with heartier dishes without losing its rosé identity. These blends echo the landscapes where they grow: rocky soils, coastal winds, summer heat, and fields of garrigue herbs.

Why People Love It

People love GSM rosé because it offers true flavour while remaining dry and refreshing. It has more presence than pale rosés but doesn't drift into heaviness. The fruit is ripe but not sweet; the acidity is balanced; the herbal and spicy notes bring savoury intrigue. It's rosé you can drink with food, grilled chicken, charcuterie, roasted vegetables, spicy dishes, or on its own, when you want something with a bit more body.

Emotionally, these rosés appeal to those who want rosé with personality and texture. They are expressive but not overwhelming, structured but still breezy. They suit late lunches, outdoor meals, warm evenings, and any moment where you want rosé that feels a little more grounded.

How This Wine Feels

Rosé of Syrah or GSM is dry, medium in body, and shaped by medium acidity. The first sip arrives with more weight than lighter rosés, showing strawberry, raspberry, cherry and citrus peel layered with gentle spice and herbs. The mid palate feels round, smooth and slightly fuller, a result of Grenache's warmth and Syrah's natural silkiness.

The finish often carries a faint savoury note such as white pepper, dried herbs or a soft impression of earth or stone. A swirl warms and deepens the aromas, bringing more complexity to the fruit and spice. After the wine leaves the palate, those same berry, spice and herbal tones return in a slow, lingering way, a reminder that this style offers depth as well as freshness.

If You Like This Wine... You May Also Like

Tavel Rosé (France)

You'll recognise the fuller body and savoury complexity, but Tavel pushes everything further with deeper colour, firmer structure, greater weight. Compared with GSM rosé, it stands out as the more muscular, concentrated expression of dry rosé.

Rosado (Spain)

Rosado matches the vibrant fruit and deeper hue but usually leans juicier and more overtly fruit-forward. GSM rosés show slightly more savoury and herbal tones. Rosado delivers a brighter, more playful, fruit-driven alternative.

Provence Rosé (France)

Provence offers a paler, more delicate counterpoint. Where GSM rosé feels warm and ripe, Provence is cool, airy, and mineral in style. It provides a lighter, subtler interpretation of dry rosé.

Sangiovese Rosé (Italy)

Both styles show acidity and red-fruit clarity, but Sangiovese rosé is leaner, more cherry-focused, and a bit more herbal.

GSM rosé tends to be rounder and warmer. Sangiovese brings a brisker, crisper edge.

Rosé of Pinot Noir

You'll see a similar sense of refinement but with reduced weight and less spice. Pinot Noir rosé is more delicate, more floral, and more transparent in texture. It offers a softer, gentler take on savoury-leaning rosé.

Stretch Wines

Light Red Grenache (served slightly chilled)

If GSM rosé appeals for its red fruit and savoury warmth, a chilled young Grenache offers added depth while keeping low tannins and generous fruit. It creates a smooth step from rosé toward red wine without adding heaviness.

Beaujolais (Gamay) or Loire Cabernet Franc Reds

These reds share GSM rosé's brightness, acidity, and red-fruit profile but add tannin and more pronounced structure. They make a natural progression for anyone looking to move into red wines with similar energy.

White Rhône Blends (Marsanne or Roussanne)

Though white, these blends echo GSM rosé's savoury warmth and Mediterranean character, shifting the palette toward waxy texture, herbs, and subtle honeyed notes. They offer a full-bodied white that resonates with the same spirit.

Myths or Misunderstandings

A common misconception is that deeper rosé is sweeter. In fact, GSM rosés are nearly always bone dry. Their colour comes from grape variety and brief skin contact, not sugar. Another myth is that structured rosé is "less refreshing." On the contrary, the acidity and herbal tones keep GSM rosé vibrant, its weight simply makes it more food-friendly.

Some assume rosé should always be pale to be high quality. GSM rosé disproves this: deeper colour can signal depth, warmth, and character, not sweetness or low quality.

Closing Reflection

Rosé of Syrah or GSM blends shows how deeply expressive rosé can be. It brings together ripe fruit, savoury herbs, warm spice, and smooth texture, a Mediterranean landscape captured in a glass. It's refreshing but also grounded; bright, but also complex. It suits relaxed meals and late afternoons, offering both comfort and character.

It teaches that rosé doesn't have to be delicate to be beautiful. It can have depth, weight, and soul while remaining fresh and inviting. For those who want rosé with richness and personality, GSM rosé is one of the most compelling expressions.

New World Rosé (South Africa, Australia, USA)

New World rosé carries the bright confidence of sunshine, juicy, expressive, and immediately friendly. The colours range from pale salmon to vibrant coral, depending on the grape variety and style, and the aromas rise easily: strawberry, ripe watermelon, cherry, guava, and sometimes a subtle tropical note. These rosés feel warm and generous, shaped by the open skies and ripening sunlight of coastal California, cool-climate Oregon, the Cape's windswept vineyards, or Australia's sunlit slopes.

What defines New World rosé is its fruit-forward character. While dry, it tends to offer more roundness and juiciness than its Old-World cousins. The flavours are approachable and vivid. The acidity is refreshing but rarely sharp. The texture is smooth, sometimes lightly silky. And beneath the fruit lies the clarity of modern winemaking, clean lines, gentle aromatics, and a comfortable ease that makes these wines perfect for relaxed occasions.

Why People Love It

People love New World rosé because it is joyful and uncomplicated in the best way. The fruit feels open and generous, strawberries, cherries, raspberries, melons, with a refreshing undercurrent that keeps the wine lively. Even the driest versions retain a softness that feels welcoming.

Emotionally, it appeals to drinkers who want wine to feel fun rather than formal. New World rosé suits picnics, barbecues, outdoor meals, poolside afternoons, and easy gatherings. It's the rosé you bring to a party and know it will make people smile. It's the rosé that doesn't demand attention; it simply shares its warmth.

How This Wine Feels

New World rosé is dry, light to medium in body, with medium acidity. The first sip brings juicy red fruit such as strawberry, watermelon and cherry, sometimes joined by subtle citrus or tropical notes depending on the climate and grape variety. It is smoother, rounder and a little more fruit forward than many Old-World styles.

The texture is soft, with a gentle mid palate. A swirl lifts ripe berry and melon aromas. After the wine leaves the palate, those impressions return with a light touch of herbs or citrus. The finish is clean, smooth and refreshing. It does not snap in the way Provence or Loire rosé often does, but instead settles into a relaxed, rounded close that encourages easy drinking.

If You Like This Wine… You May Also Like

Provence Rosé (France)

Shares the dryness and delicate fruit, but Provence shows more citrus, minerality, and finesse, with less ripe fruit and a more restrained profile. It becomes a subtler, more nuanced expression of dry rosé.

Rosado (Spain)

Rosado reflects New World rosé's ripe red fruit but adds deeper colour and greater intensity. It's livelier, fuller, and more expressive—a more robust take on fruit-forward rosé.

Rosé of Pinot Noir (Global)

You'll recognise the strawberry and cherry elements, but Pinot Noir rosé is more floral, higher in acidity, and lighter in frame. It offers a softer, more ethereal interpretation of juicy, fruit-driven rosé.

Grenache Rosé (Global GSM Styles)

Grenache-based rosés keep the red-fruit charm but introduce added warmth and gentle spice, with Syrah or Mourvèdre contributing savoury depth. The result is a more characterful style that still centres on fruit.

Sangiovese Rosé

Sangiovese rosé mirrors the red-cherry brightness but adds higher acidity and subtle herbal notes. Compared with New World rosé, it's crisper and more food-oriented—a familiar flavour profile presented in a slightly more serious, structured way.

Stretch Wines

White Zinfandel (USA)

For drinkers who enjoy fruitiness with a touch of sweetness, White Zinfandel offers soft strawberry and melon flavours with a smooth, easy finish. It stands apart by being off-dry or semi-sweet, giving a gentler, more comforting expression of the same broad appeal.

Tavel Rosé (France)

A notable contrast. Tavel is fuller, deeper, and more savoury, with firm structure and lasting flavour. Compared with New World rosé, it is more complex and food-driven—rosé with genuine depth and presence.

Loire Rosé (Cabernet Franc)

Dry like New World rosé but leaner, cooler, and more herbal. Redcurrant, cranberry, and mineral notes take the lead rather than ripe berries, offering a crisp, refreshing shift from round fruit to bright, herbal lift.

Myths or Misunderstandings

One common misconception is that New World rosé must be sweet. Most modern New World rosés are completely dry; the fruitiness comes from grape variety and warm climate, not sugar. Another myth is that fruit-forward rosé lacks quality. In fact, some of the world's most technically precise rosés come from New World regions, clean, bright, beautifully balanced wines designed for freshness.

Some also believe rosé is "just for summer." Yet, New World rosés pair beautifully with year-round dishes: roast chicken, Asian cuisine, vegetarian meals, grilled salmon, or spiced dishes. Their juicy fruit and gentle acidity make them surprisingly versatile.

Closing Reflection

New World rosé captures sunshine in liquid form. It offers fruit, freshness, and ease without heaviness or complexity. It's a wine that feels warm, open, and joyful, the kind you can serve to anyone, anywhere, and trust it will land well.

It teaches that rosé doesn't need to be austere or pale to be good. It can be generous, fruit-forward, and still beautifully dry. For drinkers who want pleasure above all else, clean, bright, unpretentious pleasure, New World rosé is one of the simplest and most satisfying choices.

---

1. Garrigue: The wild herb, shrub, and resinous scent typical of the Mediterranean landscape.
2. Savoury spice: A warm but non-sweet spice tone that leans herbal or earthy.

Chapter 7
Crisp & Light Bodied Whites
Bright wines defined by energy, lift, and refreshing precision

Chablis

Chablis feels like light made liquid, a wine shaped by clarity, freshness and quiet intensity. Lift the glass and the aromas rise gently, lemon zest, green apple, crushed shells and cool stone, all carried on a fine, pure line that seems to echo the landscape it comes from. Often a surprise to many, Chablis is made from Chardonnay. It rarely behaves like the richer, warmer styles that became famous in California. Here the grape grows in the northern reaches of Burgundy, where cold nights, long seasons and fossil rich limestone soils strip it back to its essential form. The wine that emerges feels transparent, etched with minerality and tension, a Chardonnay that reveals not weight but light.

There is something almost elemental about Chablis. It does not rely on oak for richness, nor on ripe fruit for comfort. Instead, it speaks of the Kimmeridgian soils that once formed the bed of an ancient sea, soils filled with tiny, fossilised shells that lend the wine its unmistakable precision. This geology shapes not just the flavour but the feeling of Chablis. It moves with calm focus, narrow at first, then slowly widening across the palate as delicate citrus notes mingle with hints of white flowers and mineral purity. Chablis unfolds gradually, gaining complexity with time in the glass while maintaining its sense of restraint. It is a wine that rewards attention yet never demands it.

Chablis is for moments when you want a wine that feels clean and purposeful, something that refreshes and enlightens rather than envelops. It is the taste of quiet mornings, bright afternoons and thoughtful evenings, a reminder that Chardonnay can be as much about finesse as about fullness.

Why People Love It

People love Chablis because it offers precision without severity and complexity without heaviness. There is a calm confidence to the wine, a sense of purity that feels refreshing and invigorating. For many, the discovery that Chablis is Chardonnay feels like a small revelation, an invitation to rethink the grape entirely. Its flavours are gentle yet exact, a composition of citrus, orchard fruit and stony freshness that feels both cleansing and compelling. Emotionally, Chablis appeals to those who enjoy wines that speak softly but clearly, wines that feel grounded and honest. It suits oysters and seafood, spring vegetables, simple suppers, early evening conversations and those moments when you want brightness without noise. Chablis feels like a breath taken slowly, a moment of focus in a busy world.

How This Wine Feels

Chablis is dry and lifted, with high acidity that gives the wine its signature line of energy. The first sip feels narrow, almost vertical, before unfolding gently into flavours of citrus, green apple and pear skin. The mid palate remains lean, shaped by cold climate fruit and the unmistakable presence of mineral tension. The texture is smooth but taut, and in the finest examples you may notice a faint sensation of chalk or crushed stone. Some Premier Cru and Grand Cru wines carry subtle richness from time on lees or a whisper of old oak, yet the spine of the wine remains bright and crystalline. The finish lingers with quiet persistence, a soft echo of citrus and stone that feels both refreshing and contemplative. Chablis tastes not only of fruit, but of place, a clarity that endures long after the last sip.

If You Like This Wine... You May Also Like

Muscadet (Loire)

Muscadet offers a similarly crisp and ocean kissed profile, with lemon, cool minerals and a gentle savoury depth from extended lees ageing. It feels slightly softer and more saline than Chablis, moving more quickly across the palate while retaining its sense of purity. For those who love the clean, precise structure of Chablis, Muscadet provides a lighter, maritime expression shaped by Atlantic breezes and coastal soils. It suits the same foods, the same moods and the same desire for refreshment. Where Chablis is poised, Muscadet is breezy, calm and effortlessly drinkable.

Sancerre Blanc (Loire)

Sancerre shares Chablis' clarity and fine acidity, though it speaks in the voice of Sauvignon Blanc rather than Chardonnay. Expect citrus, fresh herbs and a lifted mineral line that gives the wine its edge. The fruit feels cooler and more aromatic, while the structure remains firm and focused. For those who enjoy the tension of Chablis but want more perfume and green brightness, Sancerre offers an elegant, expressive alternative. It feels equally refined, yet it dances with lighter, more agile movement.

Soave (Italy)

Soave brings gentle orchard fruit, almond and subtle floral notes carried on a calm, mineral frame. The acidity is measured rather than piercing, creating a softer, slightly rounder feel than Chablis while maintaining a sense of quiet sophistication. The wine reflects volcanic and limestone soils, offering a composed and unhurried style that appeals to those who love delicacy. For drinkers drawn to Chablis' restraint but wanting something with a tender, more Mediterranean accent, Soave provides a graceful and harmonious companion.

Unoaked Chardonnay (Global)

Many unoaked Chardonnays share Chablis' purity of fruit and clean lines, though they vary widely in expression. Expect bright citrus, apple and pear, supported by fresh acidity and minimal winemaking influence. These wines show the grape's natural character, allowing its structure and freshness to shine. For those who seek the honesty and clarity found in Chablis but with regional variations in fruit and texture, unoaked Chardonnay offers a global journey of subtle differences within a familiar frame.

Albariño (Spain)

Albariño brings a more aromatic profile, with peach skin, citrus blossom and a touch of Atlantic salinity. It is slightly juicier and more floral than Chablis, yet it retains a brisk, refreshing feel. The wine feels lively and coastal, shaped by cool winds and maritime air that infuse it with energy. For those who appreciate the brightness and mineral tension of Chablis but want something with more perfume and fruit driven charm, Albariño provides a vibrant and uplifting choice.

Stretch Wines

Champagne Blanc de Blancs (France)

Blanc de Blancs Champagne deepens the clarity found in Chablis, offering layers of lemon, chalk and warm brioche carried by fine, persistent bubbles. The acidity is sharp yet elegant, the texture creamy, and the flavours unfolding slowly with remarkable precision. This is Chardonnay shaped by long ageing on lees, creating a wine that feels both luminous and profound. For those who love Chablis' purity and want to explore a sparkling expression with greater depth and detail, Blanc de Blancs Champagne offers a more intricate and celebratory interpretation.

Assyrtiko (Santorini)

Assyrtiko magnifies the mineral structure that Chablis hints at, delivering a wine of striking intensity and volcanic tension. Expect flavours of lemon, stone and sea spray, all wrapped in a firm, driving line of acidity that feels both powerful and precise. Assyrtiko is not gentle, yet it is deeply compelling, offering a purity that borders on elemental. For drinkers who enjoy the clarity and tautness of Chablis but want a more forceful and dramatic style, Assyrtiko provides a thrilling ascent into sharper, more sculpted territory.

German Grosses Gewächs Riesling

A dry Riesling at this level offers brilliant acidity, slate driven minerality and citrus that feels electric. The wine moves with finesse, yet it carries an energetic precision that sets it apart from the calm serenity of Chablis. With layers of lime, stone fruit and subtle herbal detail, it reveals its depth slowly and confidently. For those who value the clean architecture of Chablis and wish to explore a white wine with greater verve and aromatic lift, a Grosses Gewächs Riesling offers a beautifully complex and intellectual experience.

Myths or Misunderstandings

One common misunderstanding is that Chablis tastes like other Chardonnays. In truth, Chablis is defined less by the grape and more by the place, the climate and the soil. Another myth is that Chablis is thin or simple, yet even its lightest expressions carry depth and quiet persistence. Some assume that oak is required to create complexity in Chardonnay, but Chablis shows that precision, texture and minerality can be just as expressive. There is also a belief that all Chablis tastes the same, yet the differences between Petit Chablis, Chablis, Premier Cru and Grand Cru are significant, offering varying degrees of richness, detail and dimension.

Closing Reflection

Chablis stands as one of the clearest demonstrations of how a single grape can change entirely in the hands of place. It carries the essence of Chardonnay in its purest, most focused form, shaped by stone, climate and time. To drink Chablis is to experience a kind of quiet intensity, a wine that reveals itself slowly yet leaves a lasting impression. It reminds us that delicacy can be powerful, that simplicity can be profound, and that beauty often lies in the spaces between fruit, acidity and mineral depth. For those who appreciate purity and precision, Chablis remains one of the most enduring pleasures in the world of white wine.

Unoaked Chardonnay

There is something clarifying about a glass of unoaked Chardonnay, a sense of stepping into clean morning light. Without oak, without adornment, the grape reveals its true outline: citrus, orchard fruit, and a quiet mineral thread running beneath. Nothing distracts. Nothing rounds the edges. The wine feels like cool air hitting the skin, or the first sip of water when you're thirsty. It is Chardonnay stripped back to its essentials, showing a calm, understated beauty that many people never realise the grape can offer.

For those who believe they "don't like Chardonnay," this is often the revelation. What they disliked was the richness of *certain oaked styles*, the butter, the toast, the weight, not the grape itself.

Unoaked Chardonnay corrects that misunderstanding gently. It feels pure rather than creamy, linear rather than broad, bright rather than plush. It asks you to notice freshness instead of warmth, tension instead of depth, precision instead of opulence.

Why People Love It

People love unoaked Chardonnay because it offers clarity without sharpness. Its acidity is refreshing but not abrasive; its flavours are clean and honest. You taste lemon, green apple, and white peach, but in a way that feels grounded rather than perfumed. There is a quiet confidence to it, the sense of drinking something simple, but not simplistic.

Emotionally, it suits people who crave ease: uncomplicated meals, sunny afternoons, seafood lunches, lighter moments. The wine slips naturally into these spaces without demanding attention. It's the kind of white wine you can pour for anyone and know it will land gently, without challenge or intensity.

How This Wine Feels

Unoaked Chardonnay is dry, light to medium in body, and driven by bright, mouthwatering acidity. The first sip feels cleansing, with lemon and apple moving briskly across the palate. The fruit leans fresh rather than ripe, a reflection of cool-climate growing or careful restraint in warmer regions.

With no oak to soften the edges, the structure comes entirely from acidity and fruit. The texture feels sleek and almost crystalline[1]. A swirl lifts gentle floral and citrus notes, and once the wine has passed, those same aromas seem to drift back in a light impression of lemon zest, pear skin and a faint chalky[2] touch. The finish is crisp and quick, refreshing the palate and inviting another sip.

If You Like This Wine… You May Also Like

Chablis (France)

You'll recognise the same purity and linear freshness, but Chablis adds a stony, saline edge from its limestone soils. The acidity is usually higher, the fruit more citrus-driven. Compared with unoaked Chardonnay, it feels more structured and mineral. This is an incredibly precise wine that carries freshness into deeper, more serious territory. Chablis also commonly has lees ageing which imparts a nice silky mouth feel and some 'champagne-esque' brioche notes.

Mâcon-Villages (France)

Mâcon wines keep the unoaked clarity of style but bring a touch of warmth: ripe apple, soft peach, a gentler profile. They differ by offering more roundness in the mid-palate. Wrap yourself in comfort and sip a slightly softer and more relaxed version of the freshness you love.

Vinho Verde (Portugal)

Here the kinship is refreshment and simplicity. Vinho Verde is lighter, often with a faint spritz, and leans toward lime and green apple. Compared with unoaked Chardonnay, it's brighter, breezier, and more playful. Revel in the summer energy with this feather-light charming alternative.

Soave (Italy)

Soave mirrors the clean, citrus-and-apple palette but adds delicate almond and herbal notes. It's subtly floral and beautifully understated. Compared with unoaked Chardonnay, Soave is slightly more textural and aromatic. It demonstrates refinement as a wine that stays calm but shows more nuance.

Dry Riesling (Germany, Austria, Australia)

You'll find the same bright acidity and light body, but Riesling sharpens everything. The flavours shift to lime, white peach, and slate; the tension becomes more electric. Compared with unoaked Chardonnay, it's more aromatic and more vertically structured. It has an exhilarating freshness taken to its highest pitch.

Stretch Wines

Muscadet (France)

Muscadet shares unoaked Chardonnay's crispness but pushes it toward austerity. High acidity, salty minerality, and a lean, almost skeletal profile define the style. It's more angular and more oceanic with a sharp purity in its more focused expression of freshness.

Grüner Veltliner (Austria)

Similar in brightness and body, Grüner adds white pepper, herbs, and a savoury edge. It's earthier and slightly more complex than unoaked Chardonnay. It is refreshingly interesting and keeps freshness but brings in texture and spice.

Picpoul de Pinet (France)

Picpoul shares the lemony acidity and refreshing spirit of unoaked Chardonnay, but with a distinctly Mediterranean brightness. It's zesty, citrus-driven, and brisk with lively sunlit form of crispness.

Myths or Misunderstandings

Many people assume Chardonnay must be oaked, buttery, rich, full. Unoaked Chardonnay reveals the truth: the grape itself is clean, mineral, and beautifully structured. The 'butteriness' often associated with Chardonnay comes from stylistic choices like malolactic conversion and oak ageing, not from the grape itself. Another myth: that unoaked Chardonnay is simple. The absence of oak makes it more transparent, showing nuances of site, climate, and vintage far more clearly.

Closing Reflection

Unoaked Chardonnay teaches us to appreciate subtlety. It shows how a wine can feel refreshing without being sharp, how a grape known for richness can reveal a completely different personality in the absence of oak. It is calm, precise, and quietly expressive, a wine that reflects place with clarity and honesty.

For drinkers who value freshness, simplicity, and a sense of ease, unoaked Chardonnay offers one of the purest pleasures in the world of white wine. It reminds us that beauty can be found in restraint, and that sometimes the most revealing wines are the ones with nothing added at all.

Muscadet (Melon de Bourgogne)

Muscadet feels like a tide pulling back from the shore, clean, bracing, and quietly full of life. Lift the glass and the aromas are subtle, almost reticent: lemon zest, green apple, crushed shells[3], cool rainwater. There is nothing showy here. Muscadet speaks in a whisper shaped by the Atlantic winds of France's western edge, where vines grow close to the ocean and the climate gives everything a saline, sea-breeze clarity.

What makes Muscadet remarkable is its restraint. It offers brightness without fruitiness, minerality without weight, refreshment without hesitation. The wine glides across the palate with the straight, narrow focus of a crisp breeze or cold spring water. Some wines refresh by offering fruit; Muscadet refreshes by offering *clean lines*, a wine with nothing extra, nothing added, and nothing that distracts from the purity at its core.

Why People Love It

People love Muscadet because it is the purest form of refreshment. It's the white wine equivalent of eating oysters on a cold day or standing barefoot where the waves meet the sand. The flavours are gentle and restrained, lemon, lime, pear skin, but the sensation is vivid. The acidity is bright enough to wake the palate but not aggressive. The finish is crisp and mineral, clearing the mouth completely.

Emotionally, Muscadet appeals to drinkers who want clarity without ornamentation. It suits simple pleasures: seafood, vegetables, sunshine, quiet moments. It's a wine that fits into life the way salt fits into food, adding lift without ever drawing attention to itself.

How This Wine Feels

Muscadet is bone dry, light in body, and marked by high, firm acidity. The first sip feels quick and exact, almost like a cool blade of lemon moving straight through the palate. The fruit stays subtle and the structure feels taut. Lees ageing is what lends the wine its quiet depth, since time spent on the spent yeast adds a faint creaminess beneath the crisp exterior. It comes across more as a sensation than a flavour, a soft cushion under a sharp edge.

When you swirl the glass, the aromas rise gradually, bringing citrus, white flowers and wet stone. Once the wine leaves the palate, those scents seem to drift upward again, hinting at sea air, green herbs and lime peel. The finish lasts not through richness but through purity, as the acidity leaves the palate so clean that the mineral impression remains. It is a wine that concludes with calm, a cool, lingering clarity.

If You Like This Wine... You May Also Like

Chablis (France)

You'll recognise the same lemony brightness and mineral backbone, but Chablis adds more weight and depth. Its limestone soils create a chalky, savoury edge that Muscadet whispers rather than declares. It brings a richer form of purity, still crisp, yet more serious and structured.

Vinho Verde (Portugal)

The kinship is in refreshment. Vinho Verde is lighter, often gently spritzy, and leans toward lime and green apple. Compared with Muscadet, it feels breezier and more playful. It is effortless summer drinking, crispness with a smile.

Soave (Italy)

Soave shares Muscadet's clean lines and gentle orchard fruit but adds a floral touch and a soft almond note. It differs by feeling slightly rounder and more aromatic with subtle complexity that still shows a similar calmness with a warmer edge.

Picpoul de Pinet (France)

Picpoul matches Muscadet's citrusy energy but brings more sunshine: bright lemon, lime, and a zesty snap. It's less mineral, more Mediterranean. It brings vibrancy, a lively interpretation of the crisp, refreshing style you love.

Albariño (Spain)

If you enjoy Muscadet's ability to pair with seafood, Albariño offers the same affinity with added aromatics and peachy charm. Compared to Muscadet, it's fruitier and softer. Hang out with a friendly more aromatic expression of coastal wine.

Stretch Wines

Dry Riesling (Germany, Austria, Australia)

The structure is similar, high acidity and light body, but Riesling intensifies everything: more aromatics, more tension, more zest. It's sharper and more linear than Muscadet with a crispness taken to a thrilling extreme.

Txakoli (Basque Country Spain)

Txakoli echoes Muscadet's Atlantic freshness but adds a slight spritz and a more pronounced salty edge. It's leaner, more bracing, almost angular. It brings exhilaration and makes your palate sit up straight.

Grüner Veltliner (Austria)

Grüner shares Muscadet's clean structure but swaps citrus for herbs, white pepper, and subtle stone fruit. It's more culinary, more textured with a freshness layered with savoury detail.

Myths or Misunderstandings

A common misconception is that Muscadet is "neutral" or "simple." In fact, its subtlety is deliberate. The grape Melon de

Bourgogne naturally expresses minerality and acidity more than fruitiness. Another myth is that all light whites must be aromatic to be interesting. Muscadet proves the opposite, that purity, texture, and tension can be captivating without intense perfume.

Closing Reflection

Muscadet is a reminder that quiet wines can be deeply expressive. It shows that not all beauty announces itself loudly; some beauty is found in restraint, in simplicity, in the clean interplay of acidity and mineral freshness. It is a wine shaped by wind, water, and stone, the Atlantic translated into liquid form.

For drinkers drawn to clarity and calm refreshment, Muscadet offers one of the purest experiences in the world of white wine. It invites you to slow down and savour the elegance of understatement.

Vinho Verde

Vinho Verde feels like the first cool breeze on a warm day, gentle, refreshing, and instantly uplifting. Pour a glass and you'll notice how pale it is, almost mist-like, with aromas that rise softly: lime peel, green apple, crushed leaves, and a faint floral whisper. Sometimes there's a slight spritz, not bubbles, just a light prickle that makes the wine feel even fresher, like a splash of cold mineral water. It's the taste of northern Portugal's green, rain-washed landscapes translated into something bright and effortless.

Part of Vinho Verde's charm is how unpretentious it is. It doesn't try to impress with complexity or power. Instead, it offers the simple pleasure of refreshment, the kind that feels both casual and strangely irresistible. You don't think too hard about it; you just enjoy the way it cools the palate and lifts the mood. It's a wine that belongs as much to afternoons by the sea as to quiet evenings at home, a wine that says: relax, take another sip.

Why People Love It

People love Vinho Verde because it's joyful. Light, zesty, faintly fizzy, and low in alcohol, it feels as easy as conversation on a sunny patio. The flavours, lime, green apple, gentle white fruit, are bright but not sharp. The acidity feels like a clean rush, the spritz adds playfulness, and the low alcohol keeps everything light on its feet.

Emotionally, it appeals to anyone who wants wine to feel refreshing, uncomplicated, and fun. It's perfect for warm days, simple meals, long afternoons, or any moment when "light and lively" feels just right. Vinho Verde is the white wine equivalent of a smile, bright, friendly, and infectious.

How This Wine Feels

Vinho Verde is dry or off-dry, light in body, and driven by crisp, refreshing acidity. The first sip is brisk and citrus-led, often lifted by a faint prickle of carbonation that gives the fruit extra brightness and energy. The flavours move quickly across the palate, showing lime, lemon zest, green apple and, at times, a hint of melon or soft herbs.

The texture stays smooth but lively, never heavy or broad. A gentle swirl releases light floral and citrus notes, and once the wine has passed, those same scents return as a soft whisper of lime peel and green fruit before fading cleanly. The finish is short, bright and refreshing, much like a small wave gliding up the shoreline and then slipping back again.

If You Like This Wine... You May Also Like

Albariño (Spain)

The kinship is unmistakable: Atlantic freshness, citrus-bright acidity, and the same seafood-ready lift. Albariño simply turns up the aroma dial with hints of peach, apricot skin, soft florals and carries more mid-palate texture. It feels like a familiar coastal style given extra depth and expressiveness.

Soave (Italy)

Soave matches Vinho Verde's ease and citrus charm, but layers in pear, almond, and a gentle herbal note. It's rounder, calmer, and slightly more aromatic. If Vinho Verde offers quiet brightness, Soave provides that same calm with added nuance and softness.

Pinot Grigio (Italy)

The link here is purity and lightness. Pinot Grigio is just as clean and refreshing, though typically without the spritz. Expect lemon, apple, and delicate white flowers in a smooth, unfussy frame. It reads as a still, streamlined interpretation of Vinho Verde's breezy character.

Picpoul de Pinet (France)

Picpoul mirrors Vinho Verde's citrus-driven profile but adds Mediterranean verve with sharper lemon-lime tones, more zest, more drive. It's a touch more forceful. For anyone who enjoys Vinho Verde's brightness but craves extra vibrancy, Picpoul pushes that freshness into a livelier register.

Muscadet (France)

You'll find the same linear, refreshing acidity, but Muscadet is more mineral, more saline, more tidal in feel. It's a leaner and more serious form of crispness. Freshness becomes more focused, more chiselled, offering a sharper sense of definition.

Stretch Wines

Dry Riesling (Germany, Austria, Australia)

Riesling amplifies acidity, aromatics, and precision. It trades lime spritz for taut lime structure and digs deeper into mineral tension. Freshness becomes more electric, delivering a more charged, high-definition experience.

Txakoli (Basque Country, Spain)

Txakoli shares Vinho Verde's light frame and bright acidity but pushes the spritz and coastal salinity further. It's brisker, more cutting, almost architectural in its angles. Think of Vinho Verde reshaped into a colder, sharper ocean splash.

Grüner Veltliner (Austria)

Grüner offers similar refreshment yet adds white pepper, herbs, and a savoury twist. It's more layered, more tactile, and invites closer attention. Crispness remains, but with added dimension that unfolds as you taste.

Myths or Misunderstandings

Many assume Vinho Verde is sweet or "simple," but most high-quality examples are fully dry. Its fruitiness and low alcohol can give a gentle softness that is often misread as sweetness. Another misconception is that the spritz is artificial. It often results from a touch of captured fermentation CO_2, a natural by-product that enhances freshness.

Closing Reflection

Vinho Verde reminds us that wine can feel like movement. It is light on its feet, bright with possibility, shaped more by freshness than by weight. It offers a kind of quiet joy: a splash of coolness on a warm day, a lift of energy when the moment feels slow. Nothing about it insists. Nothing demands contemplation. It simply refreshes, brightens, and opens the palate to the ease of living.

It teaches that simplicity can be beautiful, that softness can be invigorating, and that sometimes the most memorable wines are the ones that feel like a breeze: gentle, fleeting, and unmistakably alive.

Soave

Soave feels like sunlight reflected off pale stone, gentle, warm, and quietly luminous. Lift the glass and the aromas drift up softly: white peach, lemon peel, almond blossom, a touch of fresh herbs. Nothing is loud. Nothing is sharp. Soave's beauty lies in its subtlety, the kind that reveals itself slowly as you pay attention. It feels serene, almost meditative, shaped by the volcanic and limestone soils of the Veneto hills, where the Garganega grape ripens with a calm, understated elegance.

What makes Soave compelling is its balance. It's crisp, but not angular. Fruity, but not sweet. Aromatic, but not showy. It has a clean, clear profile that reads as refreshing, yet its gentle texture and almond-like finishing note give it quiet depth. It's the kind of wine that feels woven together rather than constructed, a seamless interplay of citrus, orchard fruit, minerality, and soft herbs.

Why People Love It

People love Soave because it delivers freshness with nuance. The acidity is smooth and integrated, creating brightness without bite. The fruit is delicate, pear, lemon, white peach, framed by a faint creaminess and that signature bitter-almond flicker on the finish. It's refreshing, but it also feels complete.

Emotionally, Soave appeals to people who value subtlety. It suits peaceful meals, warm evenings, relaxed conversations, and dishes where harmony matters more than intensity: seafood pastas, grilled vegetables, risotto, salads with herbs and citrus. It's a wine that blends into life gracefully, adding a quiet shine without demanding attention.

How This Wine Feels

Soave is dry, light to medium in body, with medium acidity. The first sip feels gentle, a clear line of citrus and pear supported by a clean mineral thread. Rather than leaning on acidity alone for structure, Soave comes together through the balance of fruit, texture and minerality, creating a quiet sense of cohesion.

A swirl brings up subtle floral and herbal notes. Once the wine leaves the palate, those same impressions seem to rise again, offering hints of lemon zest, almond skin and fresh white peach before settling into a dry, slightly savoury finish. That almond note, always delicate and never intrusive, is one of Soave's signatures, adding a layer of refinement to its calm, composed profile.

If You Like This Wine... You May Also Like

Pinot Grigio (Italy)

You'll recognise the same easy-going freshness and clear citrus-pear profile. Pinot Grigio is lighter, simpler, and offers less texture, while Soave brings greater nuance, minerality, and depth. It becomes a more refined option for anyone who enjoys crisp whites but wants extra detail and subtlety.

Vinho Verde (Portugal)

The link is lightness and easy drinkability. Vinho Verde is brighter, more lime-driven, and often spritzed, while Soave leans toward smoother acidity and a softer palate. It delivers a calmer, more measured Italian expression of freshness.

Albariño (Spain)

Albariño shares Soave's balance of fruit and freshness but introduces more aromatics with peach skin, florals, citrus blossom. It feels rounder and juicier. Think of it as a familiar structure carried into a more expressive, fruit-forward register.

Gavi (Cortese Italy)

Gavi mirrors Soave's citrus-and-pear notes but adds a sharper mineral line and a gentle herbal lift. It's leaner, cooler, and more angular. For anyone who enjoys Soave's clarity yet wants increased tension, Gavi provides a beautifully precise, high-definition alternative.

Chenin Blanc (Loire Valley, dry styles)

Dry Chenin shares Soave's orchard fruit, herbal edges, and understated complexity, but with firmer acidity and more textural drive. It feels tighter and more energetic. Freshness widens into something deeper and more layered.

Stretch Wines

Muscadet (France)

You'll encounter the same citrus-led clarity, but Muscadet moves into sharper, more saline territory. It's leaner, higher in acidity, and strongly mineral. Here, crispness becomes more austere and oceanic in style.

Grüner Veltliner (Austria)

Grüner offers both crispness and complexity, bringing white pepper, herbs, and subtle stone fruit. Compared with Soave, it's spicier and slightly more assertive. It adds a savoury twist that keeps the freshness but deepens the interest.

Assyrtiko (Greece)

Assyrtiko shares Soave's minerality yet amplifies it into something saltier, more volcanic, more structured. It's intense and gripping. Choosing Assyrtiko means stepping into a bolder, more radiant form of mineral-driven white wine.

Myths or Misunderstandings

Many assume that Soave, like Pinot Grigio, is simple or neutral, a reputation shaped by years of inexpensive bottlings that overshadowed higher quality examples. Good Soave (especially Soave Classico from hillside vineyards) is one of Italy's most refined white wines. Another misconception is that Soave must be floral. While floral notes appear in some styles, classic Soave is defined more by minerality and orchard fruit.

Closing Reflection

Soave is a reminder that freshness can be gentle. It shows how delicacy, when well-structured, can be deeply satisfying. Its flavours flow softly, its texture glides, and its finish lingers with a savoury, almond-like whisper. It is a wine that seems to breathe slowly, a quiet companion to peaceful meals and warm, unhurried evenings.

It teaches that subtlety is not weakness, that nuance can be deeply rewarding, and that some wines shine brightest when they do not need to shine loudly. For those who enjoy calm refinement in their glass, Soave offers one of the most enduring pleasures in the world of crisp white wines.

Riesling (Dry Styles)

Dry Riesling enters like a clean, bright line of light, vivid, focused, and unmistakably alive. Bring the glass to your nose and the aromas feel crisp and lifted: lime zest, green apple, white peach, sometimes even a hint of jasmine or crushed slate. There is a kind of tension running through the wine, a tautness that feels almost architectural. Nothing is blurred. Nothing is soft. Every detail stands clear.

What makes dry Riesling so compelling is its purity. It doesn't sidestep acidity, it embraces it. But the acidity doesn't feel aggressive; it feels precise, like the sharpened edge of a well-honed tool. Beneath the citrus and orchard fruit lies a deeper sensation, a mineral hum shaped by the soils and stones that surround Riesling's vines. It's a wine that carries place with startling clarity, as if the landscape itself had been distilled into flavour.

Why People Love It

People love dry Riesling because it feels vibrant and refreshing in a way few wines can match. The acidity is bright and invigorating, lifting the fruit and giving the wine its signature snap. The flavours, lime, green apple, white peach, sometimes a hint of nectarine, are crisp and clean. And the mineral undertone adds depth without weight.

Emotionally, dry Riesling appeals to those who love energy in their glass. It's ideal for warm days, spicy food, seafood, or any moment that calls for brightness. For drinkers who seek precision, clarity, and a sense of motion in wine, few styles are more satisfying. It's a wine that wakes you up a little.

How This Wine Feels

Dry Riesling is immediately crisp. It is dry, light in body, and charged with high, crackling acidity. The first sip races across the palate, showing bright lime, green apple and stone fruit wrapped around a firm mineral core. It feels clean yet intense, like a citrus tone that seems to shine from within.

Riesling is also defined by its movement. Rather than spreading broadly, it seems to rise and cut upward, creating a sense of lift rather than breadth. A swirl brings citrus oil and stony aromatics into focus. After the wine leaves the palate, those scents gather again, offering impressions of lime, peach skin and slate. Despite its delicacy, the finish can be remarkably long, carrying mineral notes long after the fruit has slipped away.

If You Like This Wine... You May Also Like

Austrian Grüner Veltliner

You'll recognise the same freshness and taut acidity, yet Grüner adds white pepper, herbs, and a subtle savoury edge. Compared with Riesling, it's less citrus-led and more culinary in character. It offers a crisp white that stays lively while weaving in gentle spice and complexity.

Muscadet (France)

Muscadet echoes Riesling's dryness and mineral backbone but leans toward green apple, lemon, and salty edges rather than lime and peach. It's leaner, quieter, and distinctly oceanic. Expect a razor-clean alternative that centres purity and precise mineral focus.

Vinho Verde (Portugal)

The connection is lightness and energy. Vinho Verde is softer, lower in alcohol, and often carries a faint spritz. Next to Riesling, it's simpler and breezier. It works as an easy, uncomplicated companion for the same refreshing occasions.

Chablis (France)

You'll find the same linear precision and citrus–mineral tension, though Chablis, built on Chardonnay, offers gentler aromatics and a chalkier feel. It leans more savoury than overtly fruity. Think of it as a calmer, more composed expression of that same restrained style.

Soave (Italy)

Soave aligns with Riesling in elegance and citrus lift but brings a smoother, rounder profile with hints of almond and white peach.

It's gentler and less pointed. Crispness becomes softer and more meditative.

Stretch Wines

Alsace Riesling (Rich Dry Styles)

Still dry but carrying more texture and weight than German or Australian expressions. The fruit moves toward ripe peach, baked apple, and subtle florals. Compared with taut dry Riesling, it feels fuller and more enveloping. You get intensity and concentration without sweetness and a sense of richness that doesn't feel heavy.

Sauvignon Blanc (Sancerre or New Zealand)

You'll notice the shared acidity and lift, but Sauvignon Blanc speaks in herbs, grass, and gooseberry rather than stone fruit and citrus. It's greener, more pungent, and more overtly aromatic. Freshness shows up here with a completely different accent and attitude.

Assyrtiko (Greece)

Assyrtiko matches Riesling's intensity but drives the minerality into bolder, volcanic territory. The acidity is similarly high, yet the texture feels firmer and more commanding. It offers a striking, high-impact take on crispness, pushing the style toward the dramatic.

Myths or Misunderstandings

One persistent myth is that *all* Riesling is sweet. Many of the world's great Rieslings are fully dry, especially from Austria, Alsace, and Australia's Clare and Eden Valleys. The grape's aromatic lift and ripe fruit can create the impression of sweetness even when none is present.

Another misunderstanding is that high acidity means harshness. Riesling shows how acidity can feel electric rather than abrasive, a source of precision, length, and purity.

Closing Reflection

Dry Riesling is a reminder that clarity can be thrilling. It's a wine of angles and brightness, of citrus and stone, of energy held in perfect balance. It refreshes, invigorates, and sharpens the senses without ever feeling thin. It is both delicate and powerful, both simple and complex, a wine that rewards attention but also delights in its immediacy.

For those who love wines that move, wines that feel alive, wines that sparkle with detail, dry Riesling may be one of the most compelling expressions in the world of crisp whites.

Txakoli

Txakoli tastes like wind off the Atlantic, brisk, salty, and alive with tension. Pour it into the glass and it often shows a faint spritz, tiny bubbles tracing the surface like sea foam. The aromas are clean and sharp: lime peel, green apple, fresh herbs, wet stone. Nothing is soft, nothing is round; everything is taut and bright. It feels like the coastline distilled, the cliffs, the waves, the cold spray carried inland by the wind.

The Basque Country in Northern Spain shapes this wine with its rugged geography and maritime climate. Grapes grow on steep slopes overlooking the ocean, where cool temperatures and constant breezes preserve acidity and keep the wines lean and vivid. The result is a white wine that feels spare but thrilling, about purity, not fruit richness; about cut, not comfort.

Why People Love It

People love Txakoli because it is invigorating. It tastes like motion, quick, crisp, tangy. The acidity snaps across the palate, waking up the senses. The slight spritz adds lift and playfulness, like a squeeze of lemon on shellfish or a cold wave rushing over your feet. The flavours are simple but compelling: lime, green citrus, tart apple, slight salinity.

Emotionally, it appeals to those who crave freshness with an edge. It suits seafood, sunshine, lively gatherings, and moments when you want a wine that energises rather than relaxes. Txakoli is a wine that doesn't sit still, it brightens the moment, sharpens the mood, and feels unmistakably coastal.

How This Wine Feels

Txakoli is bone dry, very light in body, and driven by high, bracing acidity. The first sip moves fast, carrying lime and green apple sharpened by the wine's natural spritz. That faint tingle heightens the acidity and makes the fruit feel even brighter.

The texture is lean and taut, with no rounding from oak or residual sugar. A swirl lifts aromas shaped by tension rather than softness: citrus oil, herbs, a hint of sea spray. After the wine leaves the palate, those impressions rise again in a cool mineral note, like stone touched by ocean water. The finish is short and razor clean, leaving the palate refreshed and fully awake.

If You Like This Wine... You May Also Like

Vinho Verde (Portugal)

The connection is immediate: spritz, lime-bright acidity, and effortless refreshment. Vinho Verde is softer and gentler, with a mild sweetness at the edges, while Txakoli carries more sharpness and salinity. It offers a familiar feel, just lifted into a crisper, more tense register.

Muscadet (France)

Muscadet reflects Txakoli's dryness and mineral spine but trades the spritz for a savoury, lees-shaped texture. It stays equally crisp, just less tangy. Expect a quieter, more maritime take on the same coastal character.

Albariño (Spain)

The shared Atlantic imprint is clear with a refreshing citrus lift and bright acidity. Yet Albariño folds in peach, floral tones, and a rounder feel. It's more aromatic and more giving. Think of it as a friendlier, fruit-forward counterpoint to Txakoli's sharper edges.

Pinot Grigio (Lean Style)

Pinot Grigio keeps the brightness and straightforward appeal but lacks Txakoli's spritz and salinity. It's more neutral and more adaptable, offering refreshment with a gentler, less angular profile.

Dry Riesling (Germany, Austria, Australia)

Riesling shares Grüner's acidity and focus but expresses it through lime, slate, and sharper tension. Compared with Grüner, it's more aromatic and vertically structured. The payoff is electricity- a more high-toned, mineral-driven form of freshness.

Soave (Italy)

Soave mirrors Grüner's gentle orchard fruit and herbal lift but replaces pepper with almond and soft citrus. It's smoother and slightly less savoury. Linger in its calm freshness with a tender edge rather than a spicy one.

Muscadet (France)

Both wines offer crispness and mineral clarity, but Muscadet shifts toward lemon, salinity, and oceanic purity. Compared to Grüner's herbal complexity, Muscadet is leaner and more austere. Appreciate the purity of a spare, refreshing contrast.

Txakoli (Spain)

Txakoli echoes Grüner's citrus and snap, but adds spritz, stronger salinity, and more angular acidity. If you enjoy Grüner's brightness but want something sharper, this is a thrilling next step. The payoff is exhilaration.

Vinho Verde (Portugal)

The kinship is refreshing simplicity. Vinho Verde is lighter and fruitier, with spritz and easy drinkability. Grüner is more structured and savoury. Indulge in a breezier, more casual alternative.

Stretch Wines

Assyrtiko (Santorini Greece)

Assyrtiko shares Grüner's tension and minerality but turns the volume up. It's more intense, more powerful, more volcanic. Enjoy and contrast freshness expressed through force and structure rather than herbs and spice.

Sauvignon Blanc (Sancerre or New Zealand)

Sauvignon Blanc offers similar brightness but with a much greener aromatic profile- grass, gooseberry, passionfruit. It's more pungent and more aromatic with a stylistic leap into expressive, high-energy aromatics.

Verdejo (Spain)

Verdejo mirrors Grüner's herbal character but adds fennel, melon, and a soft almond finish. It's rounder and slightly more aromatic revealing a Mediterranean interpretation of herbal freshness.

Stretch Wines

Assyrtiko (Santorini Greece)

Assyrtiko matches Txakoli's citrus cut and intense minerality yet pushes everything further. It's larger in scale, more forceful, and more volcanic in tone; almost as if Txakoli's sharpness had been reinforced. It delivers a dramatic, high-impact version of mineral-driven tension.

Chablis (France)

Chablis shares the clean lines and saline accents but introduces greater depth and chalky detail. Compared with Txakoli, it feels calmer, more grounded, and more layered. It offers sophistication without stiffness, presenting crispness in a more mature, composed form.

Grüner Veltliner (Austria)

Grüner brings comparable acidity but adds white pepper, herbs, and restrained stone fruit. It's more textural and slightly more gastronomic. Expect a fresh style that encourages exploration and nuance rather than adrenaline.

Myths or Misunderstandings

A common misunderstanding is that Txakoli's spritz is artificial. It is usually a natural by-product of cool fermentation, left intentionally to preserve freshness. Another myth: that sharp acidity means poor ripeness. Txakoli's high acidity is not a flaw, it is the heart of its identity, shaped by the Basque climate. Its leanness is deliberate, not accidental.

Closing Reflection

Txakoli is a wine of motion, wind, waves, salt, citrus, and tension. It doesn't seek richness or complexity; it seeks clarity. It captures the feeling of standing on a cliff above the Atlantic, where the air is cold and full of salt, and everything feels vivid and immediate.

For those who love wines that refresh with force, wines that wake the palate and brighten the moment, Txakoli offers one of the

Grüner Veltliner

Grüner Veltliner feels like a cool breeze running through a garden- fresh, herbal, and quietly invigorating. Bring the glass to your nose and its personality emerges gently but distinctly: lime, green apple, white pepper, fresh herbs, and a faint hint of wet stone. It carries a sort of understated confidence, the kind that doesn't need bold fruit or loud perfume to make itself known. Instead, Grüner's charm lies in its sensation of freshness built on subtle complexity.

There is a natural ease to the wine. It's crisp without being sharp, aromatic without being floral, and textured without being heavy. The flavours seem to unfold in small, precise layers. At its best, Grüner feels like clean air moving across a bright landscape. It's refreshing, grounded, and unmistakably central European in character- shaped by the cool nights and warm days of Austria's vineyards.

Why People Love It

People love Grüner Veltliner because it offers refreshment with intellect. It's not showy, but it's detailed. The acidity is bright but not aggressive; the flavours are subtle but intriguing. You get citrus and green fruit, but also herbs, and a gentle peppery note that gives the wine a distinctive edge- like a small spark of energy flickering across the palate.

Emotionally, it appeals to people who want a white wine that's both easy to drink and interesting. Grüner is perfect with food- especially vegetables, herbs, white meats, and anything with a bit of spice. It's a wine that feels grounded in the natural world: crisp, clean, and quietly expressive.

How This Wine Feels

Grüner Veltliner is dry, light to medium in body, and carried by high, refreshing acidity. The first sip feels brisk and pure, with lime, green apple and stone fruit moving through a bright, lively frame. A defining feature is its gentle peppery, herbal note, a subtle savoury line that threads through the fruit and gives the wine a clear sense of shape.

The texture is smooth yet firm, sometimes showing a faint creaminess from lees contact. A swirl brings forward citrus oil, herbs and a soft hint of white pepper. Once the wine leaves the palate, those impressions return in a lift of lime zest, green herbs and a lightly mineral sensation, something reminiscent of cool stones after rain. The finish is crisp and refreshing, and it leaves a delicate herbal trace that lingers quietly.

If You Like This Wine... You May Also Like

Dry Riesling (Germany, Austria, Australia)

Riesling shares Grüner's acidity and precision but channels it through lime, slate, and a sharper, more vertical tension. It's more aromatic and more tightly focused. Freshness shows up here as electricity—a high-toned, mineral-charged expression.

Soave (Italy)

Soave reflects Grüner's orchard fruit and gentle herbal lift but trades pepper for almond and soft citrus. It's smoother, calmer, and less savoury. Expect a quieter kind of freshness, shaped by tenderness rather than spice.

Picpoul de Pinet (Languedoc France)

Picpoul de Pinet offers the same clean lines and citrus brightness found in Grüner Veltliner, but its expression feels softer and more coastal. Lemon and green apple sit beside a gentle saline note, creating a refreshing profile that feels effortless and quietly charming. The palate is brisk without sharpness and finishes with a calm, mineral clarity. For drinkers who enjoy the crisp precision of Grüner and wish to explore a sunnier, more Mediterranean interpretation of freshness, Picpoul de Pinet provides an inviting parallel.

Vermentino (Italy and Corsica)

Vermentino feels like sunlight carried on a sea breeze. The fruit is citrus led with hints of soft herbs and pale stone, and the palate has a gentle salt edged freshness that lingers without intensity. Its texture is smooth but never heavy, creating a sense of ease and brightness. For drinkers who appreciate the clean lines and lively movement of Grüner Veltliner but want to explore a style shaped by coastal warmth and Mediterranean charm, Vermentino offers a joyful and quietly refreshing alternative.

Muscadet (France)

Both wines offer crispness and mineral clarity, yet Muscadet leans into lemon, salinity, and an ocean-washed purity. It's leaner and more austere than Grüner's herbal complexity. Enjoy a pared-back, refreshing contrast built on restraint.

Txakoli (Spain)

Txakoli shares Grüner's citrus snap but adds spritz, stronger salinity, and sharper acidity. For drinkers who enjoy Grüner's brightness but want something edgier, this pushes the style into a more thrilling register.

Vinho Verde (Portugal)

The link is easy, refreshing simplicity. Vinho Verde is lighter and fruitier, often spritzed, and very casual in feel. Grüner offers more structure and savoury nuance. Choose Vinho Verde when you want breezy, uncomplicated drinking.

Stretch Wines

Assyrtiko (Santorini Greece)

Assyrtiko matches Grüner's tension and minerality but drives both harder. It's more intense, more powerful, and distinctly volcanic. Freshness appears here with force and architecture rather than herbs and spice.

Sauvignon Blanc (Sancerre or New Zealand)

Sauvignon Blanc shares the bright lift but introduces a greener aromatic spectrum—grass, gooseberry, passionfruit. It's more pungent and far more overt. Think of it as a leap toward vivid, high-energy aromatics.

Verdejo (Spain)

Verdejo mirrors Grüner's herbal streak yet adds fennel, melon, and a soft almond note. It's rounder and slightly more aromatic, giving a Mediterranean spin on herbal freshness.

Myths or Misunderstandings

Many people assume Grüner Veltliner is obscure or difficult because of its Austrian origins and savoury profile. It is one of the most versatile and accessible white wines in the world- both easy to drink and brilliant with food. Another myth: that the "peppery" note indicates spiciness or heat. In fact, it's simply an aromatic compound that gives complexity, not heat.

Closing Reflection

Grüner Veltliner proves that crisp white wine can be both refreshing and subtly profound. It offers the brightness of citrus and green fruit, the savouriness of herbs and white pepper, and a clean mineral finish that feels honest and grounded. It doesn't need boldness or opulence to express itself; its beauty lies in its quiet detail.

For those who love freshness but want something a little more thoughtful- a wine that feels alive but also composed- Grüner Veltliner is one of the most rewarding choices in the world of light-bodied whites.

Picpoul de Pinet

Picpoul de Pinet tastes like sunlight dancing on water, bright, clear, and effortlessly refreshing. Bring the glass close, and the aromatics are clean and inviting with lemon, lime zest, green apple, and a faint whisper of white flowers. Beneath that freshness sits a subtle saline note, as if someone had dragged a finger dipped in seawater across the surface of the wine. It is crisp white wine at its most joyful, simple in the best way, vibrant without being sharp.

Picpoul is grown along the Mediterranean coast of southern France, where warm days and cool breezes shape a style that feels both sunny and snappy. The grape's name translates loosely as "lip-stinger," a nod to the bright, zesty acidity that gives the wine its signature lift. Yet the acidity isn't harsh; it's lively, like citrus squeezed over chilled oysters. Picpoul is a wine that shines in warm weather, next to seafood, or in any moment that calls for bright, uncomplicated pleasure.

Why People Love It

People love Picpoul de Pinet because it feels instantly refreshing. The acidity is crisp and lively but balanced by a soft roundness beneath. The flavours are citrus-driven without being sour, and the saline undertone keeps everything feeling light, breezy, and coastal. It's the kind of wine that makes you want to take another sip before you've even set the glass down.

Emotionally, Picpoul appeals to drinkers who want brightness without intensity, something zesty, but not aggressive; simple, but not dull. It's perfect for seafood, summer afternoons, outdoor meals, and everyday moments that need a lift. It's a wine that feels like a little beam of sunshine.

How This Wine Feels

Picpoul is dry, light in body, and marked by medium-plus acidity that strikes the palate right away. The first sip delivers a sharp burst of lemon and lime, followed by a smooth, almost juicy middle that softens the acidity just enough to keep everything in balance.

The texture stays clean and streamlined. There is no oak, no added richness, nothing to distract from the bright fruit and refreshing structure. A gentle swirl lifts soft floral and citrus notes, and once the wine moves off the palate, those same impressions return in hints of citrus peel, green apple and a light mineral-saline suggestion. The finish is short but lively, a quick snap of citrus that leaves the palate tingling and ready for another sip.

If You Like This Wine... You May Also Like

Vinho Verde (Portugal)

You'll recognise the same lime-bright lift and light-bodied refreshment. Vinho Verde brings a faint spritz and a softer, more playful fruit profile. It becomes a breezier, more relaxed take on Picpoul's zesty character.

Txakoli (Basque Country Spain)

Txakoli echoes Picpoul's citrus snap and salty edge but adds extra tension and a more prominent spritz. It's leaner, more angular, and more bracing. Expect a sharper, more coastal interpretation of the style.

Muscadet (France)

The link is crispness and minerality. Muscadet leans away from citrus and toward salinity, with a leaner frame and a touch more austerity. If you enjoy Picpoul's clean finish, this offers a more serious, ocean-washed expression.

Soave (Italy)

Soave shares Picpoul's gentle orchard fruit and easy drinkability but replaces bright citrus with almond, soft herbs, and a rounder feel. It's calmer and more floral, giving a soothing, elegant alternative to Picpoul's vibrancy.

Unoaked Chardonnay

Unoaked Chardonnay brings similar clean lines but with slightly more texture and width. It swaps Picpoul's citrus spark for apples, pears, and quiet minerality. Think of it as familiar freshness delivered in a softer, more polished frame.

Stretch Wines

Dry Riesling

Riesling heightens Picpoul's citrus profile and acidity while adding aromatic lift and mineral tension. It's sharper, more expressive, and more structured. This is crispness turned up to high definition.

Assyrtiko (Greece)

Assyrtiko takes Picpoul's lemony snap and transforms it into something bolder, saltier, and more volcanic. Coastal freshness becomes raw intensity, offering a deeper, more commanding form of acidity and minerality.

Grüner Veltliner

Grüner matches Picpoul's brightness but introduces herbs, pepper, and subtle savouriness. It's more complex, more textural, and nudges the style into deeper layers while staying firmly in the refreshing camp.

Myths or Misunderstandings

A common misconception is that Picpoul de Pinet is "just a simple patio wine." While it is light-hearted and accessible, well-made Picpoul has surprising finesse, a balance of crisp citrus, soft texture, and subtle minerality. Another myth is that its acidity will be harsh. In truth, Picpoul's acidity is lively but rounded; bright enough to refresh, gentle enough to stay friendly.

Closing Reflection

Picpoul de Pinet captures the spirit of the Mediterranean coast, bright, breezy, uncomplicated in the best way. It's crisp without being sharp, sunny without being sweet, lively without being loud. It refreshes, lifts, and invites another sip.

For those who want a white wine that feels like a small, joyful burst of citrus and light, Picpoul offers one of the most effortlessly pleasurable experiences in the world of crisp whites. It reminds us that wine doesn't need complexity to charm, sometimes all it needs is honesty, brightness, and a little bit of sunshine.

Verdicchio

Verdicchio feels like cool shade on a warm afternoon, refreshing, calm, and quietly intricate. Lift the glass and the aromas drift up in soft, measured waves: lemon peel, green apple, wild herbs, almond skin, sometimes a hint of white peach. Nothing is flashy. Nothing is hurried. Verdicchio is a wine that rewards attention but doesn't demand it, carrying itself with the poised restraint that defines so many of Italy's finest whites.

What sets Verdicchio apart is its elegance. The fruit is crisp, the acidity bright, yet there's a subtle depth beneath the surface, a gentle creaminess, a faintly oily texture, a bitter-almond twist at the finish. These details give the wine dimension without weight. It's the kind of complexity that feels natural, not constructed, shaped more by hillside vineyards and ancient soils than by the hand of the winemaker.

Why People Love It

People love Verdicchio because it strikes a rare balance: refreshing yet textured, bright yet layered, clean yet quietly expressive. It offers citrus clarity without sharpness, orchard fruit without sweetness, herbal lift without greenness. And that signature almond note on the finish, a whisper of bitterness, adds sophistication that keeps the wine from ever feeling simple.

Emotionally, Verdicchio appeals to drinkers who enjoy subtlety with a little surprise. It's a wine for slow meals: seafood, risotto, grilled vegetables, delicate pastas, or anything with herbs and lemon. It suits the rhythm of Mediterranean cooking, unhurried, harmonious, and designed to be enjoyed in good company.

How This Wine Feels

Verdicchio is dry, with bright, firm acidity that gives the wine its clean, lifted shape. The first sip comes across clean and citrus-led, with lemon, lime and green apple at the forefront, yet it quickly shows more texture than you might expect. The middle of the palate softens just slightly, bringing in pear, fennel and a hint of almond.

Texture is one of Verdicchio's quiet signatures. It feels smooth and lightly viscous, almost like water moving slowly across stone. A gentle swirl lifts floral and herbal notes, along with citrus peel, almond skin and a faint mineral accent. The finish is crisp and subtly savoury, refreshing yet carrying a thoughtful, lingering complexity.

If You Like This Wine... You May Also Like

Soave (Italy)

You'll recognise the same calm citrus notes and gentle herbal lift. Soave is slightly rounder and softer, showing more peach and almond blossom with less herbal depth. It offers a serene, smoother, more floral take on Verdicchio's crisp elegance.

Pinot Grigio (Italy)

The connection lies in freshness and clean, uncluttered lines, but Pinot Grigio is simpler and more neutral. Verdicchio has greater texture, nuance, and savoury detail. Think of it as a more sophisticated step beyond an easy everyday style.

Gavi (Cortese Italy)

Gavi reflects Verdicchio's citrus, herbs, and minerality but delivers them in a cooler, sharper key. It's leaner, more angular, and more distinctly mineral. For those who enjoy Verdicchio's clarity and want extra tension, Gavi hits that mark perfectly.

Vinho Verde (Portugal)

Vinho Verde carries the same bright, refreshing spirit but adds spritz and lighter fruit. It's breezier, simpler, and more casual. This is an easygoing, softer expression of the same refreshing character.

Chenin Blanc (Loire Valley, dry styles)

Chenin shares Verdicchio's orchard fruit, herbal edges, and quiet complexity, yet brings higher acidity and a slightly waxier texture. It's more structured and more layered. Freshness becomes deeper and more dynamic in this version.

Stretch Wines

Chablis (France)

Chablis tracks Verdicchio's citrus–mineral focus but heightens the minerality into something sharper and more chalk-driven. It's less herbal and more saline. This is crispness delivered with extra precision and a firmer edge.

Grüner Veltliner (Austria)

You'll notice similar acidity and herbal lift, yet Grüner adds peppery spice and savoury depth. It's more textured and more culinary in its expression. Expect a fresh white that invites curiosity through subtle layers.

Assyrtiko (Greece)

Assyrtiko matches Verdicchio's lemony brightness but pushes everything harder—acidity, structure, minerality. It's drier, saltier, and more forceful. This is crispness reimagined with volcanic intensity and striking power.

Myths or Misunderstandings

A common misconception is that Verdicchio is simple because it's often inexpensive. In truth, many of Italy's most age worthy and characterful whites come from Verdicchio's best vineyards. Another myth is that the almond note means oxidation. On the contrary, that gentle bitter finish is a hallmark of the grape itself, a natural, defining element of its personality.

Closing Reflection

Verdicchio is a wine that rewards quiet attention. It brings together freshness, subtle texture, herbal nuance, and a whisper of almond in a way that feels balanced and effortless. It captures the character of central Italy, its hills, its herbs, its calm rhythms, and offers it in a crisp, refreshing frame.

For those who love whites that combine clarity with subtle depth, Verdicchio offers one of the most quietly compelling experiences in the world of crisp white wines. It reminds us that beauty often lives in details, and that some wines ask not to be analysed, but to be enjoyed slowly, sip by sip.

Pinot Grigio (Lean Styles)

Lean Pinot Grigio feels like the cleanest line a white wine can draw, bright, cool, and pared down to its essentials. Lift the glass and the aromas remain soft and subtle: lemon peel, green apple, pear skin, a faint floral whisper. Nothing asks for attention. Nothing overwhelms. The wine feels like a white shirt dried in the sun, crisp, fresh, uncomplicated in the best possible way.

Lean Pinot Grigio comes from the cooler corners of northern Italy, especially Alto Adige, Friuli and Trentino, where alpine air keeps the grapes crisp and focused. The wines feel bright and delicate, shaped by citrus and green apple rather than richness or spice. They carry a clean, almost weightless clarity, the kind of freshness that moves quickly across the palate and leaves the mouth feeling awake. If a bottle tastes sleek, subtle and quietly refreshing, it is likely from these higher, cooler landscapes where ripening is gentle and the fruit stays firmly in the lean and lifted style.

Where the aromatic style of Pinot Grigio carries a touch more fruit and perfume, the lean style is quieter, more restrained. It thrives in cooler climates and higher vineyards, where the grapes maintain acidity and the flavours stay tight and focused. This version of Pinot Grigio isn't trying to be expressive. It's trying to be refreshing, wine as a clear stream of light.

Why People Love It

People love Lean Pinot Grigio because it slips into life effortlessly. It's the wine you can open for anyone, at any time, with food or without, and it just works. The flavours are familiar and friendly, citrus, apple, pear, and the structure is clean and refreshing. Nothing about it feels heavy, complicated, or demanding.

Emotionally, it appeals to drinkers who want ease. It suits simple meals: salads, grilled vegetables, light seafood, casual pastas. It fits warm afternoons, picnics, and moments when you want something bright and cool but not intense. Lean Pinot Grigio is the ultimate "no fuss" white, quietly satisfying and always welcome.

How This Wine Feels

Lean-style Pinot Grigio is dry, very light in body, and carried by crisp, gentle acidity. The first sip moves quickly across the palate, citrus led, refreshing and clean. The fruit shows more as an impression than a declaration, with hints of lemon, apple and subtle pear.

The texture is sleek, almost water like, supported by a quiet mineral note. There is no oak and minimal winemaking influence, so the wine's clarity feels unfiltered and direct. A swirl lifts delicate aromatics of citrus oil and white flowers, and once the wine leaves the palate, a soft echo of green fruit and a faint herbal lift returns. The finish is short, brisk and refreshing, an easy invitation toward the next sip.

If You Like This Wine... You May Also Like

Soave (Italy)

Soave brings the same clean citrus and light orchard fruit but adds nuance—almond, herbs, and gentle minerality. It's slightly fuller and more layered than lean Pinot Grigio. What you get is subtle refinement: simplicity elevated by quiet sophistication.

Muscadet (France)

Muscadet shares the light body and bright acidity but turns drier, saltier, and more mineral-focused. Where Pinot Grigio feels soft and citrusy, Muscadet is sharper and distinctly oceanic. Expect greater clarity, a more focused seaside interpretation of crispness.

Vinho Verde (Portugal)

The connection is pure freshness. Vinho Verde stays lean and citrusy like Pinot Grigio but adds a playful spritz and lower alcohol. It's breezier, lighter, and less structured—an even more casual, summery take on easy refreshment.

Txakoli (Spain)

Txakoli echoes Pinot Grigio's brisk acidity but heightens everything: salinity, spritz, and angularity. It's more coastal and more sharply defined. This is crispness with extra tension and a tangy, energetic twist.

Dry Riesling

Dry Riesling intensifies the citrus and acidity while introducing aromatics and taut mineral tension. It remains lean in body but carries more drive and expression. If you enjoy bright, clean whites, Riesling offers a more vivid, high-definition version.

Stretch Wines

Grüner Veltliner (Austria)

Grüner matches Pinot Grigio's light body and crispness but adds herbs, pepper, and subtle earthiness. It's more complex and more textural. This is a move into savoury detail while maintaining freshness.

Chablis (France)

Chablis shares the cool, crisp profile but deepens it with chalky minerality and firmer structure. It's more serious, more angular, and more layered. Here, light-bodied refreshment becomes a more nuanced, terroir-shaped experience.

Albariño (Spain)

Albariño keeps similar acidity but amplifies the aromatics—peach, citrus blossom, gentle salinity. It's fuller and more expressive than lean Pinot Grigio. Expect an aromatic lift and extra charm while still holding onto crispness.

Myths or Misunderstandings

Many assume all Pinot Grigio is "bland" or "neutral," but this misunderstanding comes from industrially made versions that crowd supermarket shelves. Pinot Grigio made with intention, especially from Alto Adige, Trentino, or Friuli, is delicate, refreshing, and beautifully precise.

Another myth is that lean whites lack complexity. Their restraint is a choice, not a deficiency. Their complexity shows up in texture, mineral details, and balance rather than overt fruit.

Closing Reflection

Pinot Grigio celebrates clarity. It's simple in the way clean air is simple, refreshing, welcome, and quietly beautiful. It offers citrus brightness, gentle minerality, and a smooth, crisp profile that fits naturally into everyday life. It doesn't need to make a statement. Its charm lies in how effortlessly it refreshes.

For those who value purity, lightness, and ease, lean Pinot Grigio is one of the most satisfying expressions of the crisp white wine world. It teaches that sometimes the simplest pleasures are the ones we return to again and again.

---

1. Crystalline: A clean, precise clarity in flavour or acidity that feels sharp and bright.
2. Chalky: A firm, mineral sensation suggesting chalk soils, often enhancing freshness and structure.
3. A mineral note reminiscent of broken seashells, common in wines from maritime or calcareous soils.

Chapter 8
Rich & Full Bodied Whites

Broader wines shaped by warmth, texture, and depth

Oaked Chardonnay

There is a moment, when you lift a glass of oaked Chardonnay, when the outside world seems to fall away. The wine glows softly, the way late daylight warms the side of a house, and the aroma rises in a slow, steady wave, not loud, not insisting on itself, but unmistakably inviting. You sense baked apples cooling on a counter, warm pastry, a trace of vanilla left behind in an empty bowl. It feels familiar even before you sip it, as though you've stepped back into a room you'd forgotten you loved.

This generosity is exactly why some people recoil from Chardonnay altogether. Their first encounter was one of those butter-laden, heavily toasted, over-sunned wines that swept through the 1990s like a fashion trend that overstayed its welcome. They tasted one style and dismissed the whole family. What they disliked wasn't Chardonnay, it was a single interpretation, stretched too far in one direction. Oaked Chardonnay is not a monolith; it's a spectrum. It can be statuesque or restrained, savoury or creamy, sun-warmed or quietly mineral. The name is the same, but the feeling shifts dramatically from place to place.

At its best, oaked Chardonnay is not about butter or oak at all. It is about quiet richness, a fullness of presence rather than heaviness of flavour. It's a wine that slows the tempo of a meal, rounding the edges of conversation, giving everything a little more space to breathe. It is one of the few white wines that feels equally at home beside a winter roast or a summer evening. And it has that rare quality, almost emotional in nature, of making the drinker feel settled.

Why People Love It

People love oaked Chardonnay because it feels like exhaling. It offers comfort without sweetness, fullness without weight, richness without excess. The flavours themselves matter less than the *shape* they create: a sense of broadness across the palate, a gentle unfolding rather than a rush. It is a wine that seems to hold you for a moment, rather than pass through you.

For many, it is the first white wine that feels genuinely luxurious. It does not fizz with sharp edges or chase you with citrus. It wraps. It soothes. It accompanies slow meals and soft evenings. And there is a psychological comfort in its familiarity, the way it draws on flavours that are part of a domestic lexicon: baked apples, warm spices, toasted nuts, bread, cream. These are not exotic aromas; they are homely ones, grounded ones. The pleasure comes not from novelty but from resonance.

How This Wine Feels

Oaked Chardonnay feels rounded and composed. It is dry in style, yet never austere, because it is moderately fresh. It keeps the wine lively without sharpening the edges. Rather than creating narrow, linear focus, the acidity broadens the palate and gives the wine a sense of structural brightness.

The body sits in the medium plus to full range, shaped by ripe fruit, alcohol and the subtle decisions made during fermentation and ageing. Malolactic conversion softens the sharper malic acid into a gentler lactic form, smoothing the texture and shifting the citrus edge toward something closer to yoghurt or cream. Lees ageing contributes another layer of fullness, adding a quiet silkiness as the wine rests on spent yeast cells. These cells break down over time, releasing compounds that increase viscosity and add savoury depth.

Oak leaves its mark in fine, measured touches rather than heavy blocks of flavour. You may notice a hint of toast, a light frame of spice or a soft vanilla warmth. Newer barrels offer more of these notes, while older ones simply support the wine with a gentle wooden imprint. The finish lasts because the elements remain in balance, the fruit, oak and savoury richness continuing to hum together as the wine settles. When the final rise of aroma returns after the wine has left the palate, the impression feels complete, as though the wine has finished its full arc.

If You Like This Wine... You May Also Like

White Burgundy (Meursault, Puligny-Montrachet, Chassagne-Montrachet France)

You'll recognise the same calm richness—the broad, confident mid-palate and the interplay of gentle oak with ripe orchard fruit. Burgundy simply shifts the emphasis: the fruit is cooler, more citrus- and apple-driven, and the texture favours precision over opulence. The result is a wine with greater lift and minerality, offering quiet depth rather than weight. If you love the roundness of oaked Chardonnay but want a more sculpted silhouette, this is the natural next step.

Sonoma Coast & Carneros Chardonnay (California)

These wines keep the warmth, silkiness, and breadth you enjoy, but add sunnier fruit—ripe peach, baked apple, occasional pineapple—and more pronounced vanilla and toast from new oak. The difference is scale: California feels fuller, richer, more golden. If generous, comforting, almost dessert-like indulgence (without sweetness) is what you appreciate in oaked Chardonnay, these wines will feel like a welcoming embrace.

Margaret River Chardonnay (Western Australia)

Margaret River sits beautifully between richness and tension: creamy, full-bodied fruit framed by vivid acidity and a savoury, sometimes smoky undercurrent. Many winemakers employ reductive[1] techniques that introduce subtle flinty complexity beneath the fruit. This creates a wine that is both energetic and indulgent. Wonderfully full, yet refreshingly alive.

Casablanca & Limarí Chardonnay (Chile)

If you enjoy the smoothness of oaked Chardonnay but want a touch more brightness, these coastal Chilean regions offer a well-balanced middle path. Cool breezes bring freshness, limestone and granite often add hushed mineral notes, and the oak tends to be more restrained. You end up with the roundness you like, carried in a cleaner, more linear frame—generous but lifted.

South African Chardonnay (Hemel-en-Aarde, Elgin, Stellenbosch)

South Africa pairs ripe stone fruit with savoury depth, soft smokiness, a flicker of struck match, and a mineral core. Oak is applied with restraint, giving structure and spice rather than overt sweetness. For drinkers drawn to the calm sophistication of oaked Chardonnay, these wines offer the same composure with added nuance and earthy complexity.

Stretch Wines

Chablis Premier Cru (Lightly Oaked Expressions)

Chablis Premier Cru reveals how oak can support rather than shape Chardonnay. The fruit remains cool and pure, with citrus, green apple and stone, yet a gentle cloak of old oak brings subtle roundness and quiet depth. The palate feels firm and precise, guided by Chablis' familiar mineral clarity. For those who appreciate the calm richness of oaked Chardonnay but wish to explore a more restrained and finely tuned interpretation, Chablis Premier Cru provides a graceful step into a cooler, more linear world.

Blanc de Blancs Champagne (100% Chardonnay, Traditional Method)

You'll notice familiar elements—creaminess, savoury fullness, bready richness from lees ageing—but everything is elevated. Higher acidity, fine bubbles, and flavours of lemon, chalk, and toasted brioche replace the still-wine warmth with bright, elegant intensity. If oaked Chardonnay is a glowing embers warmth, Blanc de Blancs feels like stepping into clear morning light.

Viognier

This is a stretch in aromatics rather than weight. Viognier is just as full-bodied and luxuriously textured, but it trades apple and toast for apricot, peach, honeysuckle, and heady florals. The acidity is lower, the perfume more pronounced. If the generosity and silkiness of oaked Chardonnay appeal to you, Viognier offers a more sensual, aromatic expression of similar richness.

White Rioja

Here the oak influence turns savoury, not sweet. Expect chamomile, citrus peel, wild herbs, lanolin, and a faint waxiness. The body is full and the texture broad, but the flavour profile leans Mediterranean and earthy. If it's the warmth and shape of oaked Chardonnay that you love, white Rioja delivers a parallel experience spoken in an entirely different accent.

Myths or Misunderstandings

The most persistent myth is that Chardonnay is inherently buttery. But butter is a choice, a stylistic decision, not a genetic truth. Malolactic conversion and certain kinds of oak can create those flavours, but they are not required, nor are they universal. Chardonnay is one of the most transparently expressive grapes in the world; it reflects place and technique far more than any fixed aroma. Thinking all Chardonnay tastes the same is like believing all bread tastes the same because one loaf was too sweet.

Closing Reflection

Oaked Chardonnay reminds us that richness need not be loud. It teaches that generosity can be gentle, that fullness can be calming, that depth can feel like ease. It is a wine that invites the drinker to settle into themselves, to enjoy the slow unfolding of flavour, the warmth of oak used wisely, the confidence of a wine that knows how to fill a space without crowding it.

To love oaked Chardonnay is to love texture, balance, and quiet luxury. And whether you prefer it broad and sunlit or refined and mineral, the pleasure at its centre remains the same: the feeling of being held, softly, by a wine that understands comfort better than almost any other.

Chenin Blanc

Chenin Blanc is a shape-shifter, one of the most versatile grapes in the world, but in its dry, full-bodied form, it expresses a kind of quiet power. Pour a glass and the aromas unfold gradually: quince, ripe apple, pear, citrus zest, chamomile, honeycomb, and a faint whisper of wool or lanolin. Beneath the fruit lies a savoury, mineral core shaped by the ancient limestone and flint soils of the Loire. Even before tasting, you sense structure, something firm, thoughtful, and deeply rooted.

Take a sip, and the wine moves with purpose. It begins bright and taut, then broadens across the palate into waxy, textured richness. Chenin Blanc doesn't bloom all at once; it unfolds in layers. And this is what defines it: a tension between freshness and weight, acidity and texture, fruit and earth. In the Loire Valley, especially Vouvray, Montlouis, and Savennières, Chenin Blanc reaches a level of complexity that feels both ancient and evolving.

Why People Love It

People love Chenin Blanc because it offers richness without heaviness. The fruit is ripe but not tropical, the acidity firm but not sharp. It balances textures beautifully, smooth but structured, waxy but fresh. It feels grounded, with flavours that seem to echo from deep within the wine rather than sitting on the surface.

Emotionally, Chenin Blanc appeals to drinkers who enjoy both brightness and depth. It's perfect for meals with roasted poultry, root vegetables, creamy sauces, pork, mushrooms, or anything that benefits from a wine with weight and lift. It's a wine that feels intellectual without being aloof, complex, expressive, and quietly confident.

How This Wine Feels

Dry, full-bodied Chenin Blanc is shaped by high acidity, a medium plus to full frame, and a natural sense of textural richness. The first sip feels precise, with apple, pear and citrus appearing clearly before the wine widens into a slightly waxy mid palate. The acidity acts as the backbone, keeping everything lifted and focused even as the texture grows broader.

Many versions spend time on lees, which lends creaminess and a gentle savoury depth. Some are aged in neutral oak, adding quiet spice without altering the core flavours. A slow swirl brings forward honeycomb, lanolin, wet stone, white flowers and beeswax. After the wine leaves the palate, those same elements gather again, creating a lingering mineral impression that holds steady. The finish does not turn buttery or soft; it remains firm, clear and confidently persistent.

If You Like This Wine… You May Also Like

White Rhône Blends (Marsanne or Roussanne)

You'll recognise the same textural weight and savoury depth. Marsanne contributes almond and honeyed richness; Roussanne adds herbs, wax, and firmer structure. Compared with Chenin, these blends carry softer acidity and a warmer overall tone. They offer a full-bodied pleasure delivered through a different flavour palette.

Alsace Pinot Gris (Rich Expression)

Pinot Gris mirrors Chenin's honeyed texture and orchard-fruit generosity but adds more spice, ripeness, and breadth. It's rounder, fuller, and lower in acidity. This creates a more sumptuous, opulent take on the textural charm you find in Chenin.

Oaked Chardonnay (Burgundy or New World)

Chardonnay shares Chenin's sense of body and presence but channels it through creaminess, supportive oak, and subtle toasty notes. Chenin leans more mineral and structurally firm. Chardonnay offers similar weight shaped through a different architectural style.

Vouvray Sec or Montlouis Sec (Loire Valley Chenin)

These wines intensify Chenin's mineral clarity and brightness, presenting the variety in its purest, most precise form—razor-edged acidity and stone-driven detail. They provide a deeper, more transparent look into Chenin's core personality.

Chardonnay from Margaret River

You'll find the same interplay of richness and freshness, but Margaret River Chardonnay presents it with cleaner citrus and stone-fruit definition. It offers a polished, structured alternative that maintains generosity while feeling taut and composed.

Stretch Wines

Savennières (Loire Valley)

This is Chenin Blanc at its most commanding. Savennières is drier, more mineral, and notably intense—flint, smoke, quince, herbs, and wool, carried by angular structure and remarkable depth. It reveals Chenin in its most austere and powerful form.

White Rioja (Barrel-Fermented Viura)

White Rioja delivers savoury depth through oak and age: herbs, nuts, lanolin, dried flowers, gentle oxidation. Compared with

Chenin, the style feels rounder, broader, and more Mediterranean in tone. It stands as a complex variation with comparable weight but entirely different character.

Dry Furmint (Hungary)

Dry Furmint's high acidity, orchard fruit, and smoky minerality place it structurally close to Chenin, but it presents the profile in a sharper, more linear way. It offers a more vertical, intense expression of freshness and mineral drive.

Myths or Misunderstandings

A common myth is that Chenin Blanc is naturally sweet. While Chenin can make extraordinary sweet wines, dry Chenin is vibrant, structured, and powerful. The honeyed aromas come from the grape itself, not residual sugar.

Another misconception: Chenin Blanc is inconsistent. Its style varies because the grape is capable of many expressions, lean, rich, off-dry, sparkling, sweet. This is versatility, not inconsistency.

Some think its woolly or lanolin notes indicate a fault; in fact, they are classic Chenin markers, especially in aged examples.

Closing Reflection

Chenin Blanc shows how a white wine can be rich yet bright, textured yet precise. It is a wine of movement, starting crisp, expanding into waxy depth, and finishing with mineral tension. It carries its history and terroir in quiet, compelling layers.

For those who enjoy complexity without excess, and richness supported by structure, Chenin Blanc offers one of the most rewarding journeys in the world of full-bodied whites. It reminds us that depth doesn't need volume, and that some of the most remarkable wines speak softly but with remarkable clarity.

White Rhône Blends

White Rhône blends feel like warm light, golden, textural, gently aromatic, and quietly powerful. Bring the glass to your nose and the aromas seem to glow: ripe pear, apricot, almond cream, honeycomb, chamomile, yellow apple, and soft notes of dried herbs or fennel. There is a grounded, sun-soaked richness to these wines, shaped by Rhône Valley heat, stony soils, and the Mediterranean winds that temper the warmth.

The Marsanne grape provides the foundation: roundness, weight, almond, stone fruit, and a smooth, waxy texture. Roussanne grapes bring perfume and lift, flowers, herbs, spice, and a refined structure that keeps the blend from becoming too soft. Together, they create whites that are full-bodied yet subtle, generous yet composed. They feel ancient in style: wines shaped by sunlight and earth, rather than overt oak or high acidity.

Why People Love It

People love white Rhône blends because they offer richness without flashiness. The fruit is ripe and warm, the aromatics soft but complex, the texture broad without being heavy. These wines feel calming, like warm stone or late afternoon sun. They suit thoughtful meals: roasted chicken, pork, root vegetables, Mediterranean dishes, creamy sauces, autumn spices, and anything with herbs.

Emotionally, they appeal to drinkers who want fullness but not opulence, weight without sweetness, texture without butter, flavour without intensity. They are wines for quiet evenings and slow meals, offering calm depth rather than bright energy.

How This Wine Feels

White Rhône blends are dry, full-bodied, and shaped by soft, low acidity. The first sip feels soft and expansive, with pear, melon, apricot, marzipan and gentle spice unfolding in a slow, steady sweep. The mid palate is rounded and smooth, often carrying a beeswax or lanolin texture that comes from Marsanne's natural phenolics.

Roussanne contributes a touch of structure, a slight tannic grip, and added spice and floral nuance. These wines rarely come across as crisp. Instead, they travel calmly across the palate with a sense of quiet confidence. A swirl brings forward layered aromas of almond, dried herbs, honeysuckle and baked apple. After the wine leaves the palate, those impressions seem to rise again, bringing warm fruit, herbs and a gentle savoury depth that settles into a lingering, lightly nutty finish.

Lees ageing, old oak or amphora may add subtle texture or savoury accents, but overt wood is uncommon. The style centres on shape and presence rather than seasoning.

If You Like This Wine… You May Also Like

Chenin Blanc (Loire or South Africa)

You'll recognise the shared texture and savoury depth, but Chenin follows a brighter path—higher acidity, more tension, and honeyed orchard fruit. White Rhône blends feel softer and warmer by comparison. Chenin offers a fresher, more vibrant interpretation of the richness you enjoy.

Oaked Chardonnay (Burgundy or New World)

Both styles share weight, presence, and creamy texture. Chardonnay leans toward citrus, crisp acidity, and clear oak influence, while Rhône blends tend to show herbs, nuts, and waxier tones. It delivers similar body with a completely different aromatic frame.

Alsace Pinot Gris

Pinot Gris brings ripe pear, spice, and gentle acidity, echoing the weight and aromatic depth of Rhône blends. It generally offers sweeter fruit, rounder edges, and occasional oiliness, creating a warmer, silkier variation on the theme.

White Rioja

Like Rhône blends, White Rioja can be textural and savoury, with almond, herbs, and waxy nuance. It often carries more oxidative[2] character and more pronounced oak. The style brings layered, savoury depth shaped by its distinctly Spanish personality.

Grenache Blanc (Southern France, Spain)

Grenache Blanc reflects the warmth and soft acidity of Marsanne and Roussanne, showing pear, melon, and gentle herbal tones. It's typically a touch leaner and more understated, offering an easy, fresh alternative from similar regional roots.

Stretch Wines

Savennières (Chenin Blanc, Loire Valley)

Savennières represents Chenin Blanc at its most forceful—mineral, structured, and uncompromising. Compared with Rhône blends, it comes across sharper, more angular, and more layered, delivering a high-tension, deeply mineral style.

Semillon (Hunter Valley or Bordeaux)

Semillon shares the waxy texture and warm savoury elements but trades orchard fruit and herbs for lemon, lanolin, toast, and a broad range of acidity depending on region. It offers a full-bodied experience from an entirely different stylistic direction.

Viognier (Northern Rhône or New World)

Viognier brings apricot, honeysuckle, and lush aromatic richness. It's more floral, more expressive, and often more voluptuous than Rhône blends. This style explores the luxurious, perfume-driven side of full-bodied whites.

Myths or Misunderstandings

One myth is that white Rhône blends are heavy. They are full-bodied, yes, but their weight is gentle, more waxy than creamy, more earthy than rich. Another misconception: that low acidity means flabbiness. These wines gain structure from phenolics (grape-derived texture) rather than from acidity, leading to a unique, tactile balance.

Some assume these wines must be oaky because of their body. In fact, many top examples use neutral vessels or very restrained wood, keeping the focus on grape character and texture.

Closing Reflection

White Rhône blends reveal that richness can be calm rather than loud. These wines offer weight without opulence, complexity without intensity, and texture without heaviness. They feel elemental, shaped by sun, stone, and quiet craftsmanship.

They teach that full-bodied whites don't need to be buttery or tropical to be profound. And for those who love wines that move slowly and unfold gently, Marsanne and Roussanne offer one of the most rewarding experiences in the entire white wine world.

White Rioja

White Rioja feels like a warm breeze carrying the scent of herbs, orchard fruit, and sun-dried grass. It is a wine built not around brightness or flamboyance, but around depth, texture, and quiet savoury beauty. Bring the glass to your nose and you'll sense apple, pear, quince, chamomile, almond, vanilla, toast, and a subtle waxy note that speaks of time, whether in barrel or bottle. There is something nostalgic about its aroma, something that feels both ancient and enduring.

Made primarily from **Viura** (also known as Macabeo), sometimes blended with Garnacha Blanca or Malvasía Riojana, White Rioja has travelled through stylistic eras. Modern versions tend to be fresher and more fruit-driven; traditional styles are aged in old oak barrels for years, developing a distinctive nutty, honeyed depth. But across all expressions, one characteristic remains: a balance of richness and savouriness, with persistent acidity and a texture that feels almost architectural.

Why People Love It

People love White Rioja because it offers complexity that feels natural rather than constructed. The fruit is gentle, apple, pear, citrus, but the savoury elements feel woven into the wine: herbs, nuts, dried flowers, lanolin, beeswax, a whisper of oxidative character in more traditional styles. The wine has weight without heaviness, flavour without sweetness, and a long, thoughtful finish.

Emotionally, it appeals to drinkers who enjoy wines shaped by time, wines with stories in them. It suits roasted poultry, aged cheeses, creamy sauces, mushrooms, seafood in rich preparations, and dishes that echo its savoury depth. It feels both grounded and refined, like an old wooden table polished smooth by use.

How This Wine Feels

White Rioja is dry, medium plus to full in body, with medium acidity and a broad, layered texture. The first sip feels rounded and savoury, with baked apple, citrus peel, almond, honeycomb and touches of herbs or hay. The acidity arrives gently but with purpose, lifting the richness and keeping the wine balanced rather than heavy.

Barrel fermentation and ageing define much of its character. Contemporary styles rely on neutral oak for subtle texture, while traditional versions spend long periods in older barrels, gaining oxidative nuances that register as nutty, waxy or lightly sherried. Viura's natural phenolics add a quiet grip on the palate, creating structure without overt tannin.

A swirl deepens the aromatics, bringing vanilla, chamomile, dried flowers, toast and warm stone into view. After the wine leaves the palate, those savoury and citrus notes seem to rise again, leading into a long, dry and gently complex finish.

If You Like This Wine… You May Also Like

White Rhône Blends (Marsanne or Roussanne)

These wines share White Rioja's savoury warmth, waxy texture, and herbal depth. Rhône whites are often richer, rounder, and softer in acidity, but the stylistic kinship is unmistakable. They offer a Mediterranean expression of the same calm, layered complexity.

Chenin Blanc (Loire, dry styles)

You'll recognise honeycomb, chamomile, and orchard fruit, now paired with a sharper mineral line and higher acidity. Chenin feels more vertical, more focused, and more precise, while Rioja is broader and more textural. This gives a fresher, brighter alternative with comparable depth.

Oaked Chardonnay (Burgundy France or New World)

The link comes from texture and oak-derived richness. Chardonnay leans more citrus-driven and firmly structured; White Rioja is more savoury, herbal, and mellowed by oxidative notes. It delivers similar body but through a distinctly different personality.

Godello (Valdeorras Spain)

Godello echoes Rioja's savoury complexity and generous mid-palate, showing stone fruit, herbs, and a creamy glide. It tends to be a touch fresher and more mineral, offering a contemporary Spanish white that balances Rioja's soul with Atlantic lift.

Aged White Bordeaux (Semillon or Sauvignon blends)

Aged Semillon brings wax, lanolin, lemon curd, and gentle oxidative detail, paralleling White Rioja's depth. It often carries slightly higher acidity and more citrus drive. This provides a nuanced pathway into wines shaped as much by time as by fruit.

Stretch Wines

Traditional Aged White Rioja (10+ years in barrel and bottle)

This is Rioja at its most resonant: deep gold colour, nutty savour, oxidative richness, honey, herbs, and layers of maturity. Compared with modern styles, it is less fruit-led and far more contemplative—an immersion into old-world winemaking tradition.

Fiano or Greco di Tufo (Southern Italy)

These southern Italian whites deliver savoury richness, mineral weight, and gentle phenolic grip, with citrus and stone fruit taking the lead. They are textural, expressive, and volcanic in tone—complex wines that speak the same structural language through a different regional accent.

Grüner Veltliner Smaragd (Austria)

In its richest form, Grüner offers weight, spice, herbs, and savoury depth. It differs with higher acidity and a distinctive peppery lift. This creates a more structured, high-tension interpretation of full-bodied white wine.

Myths or Misunderstandings

A frequent misconception is that all White Rioja is oxidised or old-fashioned. In fact, the region produces a spectrum: from fresh, clean, modern styles to deeply traditional, long-aged wines. Another myth is that White Rioja must be oaky. While oak plays a role, many contemporary producers use it with great restraint to highlight texture rather than flavour.

Some drinkers confuse the honeyed aromatics with sweetness; White Rioja almost always remains dry, even when aged.

Closing Reflection

White Rioja captures the beauty of time, texture, and savoury complexity. It brings together gentle fruit, subtle oak, herbal nuance, and a layered richness that seems to deepen with every sip. It is a wine of patience and presence, one that reveals itself gradually, like pages of a well-worn book.

For those who enjoy whites that are full-bodied yet thoughtful, rich yet dry, expressive yet understated, White Rioja offers one of the most soulful and distinctive experiences in the world of white wine. It teaches that maturity, nuance, and savoury depth can be just as captivating as brightness or intensity.

Alsace Pinot Gris (Rich Expression)

Alsace Pinot Gris feels like autumn sunlight, warm, golden, and quietly expansive. Lift the glass and the aromas bloom slowly, like fruit ripening on the branch: pear, ripe apple, quince, baked peach, honey, ginger, soft spice, and a gentle smokiness that drifts in like distant woodsmoke. The wine has presence. Not loudness, presence. A quiet fullness that feels comforting and grounded.

In Alsace, Pinot Gris ripens deeply, building layers of fruit, spice, and texture. The cool nights preserve acidity, but the warm days coax richness from the grapes, giving the wine both weight and lift. It often feels slightly oily or waxy on the palate, not heavy, but textural, like silk brushed one way and suede the other. This is Pinot Gris at its most expressive, far removed from the crisp neutrality of Italian Pinot Grigio.

Why People Love It

People love Alsace Pinot Gris because it bridges fruit, spice, and savoury nuance in a way few white wines can. The flavours are generous, layered, and inviting: pear tart, baked apple, ginger, almond, honeycomb. The acidity is gentle, giving the wine a soft, rolling feel across the palate.

It's a comforting wine, soothing, warm, and subtly aromatic. Emotionally, it appeals to drinkers who enjoy depth but not sharpness, richness but not heaviness. Its gentle sweetness (when present) is usually balancing, not dominating, and even dry examples feel lush and textural. It fits autumn meals, candlelit evenings, reflective moods, and dishes that lean toward spice, cream, or richness.

How This Wine Feels

Alsace Pinot Gris can be dry or off dry, but the richer style sits in a medium plus to full body with gentle acidity and a broad, generous texture. The first sip spreads slowly across the palate, showing ripe orchard fruit, soft spice and a quiet honeyed note. The acidity stays subtle yet steady, giving shape to the wine's weight.

A light phenolic grip is common, adding structure and keeping the softness from feeling loose or heavy. With a swirl, the aromas grow deeper and more layered: ripe peach, ginger, almond, a touch of smoke and at times a hint of mushroom or earth. Once the wine moves off the palate, those impressions gather again, carrying fruit and spice back through the senses before settling into a long, warm, slightly savoury finish.

Alsace Pinot Gris is one of the rare white wines that can feel almost red in texture, which is part of why it works so well across a wide range of foods.

If You Like This Wine... You May Also Like

White Rhône Blends (Marsanne or Roussanne)

You'll recognise the waxy texture, gentle acidity, and savoury warmth. Rhône whites tend to be more herbal and nuttier, while Pinot Gris leans fruit-driven and spicy. They offer similar richness expressed through a different flavour spectrum.

Chenin Blanc (Loire or South Africa)

Chenin shares Pinot Gris's orchard fruit, honeyed hints, and layered texture, but shows higher acidity and clearer mineral tension. It provides a brighter, more finely balanced interpretation of savoury, textured richness.

White Rioja

You'll find familiar savoury notes—almond, honeycomb, subtle oxidative edges. White Rioja is more herbal, more earthy, and shaped strongly by place. It delivers comparable weight with a distinctly Spanish sense of nuance.

Oaked Chardonnay

Similar in body and warmth, but Chardonnay expresses itself through oak spice, toast, and citrus lift. Alsace Pinot Gris remains fruitier and more overtly aromatic. Chardonnay offers a rich white with a different structural and textural centre.

Gewürztraminer (Alsace)

If the aromatic side of Pinot Gris appeals to you, Gewürztraminer raises the intensity—rose, lychee, spice, gingerbread. It's fuller in perfume and more assertive, giving an amplified, exotic expression while still carrying weight.

Stretch Wines

Vendanges Tardives Pinot Gris (Late Harvest, Alsace France)

A sweeter, richer, far more opulent take on the same grape—honeyed, exotic, deeply layered. Compared with the richest dry Pinot Gris, this moves toward dessert-wine territory, embracing decadence and concentration.

Savennières (Chenin Blanc, Loire France)

Taut, mineral, and powerful, Savennières offers a striking contrast to Pinot Gris's softer warmth. It shifts the conversation from plushness to precision, showing structure over suppleness.

Fiano (Southern Italy)

Fiano delivers waxy texture, honey, herbs, and smoky minerality, paired with higher acidity than Pinot Gris. It's a savoury, volcanic interpretation of full-bodied white wine, bringing deeper, earthier layers of richness.

Myths or Misunderstandings

Many assume Pinot Gris must be light and neutral because they associate it with Pinot Grigio. In truth, Alsace expressions are some of the most richly textured, layered white wines in the world. Another misconception is that any sweetness is a flaw. In fact, slight residual sugar is part of the classic style, balancing phenolic grip and spice.

Some also believe richness must come from oak. Alsace Pinot Gris shows that grape ripeness and lees contact can produce fullness and warmth without pronounced wood influence.

Closing Reflection

Alsace Pinot Gris is a reminder that richness can be gentle, aromatic, and nuanced. It offers warmth without heaviness, texture without weight, sweetness without sugariness, and spice without heat. It moves across the palate with the soft certainty of something well-made and deeply rooted in its place.

For those who love white wines that feel layered, textural, and quietly expressive, wines that resonate rather than shout, Alsace Pinot Gris offers one of the most comforting and profound experiences in the world of full-bodied whites. It teaches that complexity can feel soothing, and that generosity can be subtle.

---

1. Reductive: Aromas that develop when wine making is kept in low oxygen conditions, often showing notes such as struck match, smoke, rubber or flint.

2. Oxidative: A wine making style shaped by air exposure that creates flavours of nuts, caramel, and dried fruit.

Chapter 9
Sparkling Wines

Wines driven by brightness, tension, and celebration

Champagne

Champagne feels like light captured under pressure, precise, energetic, and quietly luxurious. Pour a glass, and the bubbles rise in fine, steady streams, carrying aromas of lemon zest, crisp apple, pear, white peach, brioche, toasted almonds, and a faint whisper of chalk or seashell. Nothing else in the world smells quite like this. Even before tasting, you sense tension, elegance, and depth, a wine shaped by cold air, long patience, and underground chalk.

What makes Champagne extraordinary is not just its bubbles, but the feeling they create. The first sip is bright and linear, the acidity cutting cleanly through the palate like a beam of light. Then the texture arrives, creamy, silky, shaped by years of resting on lees. Champagne balances contrast with extraordinary finesse: sharpness and softness, citrus and brioche, delicacy and intensity. It is a wine of opposites resolved into harmony.

Why People Love It

People love Champagne because it feels like an occasion in itself. The aromatics are layered, the bubbles fine, the palate long and precise. Even without food, Champagne feels complete. With food, it becomes transformative, pairing with oysters, fried dishes, caviar, cheese, roast chicken, sushi, and nearly everything in between.

Emotionally, Champagne appeals to those who love clarity and elegance. It feels timeless and celebratory, but also contemplative, a wine that rewards attention but offers joy even without it. Champagne makes ordinary moments feel elevated, and special moments unforgettable.

How This Wine Feels

Champagne is dry in its Brut style, light to medium in body, with high acidity and exceptionally fine bubbles. The first sip feels electric, showing sharp citrus, green apple and chalk, all carried upward by bubbles that register more as texture than fizz. As the wine moves across the palate, the flavours broaden into brioche, nuts, pastry, cream and gentle spice. These notes come from autolysis[1], the slow breakdown of yeast during extended lees ageing.

The mousse is fine and steady, offering lift rather than a noticeable tickle. A swirl releases aromas of bread dough, citrus oil, hazelnut, white flowers and a hint of chalk dust. After the wine leaves the palate, those impressions return in a long, quiet echo of toast, citrus and savoury depth. The finish is lengthy, cleansing and quietly powerful, built on the interplay of fruit, acidity and minerality that continues well after the sip has passed.

If You Like This Wine... You May Also Like

Blanc de Blancs Champagne

Made entirely from Chardonnay, this style shows even greater precision showing more chalk, more citrus lift, and a lighter, more linear frame. It represents Champagne at its most crystalline and finely etched.

Blanc de Noirs Champagne

Produced from Pinot Noir or Pinot Meunier, these wines offer richer fruit, deeper texture, and notes of red apple and berry. They deliver intensity and weight while remaining refined and balanced.

English Sparkling Wine

You'll notice the same high acidity, mineral tension, and fine bubbles, but in a cooler, more sharply defined style. English sparkling often feels even brighter and more electric than Champagne.

Crémant (France)

Traditional-method sparkling from regions such as Alsace, Loire, and Burgundy. Expect finer bubbles, gentle toastiness, and elegant structure but often at a more accessible price point. A refined option that offers complexity without Champagne's cost.

Franciacorta (Italy)

Italy's traditional-method counterpart to Champagne. Richer, creamier, and slightly riper in fruit profile, it brings a sophisticated texture warmed by Italian sunshine.

Stretch Wines

Cava Gran Reserva or Cava de Paraje (Spain)

Extended lees ageing adds autolytic depth that can approach Champagne's complexity. Cava remains a touch warmer and more Mediterranean in fruit character, creating a structured style expressed in a sunnier voice.

Traditional-Method Sparkling Rosé (Global)

Red-fruit aromatics, deeper complexity, and firmer texture define these wines. They're bolder and more expressive than many Champagnes while retaining similar precision and structure.

Grower Champagne or Récoltant-Manipulant (RM)

Champagne made by the growers themselves, often emphasising terroir, individuality, and pronounced character. These cuvées tend to be more distinctive and place-driven, offering a sharper sense of origin within the Champagne category.

Myths or Misunderstandings

One myth is that Champagne is always expensive. While top cuvées are costly, many non-vintage Champagnes offer remarkable quality at accessible prices. Another misconception is that Champagne is meant only for celebrations. In truth, its acidity and complexity make it one of the greatest food wines in the world.

Some also believe Champagne's bubbles are "stronger" because of carbonation, but the fine mousse comes from the traditional method, where bubbles form naturally in the bottle during a second fermentation.

Finally, sweetness confuses many drinkers: "Brut" does not mean no sugar; it means dry. Champagne can range from bone-dry "Brut Nature" to lusciously sweet "Doux."

Closing Reflection

Champagne is more than sparkling wine; it is elegance made liquid. It embodies precision, patience, and the art of creating harmony from contrast. It is at once celebratory and reflective, joyful and contemplative, timeless and alive.

For those who love wines that feel graceful yet powerful, Champagne offers one of the most profound experiences in the world of wine. It reminds us that beauty can be both bright and deep, and that some wines carry the soul of the earth in every shimmering bubble.

Crémant

Crémant is the quiet elegance of French sparkling wine, a style that glimmers rather than shouts, offering all the refinement of the traditional method without the weight of expectation that often surrounds Champagne. Made in the same labour-intensive way, with a second fermentation in the bottle and long ageing on the lees, Crémant carries the same gentle creaminess, the same fine bubbles, the same slow unfurling of flavour. What it does differently is the mood. Crémant feels approachable, generous, calm. It brings celebration into the room without insisting on an occasion.

Pour a glass and the bubbles rise like a soft sigh. Aromas drift up in delicate threads, citrus peel, orchard fruit, blossom, sometimes almond or warm pastry from time spent resting quietly on its lees. Nothing feels hurried, nothing feels forced. Crémant moves with ease across the palate, bright but not sharp, creamy but not rich, balanced in a way that makes it feel comfortable from the very first sip.

Part of its charm is its breadth. Crémant is not from one place, but many. Each region brings its own accent, shaped by its grapes, its soils and its sense of light. Crémant from Alsace feels floral and airy. Crémant from the Loire is crisp and mineral. Burgundy brings precision. Limoux brings warmth. Jura brings quiet intensity. Bordeaux brings generosity. Together, they create a landscape of sparkling wines that feel related yet distinct, each one offering something to discover.

And while Crémant is often more affordable than Champagne, it does not ask you to compromise. It offers craftsmanship and beauty in a gentler register, making it one of the most rewarding sparkling wine styles for everyday celebration.

Crémant tastes like ease, like clarity, like the soft glow that begins a gathering before the meal has even reached the table. It is a wine that brings people closer simply by being poured.

Why People Love It

People love Crémant because it feels both refined and relaxed. It carries the elegance of Champagne, yet presents it in a more welcoming way. The bubbles are fine, but never aggressive. The fruit feels fresh, but never sharp. The flavours are detailed but not demanding. Crémant feels like a kind conversation rather than a grand announcement.

There is pleasure in its versatility. It suits quiet dinners, lively afternoons, early evenings when the light begins to soften and even the moments when you simply want something beautiful to share. Crémant does not rely on luxury to make its case. Its charm lies in balance, in softness, in a sense of proportion that makes it as appropriate for a picnic as it is for a celebration.

There is also a quiet confidence to Crémant. It does not borrow prestige from Champagne. It does not imitate. Instead, each bottle reflects its own region and its own style, offering its own expression of craftsmanship. For many drinkers, this sense of individuality feels refreshing. Crémant invites curiosity without demanding knowledge.

Emotionally, Crémant appeals because it feels like a gentle uplift. It brightens the moment without transforming it. It adds sparkle to the everyday as naturally as it adds polish to special occasions.

How This Wine Feels

Crémant is dry, light to medium in body, and carried by crisp acidity that sharpens the bubbles just enough to make the wine feel alive. The mousse is fine and persistent, more of a soft texture than a foamy rush, giving the wine a subtle creaminess without weight.

The first sip is usually bright with lemon zest, green apple or pear. As the bubbles settle, the flavours widen into peach, almond, white flowers, gentle spice or a hint of brioche from the lees that cradle the wine as it ages. Everything unfolds gradually. Nothing overwhelms.

Crémant finishes with quiet clarity. Aromas drift back in a soft echo, often citrus peel, pastry or clean minerality that lingers longer than expected. It feels serene, composed, balanced, like a deep breath after a long day.

Understanding the Different Styles of Crémant

One of Crémant's greatest strengths is its diversity. Each region brings its own grapes, climate and character, shaping wines that feel unified in method but varied in expression. These are not technical distinctions. They are differences you can feel in the glass.

Crémant d'Alsace

Alsace offers the lightest and most floral expression of Crémant. It often tastes of pear, white peach, blossom and gentle spice, carried by softness and calm freshness. Pinot Blanc and Auxerrois give roundness, while Pinot Noir adds quiet structure. Crémant d'Alsace feels like spring air, delicate and uplifting.

Crémant de Loire

The Loire Valley brings brightness, energy and a vivid mineral line. Chenin Blanc gives apple and quince, along with a fine thread of waxy depth, while Chardonnay and Cabernet Franc add clarity and definition. This is Crémant with a clean, purposeful edge, refreshing and quietly complex.

Crémant de Bourgogne

Burgundy's Crémant is precise and finely shaped. Chardonnay brings citrus and chalk, Pinot Noir brings red apple and subtle fruit bite. The result is a sparkling wine with tension, detail and a soft echo of Burgundy's still wines. It often feels the most refined in structure.

Crémant de Limoux

Limoux offers warmth and gentle richness. Mauzac brings apple peel and soft herbal notes, Chardonnay and Chenin Blanc add breadth and freshness. The wine feels sunny yet balanced, with a smooth, rounded mid palate that makes it one of the most comforting styles of Crémant.

Crémant du Jura

Jura creates a sparer, more mineral interpretation. Chardonnay brings citrus and almond, Savagnin adds quiet savouriness and subtle nutty tones. The wines feel poised and contemplative, with a lifted, almost Alpine purity.

Crémant de Bordeaux

Bordeaux offers a fruit led style, often softer and more approachable. Sémillon adds honeyed charm, Sauvignon Blanc brings lightness and freshness, and Cabernet Franc or Merlot can add gentle berry notes in rosé versions. These are generous, easy going Crémants that feel friendly from the first sip.

If You Like This Wine... You May Also Like

Champagne (France)

You will recognise the same traditional method craftsmanship, but Champagne carries more drive, more tension and more chalky depth. Its flavours layer themselves with greater intensity. For anyone who loves Crémant's elegance but wants to explore a more concentrated, more architectural style, Champagne is the natural next step.

Franciacorta (Italy)

Franciacorta takes the energy of Chardonnay and Pinot Noir and gives it warmth and gentle richness. The bubbles glide smoothly. The fruit feels ripe and polished. It is a refined, almost serene sparkling wine that mirrors Crémant's softness while adding depth.

English Sparkling Wine

A vivid, high-toned expression shaped by cool climates. Lemon, green apple and chalk define the palate. It is crisper, brighter and more linear than most Crémant, perfect for those who enjoy precision and clarity.

Cava Gran Reserva (Spain)

Long ageing brings savoury depth, toasted notes and subtle spice. This is a Mediterranean expression of the traditional method that shares Crémant's calmness while offering more warmth and layered complexity.

Trentodoc (Italy)

Trentodoc expresses mountain freshness with orchard fruit, delicate florals and a refined mineral core. It feels poised, uplifting and deeply pure. An ideal bridge between Crémant's gentleness and Champagne's tension.

Stretch Wines

Grower Champagne (RM)

Crémant drinkers who are drawn to nuance and subtle complexity often find themselves captivated by Grower Champagne. These wines express single vineyards, specific soils and a thrilling sense of place. They feel chiselled, detailed and quietly profound.

Sekt (Traditional Method, Germany)

A fresher, more aromatic expression of sparkling wine. Riesling based Sekt offers citrus, blossom and electric acidity, while Pinot based versions feel elegant and understated. This is a move into cooler, more lifted territory.

Sparkling Rosé (Traditional Method)

Adds colour, strawberry tones and gentle red fruit. The texture remains refined, but the flavour expands. For those who enjoy

Crémant's calmness yet want something a little more expressive, sparkling rosé offers a vibrant next step.

Pet Nat

A completely different rhythm. Cloudy, lightly fizzy and often playful, Pet Nat feels spontaneous and rustic beside the composure of Crémant. It offers freedom rather than discipline while retaining the joy of bubbles.

Myths or Misunderstandings

A common misconception is that Crémant is simply a lower cost version of Champagne. While it is often more affordable, the difference lies not in quality but in character. Crémant reflects different grapes, different climates and different regional traditions. It is not trying to be Champagne. It is offering its own voice.

Another myth is that Crémant is simple or fruit driven. Many Crémants spend extended time on their lees and develop flavours of pastry, toasted nuts, warm bread and subtle spice. There is a spectrum of expression, ranging from light and floral to structured and savoury.

Some people assume that a gentle mousse means less craft. In truth, the traditional method is identical to that of Champagne, with every bottle undergoing a second fermentation inside the glass. The softness comes from intention, not inferiority.

Closing Reflection

Crémant is sparkling wine at its most gracious. It offers beauty without insistence, complexity without weight and celebration without complication. It is a wine that invites you to enjoy the moment as it already is, rather than urging you to turn it into something more.

In its finest expressions, Crémant tastes of calm brightness, of fruit softened by light, of gentle bubbles rising through citrus and blossom and pastry. It lingers with quiet clarity, leaving space for conversation, for connection, for ease.

Crémant teaches that refinement does not need to be loud and that joy does not need to be extravagant. Sometimes the most memorable glasses are the ones that simply feel right the moment you lift them.

Traditional Method Sparkling

(Franciacorta • Cava Gran Reserva or Paraje • English Sparkling • Trentodoc)

Traditional-method sparkling wines made outside Champagne feel like familiar music played on different instruments, recognisable in structure and elegance, yet full of regional personality. Lift the glass and the aromas rise with precision: citrus zest, green apple, pear, toasted brioche, roasted nuts, white flowers, sometimes a touch of creaminess or a mineral spark. The bubbles are fine, tight, persistent, unmistakably the result of the 'méthode traditionnelle,' where the second fermentation happens in the bottle just like Champagne.

But while the method is the same, the expression varies. Franciacorta leans warm and silky, shaped by Italian sunshine. Cava Gran Reserva or Cava de Paraje feels Mediterranean, savoury, with herbal edges and long lees richness. English Sparkling Wine crackles with acidity and chalk-driven precision. Trentodoc balances Alpine freshness with northern Italian fruit purity. These wines show that complexity, finesse, and autolytic depth are not exclusive to Champagne, they flourish wherever climate, soil, and craft converge.

Why People Love It

People love traditional-method sparkling wines because they offer Champagne-like texture and depth at often friendlier prices. The bubbles are refined, the flavours layered, and the styles diverse. These wines feel elegant without being exclusive, serious without being austere.

Emotionally, they appeal to drinkers who want sophistication with individuality, wines that reflect place as clearly as they reflect method. They suit special occasions, dinners, celebrations, thoughtful evenings, and quiet moments where you want a wine with presence. They feel both luxurious and approachable.

How This Wine Feels

These wines are dry in Brut or Extra Brut styles, light to medium in body, with high acidity and a creamy, persistent mousse. The first sip usually shows citrus brightness such as lemon, lime and green apple, carried by bubbles that feel fine and silky. As the wine moves across the palate, the influence of lees ageing becomes clear, adding layers of brioche, biscuit, toasted nuts, cream and quiet savoury tones.

Extended time on the lees is central to the style. Contact with the yeast cells builds texture and depth, giving the mid palate richness and allowing the finish to stretch out with poise. A gentle swirl brings new aromas to the surface, including white flowers, citrus oil, almond and fresh bread. After the wine leaves the palate, those flavours return in an elegant echo of toast, citrus and minerals that lingers with calm precision.

Different regions express these qualities in their own way:

- Franciacorta feels creamy, soft and subtly nutty.

- Cava Gran Reserva shows a savoury, herbal, Mediterranean character.

- English sparkling wine is razor sharp, chalky and driven by lemon.

- Trentodoc feels crisp, orchard fruited and distinctly Alpine in purity.

If You Like This Wine... You May Also Like

Champagne (France)

The closest stylistic match. Champagne brings greater tension, chalky detail, and layered depth, especially when aged for longer on the lees. It represents the most refined and classical expression of the traditional method.

Crémant (France)

Offers similar finesse but tends to be fruitier and softer, depending on the region. It emphasises brightness rather than profound depth. A polished, elegant option that carries its own regional personality.

Alta Langa (Piedmont, Italy)

Alta Langa delivers a refined traditional method expression with a distinctly Italian voice. The fruit is cool and precise, the mousse fine, and the palate shaped by long lees ageing that adds gentle richness to its citrus and orchard notes. There is often a calm mineral thread beneath the fruit, lending poise and quiet structure. For those who enjoy the elegance of traditional method sparkling wine and wish to explore an Italian style with depth, freshness and graceful balance, Alta Langa provides a beautifully composed option.

Prosecco (Italy)

Made differently and tasting different as a result—softer bubbles, gentler fruit, and an easy, friendly character. A straightforward, relaxed approach to sparkling wine suited to informal occasions.

Sparkling Rosé (Global)

Built on traditional-method structure but enriched with red-fruit charm. It's a more expressive, more colourful variation on refined bubbles, adding vibrancy without losing elegance.

Lambrusco (Dry styles)

An unexpected direction: sparkling red with savoury berry flavours and a frothy, lively mousse. Less about finesse, more about fun—a bold, characterful take on fizz.

Stretch Wines

Grower Champagne (RM)

Made by the growers themselves and shaped strongly by terroir. Compared with polished non-Champagne sparklers, it feels sharper, more mineral, more intense. A style defined by individuality and vineyard expression.

Sekt (Germany, Traditional-Method)

Riesling Sekt delivers citrus and stone fruit with high, racy[2] acidity; Pinot-based versions lean delicate with orchard fruit purity. All share a cooler-climate tension that sets them apart, giving a vivid, energetic profile.

Pet-Nat (Naturally Sparkling Wines)

Unfiltered, lightly fizzy, often slightly rustic. These wines can be cloudy, fruity, gently funky, always lively. Less structured than traditional-method bottles, they offer a spontaneous, free-form expression of bubbles with plenty of personality.

Myths or Misunderstandings

A common misconception is that Champagne is the only fine traditional-method sparkling wine. In fact, Franciacorta, Trentodoc, high-end Cava, and English sparkling often match or exceed Champagne in quality. Another myth: that all Cava is inexpensive and simple. Top-tier Cava categories (Gran Reserva, Paraje Calificado) undergo long lees ageing and show remarkable complexity.

Some assume all non-Champagne sparkling wines are sweeter or fruitier when in fact most traditional-method styles are fully dry and deeply structured.

Finally, many believe bubbles are "just bubbles," but the size, texture, and persistence of mousse are defining markers of quality, and traditional-method wines excel in this regard.

Closing Reflection

Traditional-method sparkling wines beyond Champagne remind us that excellence is not confined to borders. These wines capture elegance, craft, and patience, bubbles shaped by terroir, climate, and time. They bring together citrus, minerality, savoury depth, and fine-textured mousse in a way that feels both familiar and distinct.

For drinkers who love sparkling wine and want to explore its diversity, these bottles offer some of the most rewarding journeys, sophisticated, expressive, and deeply satisfying. They teach us that beauty comes in many accents, and that the language of bubbles speaks differently in every landscape.

Prosecco

Prosecco feels like celebration made effortless. The moment the bubbles rise, the aromas come forward lightly and happily: fresh pear, green apple, white peach, wildflowers, and a touch of citrus. Nothing is heavy. Nothing is intense. Prosecco's charm lies in its brightness, its easy sweetness of fruit, and the gentle way its bubbles glide across the tongue, more soft sparkle than sharp fizz.

Made primarily from Glera, the grape naturally produces wines with delicate aromatics and soft textures. Fermented in large tanks rather than individual bottles, Prosecco keeps its freshness and fruitiness at the forefront. This is why Prosecco feels so welcoming: it's bubbly, but friendly; energetic but not demanding; lively, but soft around the edges.

It is the sparkling wine people reach for without overthinking, the one that fits sunny afternoons, casual gatherings, uncomplicated pleasures. Where Champagne is all tension and precision, Prosecco is all ease and charm.

Why People Love It

People love Prosecco because it is joyful and accessible. The flavours are familiar, pear, peach, citrus, elderflower, and the mousse is gentle rather than prickly. The acidity is refreshing but not sharp, making it easy to drink even for those who rarely reach for bubbles.

Emotionally, Prosecco appeals to people who want a sparkling wine that feels relaxed and fun rather than formal. It suits brunches, celebrations, picnics, spritz cocktails, and moments when simplicity is part of the pleasure. It's the sparkling wine that says, "come as you are."

How This Wine Feels

Prosecco is dry to off dry, light in body, with medium acidity and soft, creamy bubbles. The first sip brings a gentle burst of orchard fruit such as pear, apple and peach, all lifted by the mousse. The bubbles are finer than soda yet softer than those in Champagne, rising in a quiet, steady stream that makes the wine feel airy rather than tight.

The palate moves quickly, with the fruit gliding across before finishing in a clean, lightly floral impression. A swirl brings delicate aromatics into focus. After the wine leaves the palate, white peach, citrus blossom and a touch of honeydew seem to return in a soft second wave. The finish is short, crisp and refreshing, made to encourage the next sip rather than hold the spotlight.

If You Like This Wine... You May Also Like

Cava (Spain)

You'll recognise the bubbles and easy freshness, but Cava's traditional-method production brings finer mousse, more structure, and a leaner, more mineral feel. Prosecco remains fruitier and softer. Cava offers a more layered, serious style while keeping the celebratory energy intact.

Champagne (France)

Champagne shares Prosecco's sparkle but delivers far greater structure, toastiness, and complexity thanks to long lees ageing.

Where Prosecco leans peachy and floral, Champagne is biscuity, precise, and deeply refined—sparkling wine at its most elegant.

Moscato d'Asti (Italy)

A sweeter, low-alcohol option with soft bubbles and floral lift. Its peach, honey, and orange blossom flavours appeal to drinkers who enjoy Prosecco's fruitiness but want something even more playful and frothy.

Lambrusco (Italy)

Lambrusco brings red fruit, gentle bubbles, and styles ranging from dry to lightly sweet. It's richer and more savoury than Prosecco but just as refreshing, offering a darker, berry-driven take on sparkling wine.

Crémant (France)

Crémant uses the same traditional method as Champagne, offering finer bubbles, toastier notes, and more structure than Prosecco, often at a more accessible price. It provides complexity and finesse without the premium Champagne tag.

Stretch Wines

English Sparkling Wine

Expect higher acidity, sleeker structure, and Champagne-like precision. It's far cooler and more linear than Prosecco, offering a sharp, high-definition style of crispness.

Traditional-Method Rosé (Global)

These rosé sparklers bring red fruit, firmer bubbles, and more texture. Compared with Prosecco's soft stone-fruit charm, they feel brighter, more energetic, and more characterful, adding colour and depth to the experience.

Franciacorta (Italy)

Italy's traditional-method equivalent to Champagne—deeper, toastier, and more structured than Prosecco. It offers a polished, luxurious expression of Italian sparkling wine, showing just how elevated the style can become.

Myths or Misunderstandings

Many assume Prosecco is always sweet. Most high-quality Prosecco is Brut (dry), though the fruitiness can create a soft impression of sweetness. Another myth: that Prosecco is "cheap Champagne." It is not trying to be Champagne. It is an entirely different style built on softness, fragrance, and approachability.

Some believe the bubbles are artificial; in fact, Prosecco is naturally sparkling, the bubbles form during the Charmat method's pressurised fermentation.

Closing Reflection

Prosecco is a reminder that sparkling wine can be joyful without being serious, refreshing without being complex, celebratory without formality. It offers fruitiness, gentle bubbles, and easy charm, a wine that feels like laughter or a shared toast.

It teaches that pleasure doesn't need tension, length, or complexity. Sometimes the simplest wines carry the clearest happiness. And for those who want bubbles that feel welcoming and bright, Prosecco is one of the most delightful choices in the world.

Cava

Cava feels like sunlight captured in bubbles, a sparkling wine shaped by Mediterranean warmth, patient craftsmanship and the calm precision of the traditional method. Pour a glass and the colour settles in pale gold, bright enough to reflect the light, yet gentle in its glow. Lift it to your nose and the aromas rise with poised clarity: lemon peel, orchard fruit, almond, white blossom and a soft savoury thread that hints at the slow transformation taking place inside the bottle. The bubbles feel fine and steady, moving with quiet confidence rather than exuberance. Cava is made using the same traditional method as Champagne, with the second fermentation taking place in the bottle and the wine resting on its lees. Yet the warmth of its climate and the unique character of its native grapes give it a personality that feels more relaxed, more open and more Mediterranean in spirit.

Cava's identity is shaped partly by its grapes, particularly Macabeo, Xarel lo and Parellada. These varieties do not chase richness. They give brightness, herbal lift and gentle savoury tones that add depth without weight. They carry the warmth of the region but also the clarity that comes from higher altitudes and coastal winds. Cava's quality levels, especially Reserva and Gran Reserva, introduce extended lees ageing that adds layers of brioche, toasted nut and soft spice while retaining the wine's underlying freshness. At its heart, Cava feels composed and balanced. It offers refinement without austerity, warmth without heaviness and complexity without insistence.

Cava is a wine that suits easy gatherings, long afternoons, generous meals and celebratory moments that do not require fanfare. It brings people together without demanding attention, a sparkling wine that enhances the atmosphere rather than defining it. There is a serene confidence to Cava, a sense that it knows exactly what it wants to be.

Why People Love It

People love Cava because it offers the refinement of traditional method sparkling wine with a softness that feels instantly inviting. The bubbles carry flavours gracefully, never overwhelming the senses, and the aromas unfold with a quiet charm that lingers gently in the air. Cava feels structured yet comfortable, shaped by time on the lees but lifted by Mediterranean fruit. It suits those who want elegance without formality, who appreciate craft without ceremony and who enjoy wines that reveal their depth without needing to be studied.

Emotionally, Cava feels warm, sociable and content. It mirrors long lunches, evening terraces and the easy rhythm of southern light. It pairs naturally with food but stands beautifully on its own, a companion rather than a centrepiece. For many drinkers, Cava becomes the sparkling wine they return to when they want something delicious yet uncomplicated, something generous yet refined. It feels refreshing in spirit as much as in taste.

How This Wine Feels

Cava is dry, bright and finely textured, with bubbles that feel persistent rather than energetic. The first sip often brings lemon zest, green apple and pear, followed by subtle herbal tones and a gentle savoury line from the native grapes. Reserva and Gran Reserva expressions carry deeper layers of pastry, toasted nut and soft spice, a richness gained from long ageing on the lees. The wine moves smoothly across the palate, guided by fresh acidity and a calm, balanced mid palate.

The finish lingers with quiet clarity, offering a soft echo of citrus, almond and delicate yeast. Cava rarely feels sharp or forceful. Instead, it settles into a place of lightness and ease, leaving the senses refreshed and ready to enjoy another sip. It has the poise of Champagne but expresses it in a warmer, more relaxed voice.

If You Like This Wine… You May Also Like

Prosecco (Italy)

Prosecco offers a softer, fruit led style that feels gentle and lightly floral, with ripe pear, apple and a smooth, rounded texture. Its bubbles are more tender, creating a playful and easy drinking experience. While it does not carry the savoury depth of Cava, it offers a sense of charm and approachability that suits similar occasions. For drinkers who appreciate Cava's friendliness and want a sparkling wine with a more playful, fruit centred personality, Prosecco provides a joyful and uncomplicated alternative.

Crémant de Limoux (France)

Crémant de Limoux offers a fuller, warmer expression of traditional method sparkling wine, shaped by southern French sunshine and a blend of Chardonnay, Chenin Blanc and Mauzac. Expect ripe orchard fruit, lemon curd, subtle toast and a smooth, generous mid palate. The wine shares Cava's balance of freshness and quiet richness, making it an excellent choice for those who enjoy the Mediterranean character of Cava but want something with slightly deeper fruit and calm savoury tones. It feels welcoming, composed and beautifully rounded.

Crémant de Loire (France)

Crémant de Loire brings bright acidity, citrus and apple fruit, and a clear mineral thread, shaped largely by Chenin Blanc. It feels tauter and more linear than Cava, offering a cooler and more pointed style while maintaining the same refined texture of traditional method bubbles. For drinkers who enjoy Cava's clarity and structure but want a sparkling wine with more tension and a touch more brightness, Crémant de Loire provides a refreshing and elegant experience.

Franciacorta (Italy)

Franciacorta takes traditional method winemaking into a richer, more polished register. The fruit leans towards ripe citrus, peach and light pastry, supported by fine bubbles and a creamy texture from extended lees ageing. It feels more layered and more concentrated than Cava, yet it retains a sense of balance and calm. For those who enjoy Cava's refinement and wish to explore a more luxurious interpretation, Franciacorta offers an indulgent but composed alternative.

English Sparkling Wine

English sparkling wine brings vivid acidity, citrus brightness and chalky tension shaped by a cool climate. The bubbles feel brisk, the fruit compact and the finish taut and mineral. It is a sparkling wine of energy and precision, offering a dramatic contrast to Cava's softer warmth. For drinkers who enjoy the traditional method style but desire something sharper, cooler and more exhilarating, English sparkling wine provides a thrilling step outward.

Stretch Wines

Champagne (France)

Champagne deepens the conversation begun by Cava, offering layers of citrus, brioche, toasted nut and mineral length shaped by long ageing on the lees. The bubbles feel finer and the structure more defined, with flavours that build slowly through the glass. There is both delicacy and authority in Champagne, a sense of quiet depth beneath its elegance. For drinkers who enjoy Cava's refinement but want a more intricate, more resonant expression of the traditional method, Champagne offers a profound and memorable progression.

Trentodoc (Italy)

Trentodoc carries mountain freshness, with bright citrus, Alpine herbs and a fine mineral spine. The bubbles rise with precision, and the palate feels cool, pure and linear, shaped by Chardonnay and Pinot Noir grown at high altitude. It is a sparkling wine that feels both delicate and firm, offering a vivid contrast to Cava's Mediterranean warmth. For those who appreciate Cava's clarity and want to explore something with more chiselled edges and lifted tension, Trentodoc offers a captivating shift in tone.

Aged Cava Gran Reserva (Spain)

Extended ageing transforms Cava into a more contemplative wine, with deeper flavours of toasted almond, brioche, warm spice and savoury depth that stretch across the palate. The bubbles feel more integrated, the fruit more concentrated and the finish longer and more layered. This is Cava at its most serious and complex, a style that rewards slow sipping and thoughtful moments. For drinkers who enjoy the structure and calm richness of Cava and wish to explore its most expressive form, Gran Reserva offers a beautifully mature and resonant experience.

Myths or Misunderstandings

A common misunderstanding is that Cava is simply a cheaper version of Champagne. While the wines share the same method, they express entirely different landscapes, grapes and personalities. Another misconception is that Cava is always simple or light, yet Reserva and Gran Reserva styles offer remarkable depth and ageing potential. Some believe that all Cava tastes alike, but the variations between altitudes, ageing periods and grape blends create a wide spectrum of styles. It is also assumed that sparkling wine from warmer regions must be soft, yet the best Cava balances warmth with freshness through thoughtful vineyard selection and long maturation.

Closing Reflection

Cava is a celebration of balance, a sparkling wine that brings refinement into everyday life with grace and ease. It offers the beauty of the traditional method shaped by Mediterranean light, combining freshness with warmth and structure with calm generosity. It suits both lively gatherings and quiet moments, always offering a sense of uplift. Cava reminds us that elegance does not need to be reserved for grand occasions. Sometimes it is the subtle, gentle pleasures that stay with us the longest, rising softly through the glass and settling in memory with a quiet, joyful glow.

Sparkling Rosé

Sparkling Rosé looks like celebration dressed in colour, a glass of soft ruby or coral, alive with bubbles that rise in delicate, steady streams. Bring it to your nose and the aromas bloom with both freshness and charm: wild strawberry, raspberry, pomegranate, cherry blossom, citrus peel, and sometimes a hint of pastry, herbs, or spice depending on the method used. It carries the brightness of sparkling wine and the joy of red fruit, a combination that feels instantly festive.

Unlike still rosé, sparkling rosé brings texture and lift. The bubbles give red fruit a buoyant, dancing quality. And unlike many sparkling whites, sparkling rosé feels slightly fuller, rounder, and more expressive. It is the wine of summer brunches, celebrations, special dinners, and joyful spontaneous moments. There's something about that colour, that glimmer, that feels emotionally uplifting before you even take a sip.

Why People Love It

People love sparkling rosé because it blends refreshment with romance. It has the crispness of a sparkling white and the gentle fruit of a rosé, making it one of the most universally appealing styles of bubbly. The acidity is lively, but the fruit softens the edges. The bubbles sparkle without sharpness. The flavours feel familiar, strawberries, cherries, citrus, but carried upward by the elegance of effervescence.

Emotionally, sparkling rosé appeals to drinkers who want something festive but not formal. It suits birthdays, dinners, anniversaries, picnics, brunches, or any moment that feels like it deserves a little colour. It's sophisticated enough for evening, but playful enough for afternoon.

How This Wine Feels

Sparkling rosé can be dry to off dry, light to medium in body, with crisp acidity and fine, elegant bubbles. The first sip feels lifted, showing strawberry, raspberry and citrus zest, often with a faint creaminess in traditional-method styles that comes from time spent on the lees. The mousse acts as a soft cushion for the fruit, giving the flavours a rounder feel than in a still rosé.

The wine usually carries more mid palate weight than a white sparkling wine, especially when Pinot Noir or Grenache forms the base. A swirl brings out red fruit, floral notes and, depending on the style, hints of pastry or spice. After the wine leaves the palate, the aromas gather again, returning strawberry and cherry with a light touch of brioche or herbs. The finish is crisp, refreshing and lightly fruity, cleansing the palate without turning austere.

If You Like This Wine... You May Also Like

Prosecco Rosé

Soft bubbles and approachable fruit carry through here, with a little extra peach and floral lift. Compared with traditional-method sparkling rosé, Prosecco Rosé stays lighter, gentler, and more playful. It is an easy, everyday style built for uncomplicated enjoyment.

Crémant Rosé (France)

Dry, refined, and traditionally made, with fine bubbles and subtle toast. It echoes the structure of Champagne Rosé but with softer fruit and a more understated complexity. A polished, sophisticated option that remains comfortably priced.

Champagne Rosé

You'll recognise the bubbles and red-fruit brightness, but Champagne Rosé deepens everything—brioche richness, chalky tension, layered precision. It stands as a more powerful, more expressive, more finely structured form of sparkling rosé.

Lambrusco Rosato (Italy)

Sparkling, fruity, and full of charm. Lambrusco Rosato is juicier and sometimes lightly sweet, offering bright berry flavours with lively energy. A spirited, flavourful spin on rosé bubbles.

Cava Rosado (Spain)

Traditional-method sparkle with strawberry and cherry notes supported by herbal, savoury touches. More structured than

Prosecco Rosé yet gentler than Champagne. It sits comfortably between crisp freshness and layered complexity.

Stretch Wines

Still Rosé (Provence style)

For those who love sparkling rosé but want to explore still wine, Provence offers the cleanest, most delicate shift. Without bubbles, the focus moves to purity, texture, and quiet elegance—a serene counterpart to sparkling styles.

Red Lambrusco (Dry styles)

A bold step into sparkling red. Dry Lambrusco brings red fruit with tannin, weight, and a frothier mousse, creating a darker, more savoury, more tactile experience—an entirely different way to approach fizz.

Blanc de Noirs Champagne

Dry, structured, and made entirely from Pinot Noir (or Meunier). Even without colour, it carries red-fruit depth shaped by chalky precision. A focused, serious expression of Champagne rooted firmly in red-grape character.

Myths or Misunderstandings

A common myth is that sparkling rosé is sweet. Most quality examples are Brut or Extra Brut, dry, crisp, and structured. The fruitiness comes from the red grapes, not sugar.

Another misconception is that colour indicates sweetness or heaviness. Sparkling rosé gets its hue from brief maceration or blending with a little red wine, neither of which determines sugar level or weight.

Some believe sparkling rosé is less serious than Champagne Blanc de Blancs or Blanc de Noirs. In truth, some of the world's most complex sparkling wines are rosé, especially when Pinot Noir takes centre stage.

Closing Reflection

Sparkling Rosé brings together the elegance of bubbles and the charm of red fruit. It is both refreshing and expressive, both celebratory and comforting. The colour brings joy, the bubbles bring energy, and the flavours bring a sense of ease.

For drinkers who want something beautiful, versatile, and uplifting, sparkling rosé offers one of the most emotionally resonant experiences in the sparkling world. It reminds us that celebration isn't only about precision, sometimes it's about colour, fruit, and the quiet thrill of tiny bubbles rising through something pink.

---

1. Autolytic: Flavours and textures that come from yeast breakdown during extended lees ageing, often showing bread, dough, or nutty tones.
2. Racy: A wine with lively, high acidity that creates a sense of speed and energy.

Chapter 10

Sweet Wines

Wines where richness meets balance and sweetness carries structure

Moscato d'Asti

Moscato d'Asti feels like sunlight caught in bubbles, bright, fragrant, softly sweet, and wonderfully light. Bring the glass close and the aromatics rise in a way few wines can match. You'll savour white peach, apricot, orange blossom, honeysuckle, pear sorbet, and a gentle lift of citrus. It smells like summer fruit perfumed with flowers, delicate yet exuberant.

The wine itself is lightly sparkling, not fully fizzy, a soft, frothy, playful mousse that feels more like a whisper than a fizz. Everything about Moscato d'Asti expresses ease: low alcohol, gentle sweetness, airy bubbles, and the impression of biting into a perfectly ripe peach.

Why People Love It

People love Moscato d'Asti because it brings joy without heaviness. The sweetness is tender, not syrupy. The alcohol is low, usually around 5–6%, making it feel refreshing rather than indulgent. The bubbles lift the fruit, keeping the wine lively and bright.

Emotionally, it appeals to those who want a wine that feels happy, a wine that flatters fruit desserts, celebrates casual occasions, and welcomes even the most hesitant wine drinker. It makes people smile.

It's perfect for brunch, birthdays, picnics, toasts, and moments when you want sweetness without weight.

How This Wine Feels

Moscato d'Asti is lightly sparkling, sweet, and delicately textured. The first sip brings an immediate rush of fruit such as peach, pear, grape and citrus, all wrapped in frothy, creamy bubbles. The acidity is bright enough to balance the sweetness, so the wine feels lively rather than sticky.

The sweetness moves gently across the palate, carried by the wine's natural aromatic intensity. The texture is silky, soft and buoyant. A swirl lifts floral and fruit notes even higher, and once the wine leaves the palate, those aromas return with blossomy sweetness and touches of citrus peel.

The finish is lightly sweet, refreshing and clean, leaving a soft echo of peach and orange blossom.

If You Like This Wine... You May Also Like

Brachetto d'Acqui (Italy)

Also lightly sparkling and sweet, but with red fruit—strawberry, raspberry, rose. It's fruitier, more aromatic, and just as gently bubbly. A red-fruited counterpart to Moscato's peachy lightness, full of effortless charm.

Asti Spumante (Italy)

Fully sparkling, more effervescent, and slightly sweeter than Moscato d'Asti. It feels brighter, bubblier, more overtly festive—Moscato's joy turned up and set alight.

Late-Harvest Riesling

Shares sweetness and fruit purity but adds higher acidity and flavours of lime, apricot, and floral spice. It's more intense, less frothy, and shaped by sharper structure that brings added complexity.

Off-Dry Rosé or White Zinfandel

These wines echo Moscato's soft sweetness and easy fruit, just without the bubbles and with gentler aromatics. A simple, relaxed still-wine expression of the same sweet-leaning charm.

Prosecco (Extra Dry)

Not sweet, but fruit-forward and lightly floral with soft mousse. It's drier, cleaner, and less aromatic than Moscato, offering a more refreshing, lightly sparkling alternative.

Stretch Wines

Sauternes (France)

Far richer and more honeyed, showing apricot, saffron, vanilla, and botrytis[1] spice. Compared with Moscato, this is deeper, weightier, and unmistakably luxurious—sweetness taken to its most decadent dimension.

Tokaji Aszú (Hungary)

Intensely sweet yet lifted by electric acidity, with flavours of apricot, marmalade, tea, and honey. More structured and dramatically long on the palate, taking sweetness into a vivid, high-definition realm.

German Auslese or Spätlese Riesling

Sweetness balanced by vibrant acidity and firmer mineral drive. Where Moscato is airy and gentle, these Rieslings are richer, more layered, and shaped with a sense of poised elegance.

Myths or Misunderstandings

One myth: that Moscato d'Asti is "simple" or "unsophisticated." In truth, the finest examples show remarkable purity and aromatic precision, capturing freshness that would be lost in a more powerful style.

Another misunderstanding: that Moscato must be sugary-sweet. Because of its low alcohol and bright acidity, Moscato d'Asti often tastes lighter and less sweet than its sugar level would suggest.

Some also think Moscato is only for desserts. While perfect with fruit, it's also excellent with spicy foods, salty snacks, soft cheeses, and moments where sweetness offers comfort.

Closing Reflection

Moscato d'Asti is a reminder that wine can be charming, joyful, and light. It offers fruitiness, sweetness, and delicacy without intensity or weight, a wine that feels playful and welcoming. Its low alcohol and gentle bubbles make it feel like a celebration you can sip easily.

It teaches that sweetness can be refreshing, that aromatics can feel like a breeze, and that some wines exist simply to give pleasure. For anyone who wants a wine that feels bright and joyful, Moscato d'Asti is one of the purest expressions of happiness in a glass.

Ice Wine

Ice Wine feels like winter fruit concentrated into liquid gold, pure, radiant sweetness balanced by electrifying acidity. Bring the glass to your nose and the aromas shine intensely: apricot, peach nectar, candied citrus, ripe pineapple, honey, and sometimes a hint of fresh herbs or a cool, crystalline lift. It smells like fruit preserved by frost, heightened rather than muted, bright even in its richness.

Made in cold climates, Canada, Germany, Austria, occasionally the Finger Lakes, N.Y., Ice Wine exists only because grapes are allowed to freeze naturally on the vine. At temperatures around −8°C (17°F) or below, water inside each grape turns to ice. When the grapes are pressed while still frozen, only the tiny, concentrated droplets of sugary juice escape, leaving the ice behind. The yield is tiny. The flavour is immense.

Why People Love It

People love Ice Wine because it delivers purity with intensity. The sweetness is rich but not cloying, lifted by acidity that keeps everything bright. It feels luxurious and precise at the same time, like fruit transformed, not overwhelmed. Its flavours are vivid, almost luminous: apricot, peach, lemon curd, honey, lychee, tropical fruit, crystalline citrus.

Emotionally, it appeals to those who want a dessert wine that feels alive rather than heavy. It suits special occasions, quiet winter evenings, fruit-based desserts, and meals that end with something small but spectacular. There is something magical in the idea of grapes frozen on the vine, nature's intervention creating sweetness through hardship.

How This Wine Feels

Ice Wine is sweet, medium to full in body, and driven by very high acidity. The first sip feels luxurious, with thick, honeyed fruit gliding across the palate. Soon after, the acidity steps in, bright and sharp, lifting the richness and turning the sweetness into something elegant rather than heavy.

The texture is silky but deeply concentrated. A swirl intensifies the aromas, bringing forward apricot jam, marmalade, honeysuckle, peach and tropical fruit. After the wine leaves the palate, those scents return in a vivid mix of citrus zest, candied fruit and honeyed brightness. The finish is long, shimmering and mouthwatering, the interplay of acidity and sweetness lingering long after the sip has passed.

If You Like This Wine… You May Also Like

Sauternes (France)

Sauternes shares Ice Wine's sweetness and richness but adds botrytis-driven layers of saffron, vanilla, honey, and warm spice. It's creamier, deeper, and far more luxurious—dessert wine at its grandest, shaped by complexity as much as by sweetness.

German Beerenauslese Riesling (BA)

BA delivers comparable sweetness but with electric acidity and concentrated apricot, citrus, and honey. Botrytis brings added spice and nuance, creating a high-sweetness style defined by precision and layered detail.

Tokaji Aszú (Hungary)

Tokaji parallels Ice Wine's intensity yet introduces apricot paste, tea, orange peel, and volcanic minerality. Its acidity is razor-sharp, giving the wine an architectural, finely chiselled form of sweetness.

Late-Harvest Riesling

Shares Ice Wine's sweetness and fruit purity but offers softer contours, rounder flavours, and less concentration. A gentler, more relaxed take on the style, ideal for a lighter, easier expression of sweetness.

Moscato d'Asti

For drinkers who enjoy sweetness but prefer minimal alcohol and soft bubbles, Moscato offers joyful, fragrant charm without the intensity of Ice Wine. Sweetness comes in a lighter, airy frame.

Stretch Wines

Eiswein (Germany or Austria)

Traditional Eiswein reflects Ice Wine's purity but tends to be lighter, more mineral, and more lime-driven. Now rare due to climate, it shows sweetness carried with delicacy and clarity rather than weight.

Vin Santo (Italy)

A completely different style of richness—caramel, dried fruit, nuts, and warm oxidation. Lower acidity and greater warmth create a contrasting but equally powerful expression of dessert wine rooted in tradition.

Recioto della Valpolicella (Italy)

A sweet red wine offering cherry, chocolate, and spice. It shifts from sweet white to sweet red while retaining similar textural generosity, opening a distinctive path for those who love dessert wines with deeper, darker flavour.

Myths or Misunderstandings

One frequent misunderstanding is that Ice Wine is syrupy or heavy. Its defining trait is acidity, the brightness that prevents sweetness from becoming cloying. Another myth: that Ice Wine can be made artificially by freezing grapes after harvest. True Ice Wine (or Eiswein) must freeze *naturally on the vine*.

Some also assume Ice Wine is only for desserts. While perfect with fruit-based sweets, it also pairs beautifully with blue cheese, foie gras, citrus tarts, or simply enjoyed on its own, a small glass of concentrated beauty.

Closing Reflection

Ice Wine reveals sweetness at its most luminous. It brings together the richness of honeyed fruit and the brilliance of cutting acidity in a balance that feels almost crystalline. It is nature's gift: a wine made through cold, patience, and precision.

For those who want dessert wine that feels both luxurious and vibrant, Ice Wine offers one of the clearest expressions of sweet purity in the world. It teaches that sweetness can be fresh, that richness can be bright, and that some of the most extraordinary wines come from the harshest conditions.

Sauternes

Sauternes feels like a golden tapestry, a wine woven from honey, light, and time. Pour it and the colour alone tells a story: deep gold, sometimes shading toward amber, shimmering with richness. Bring the glass to your nose and the aromas rise in slow, complex layers: apricot and peach compote, candied citrus peel, saffron, honeycomb, toasted almonds, vanilla, quince, and the unmistakable fragrance of botrytis, noble rot, which adds a spicy, almost incense-like perfume.

There is nothing else quite like it. Sauternes is one of the world's great sweet wines, crafted from grapes affected by *Botrytis Cinerea*, a fungus that concentrates sugars, acids, and flavours while transforming the fruit's character. Made primarily from Sémillon, with Sauvignon Blanc for lift and Muscadelle for perfume, it is a wine of both richness and radiance, a paradox of decadence and purity.

Why People Love It

People love Sauternes because it offers sweetness with architecture. It is rich, luscious, and intensely flavoured, but never heavy. The acidity acts like a beam of light through stained glass, illuminating the honeyed layers and keeping the wine vibrant.

Emotionally, Sauternes appeals to those who enjoy wines that feel luxurious, contemplative, and almost otherworldly. It elevates meals, enhances desserts, and creates moments of calm indulgence. It's a wine for evenings when time seems to slow, a wine that invites you to linger.

How This Wine Feels

Sauternes is sweet, full bodied and unctuous, yet carried by vivid acidity. The first sip coats the palate with concentrated fruit such as apricot jam, marmalade, peach nectar and dried pineapple. Soon after, the brightness arrives. Lemon peel and crisp acidity cut through the richness, lifting the wine and keeping it in motion.

The texture is silky, thick and luxurious. Time spent in oak adds gentle layers of spice, vanilla and warmth. A swirl deepens the aromatics, bringing forward honeycomb, toasted nuts, golden raisins, saffron and crème brûlée. Once the wine leaves the palate, those notes gather again, returning with ripe fruit, spice and a faint nuttiness that stretches through a long, glowing finish.

Sauternes also changes beautifully with age. Young bottles are vibrant and fruit driven. With time, the wine develops caramel, toffee, dried fruit and mushroom tones that add remarkable depth and complexity.

If You Like This Wine… You May Also Like

Tokaji Aszú (Hungary)

You'll recognise the sweetness and botrytis richness, but Tokaji is sharper, more acidic, and more tea-like, with flavours of apricot paste, orange peel, and honeyed spice. It delivers sweetness with electrifying tension and a finely etched sense of brilliance.

German Beerenauslese (BA)

BA wines are similarly sweet and luscious but lean more toward citrus, stone fruit, and floral delicacy. They rely on acidity and purity rather than oak or deep spice, giving a cleaner, more crystalline expression of botrytised sweetness.

Recioto della Valpolicella (Italy)

Where Sauternes glows with honey, apricot, and saffron, Recioto moves into darker territory with cherry liqueur, cocoa, dried fruit, velvety richness. The tone is different, but the sense of luxury is the same. For anyone drawn to Sauternes' opulence who wants to explore a red-fruit, soft-chocolate style of sweetness, Recioto offers a beautifully contrasting path.

Ice Wine (Canada, Germany)

Ice Wine brings purity, brightness, and intense sweetness without botrytis spice. It focuses on peach, apricot, and citrus, giving a cleaner, frost-shaped clarity rather than a fungus-driven richness.

Vin Santo (Italy)

Vin Santo channels oxidative richness—caramel, dried fruit, nuts—rather than botrytis character. It's less bright, more meditative, and deeply traditional, offering indulgence expressed through warmth and age.

Late-Harvest Riesling

Shares sweetness and fruit purity but with higher acidity and a lighter, cooler texture. Compared to Sauternes, it comes across more delicate and more refreshing, giving sweetness with greater agility.

Stretch Wines

Aged Sauternes (15–30 years)

A further journey into Sauternes itself. Age transforms the wine into something deeper and more intricate: toffee, dried apricot, chai spice, toasted hazelnut, tobacco leaf, mushroom. It becomes a slow-unfolding, profoundly expressive form of sweetness.

Rutherglen Muscat (Australia)

Extremely rich and intensely sweet, with flavours of raisin, coffee, caramel, and chocolate. Heavier and more viscous than Sauternes, offering a level of decadence that pushes sweetness to its outer limits.

Madeira (Boal or Malmsey)

Madeira delivers sweetness shaped by volcanic acidity and long oxidative development with burnt sugar, citrus peel, coffee, sea-spray salt. It stands as a dramatic, fire-and-earth alternative to honey-and-fruit styles, with a structure entirely its own.

Myths or Misunderstandings

A common myth: Sauternes is only a "dessert wine." While perfect with fruit tarts, custards, or pear desserts, it also pairs brilliantly with savoury dishes, especially foie gras, pâté, blue cheese, roasted nuts, and even spicy Asian cuisine. In France, Sauternes is considered an *aperitif*.

Another misconception: all Sauternes tastes the same. In truth, each château has its own signature, some lean more honeyed, others more citrusy or spicy, others more mineral and lifted.

Some drinkers assume its sweetness makes it heavy. Acidity and botrytis give Sauternes remarkable lift, it's rich, certainly, but rarely cloying.

Closing Reflection

Sauternes is a testament to patience, nature, and craft. It takes risk, waiting for noble rot, and extraordinary labour to produce a single bottle. The result is one of the most captivatingly sweet wines in the world: rich yet balanced, luxurious yet bright, complex yet comforting.

It teaches that sweetness can be profound, that time can shape beauty, and that wine can feel both indulgent and illuminated. For those who want a sweet wine that carries history, complexity, and emotional resonance, Sauternes offers an experience like no other.

Tokaji Aszú

Tokaji Aszú feels like sweetness shaped into architecture, luminous, structured, and profoundly expressive. As you lift the glass, the aromatics rise in waves both delicate and intense: apricot paste, dried peach, orange marmalade, candied citrus peel, honeycomb, saffron, chamomile, toasted nuts, and a thread of black tea or tobacco leaf. These aren't simple fruit notes. They carry depth, warmth, and a quiet sense of centuries-old tradition.

Made in Hungary's Tokaj region, Tokaji Aszú is one of the world's great sweet wines, crafted from grapes touched by *noble rot* (*Botrytis cinerea*). The shrivelled, botrytised berries, called "aszú" berries, are painstakingly hand-picked, then macerated in a base wine or must. The result is a wine of breathtaking concentration, shimmering acidity, and a balance that feels almost impossible: sweet, yet taut; rich, yet never heavy.

Why People Love It

People love Tokaji Aszú because it is sweet wine with spine, sweetness held in tension by laser-bright acidity. The flavours are vivid and layered: apricot, citrus, tea, spice, dried fruit, honey, ginger. But what makes Tokaji unforgettable is its energy. Beneath the richness shines a piercing acidity that keeps every sip lively and breath-catching.

Emotionally, Tokaji appeals to those who want sweetness that feels alive, not languid. It suits contemplative evenings, winter warmth, holiday tables, cheese courses, fruit desserts, and any moment that deserves a wine with history and soul. Tokaji is a wine to savour slowly, with a kind of reverence.

How This Wine Feels

Tokaji Aszú is sweet, full bodied and shaped by very high acidity. The first sip feels luxurious, with dense apricot, marmalade, citrus oil and honeyed spice rolling across the palate. Soon after, the acidity comes forward, sharp and clean, lifting the wine's weight and making the sweetness feel bright rather than heavy.

The texture is silky and concentrated, with a slight firmness from the botrytis that gives the wine a gentle grip. A slow swirl deepens the layers, bringing out orange blossom, ginger, beeswax, dried fruit and tea leaves. Once the wine leaves the palate, those flavours gather again, revealing apricot jam, black tea, spice and citrus peel, leading into a finish that seems to glow for minutes. The balance of sweetness and acidity is so harmonious it can feel almost otherworldly.

Tokaji also ages exceptionally well. Young bottles are vivid with fruit and citrus. Over time, the wine broadens into caramel, tea, tobacco, dried apricot and savoury complexity, becoming deeper and more intricate with each passing year.

If You Like This Wine… You May Also Like

Sauternes (France)

Both wines are botrytised and luxurious, but Sauternes is richer, warmer, more honeyed, with vanilla and spice from oak. Tokaji is sharper, more tea-like, more citrus-driven. It becomes a study in contrast—the French expression of opulence beside the Hungarian expression of brilliance.

Recioto della Valpolicella (Italy)

Tokaji's electric acidity and citrus lift meets its opposite in Recioto's plush, fruit-heavy sweetness. Both wines are complex and age beautifully, yet their voices diverge completely. For those who admire Tokaji's depth but want something softer, rounder, and more comforting, Recioto brings warmth where Tokaji brings radiance.

German Beerenauslese (BA)

BA shows similar sweetness and high acidity, centred on apricot, peach, citrus, and floral clarity. It tends to be silkier, gentler, and less spicy than Tokaji. A delicate, crystalline counterpart to Tokaji's more intense, tea-inflected richness.

Ice Wine (Canada, Germany)

Ice Wine shares Tokaji's purity and intense sweetness but without botrytis influence. It leans fruitier, brighter, more linear, focusing on frozen concentration rather than noble rot. A cleaner, frost-shaped interpretation of sweetness.

Vin Santo (Italy)

Vin Santo mirrors some of Tokaji's nuttiness and dried-fruit depth, but achieves it through oxidative ageing. It is warmer, less acidic, and more meditative, offering richness shaped by air and time rather than fungus.

Late-Harvest Riesling

A lighter, fresher approach to sweet wine—higher acidity, softer texture, and a fruit-driven profile. Compared to Tokaji's structure and spice, it feels gentler, offering sweetness with more lift and agility.

Stretch Wines

Essencia (Tokaj)

Essencia represents Tokaji at its most extreme: intensely sweet, nectar-thick, and profoundly concentrated. With almost no alcohol and near-pure botrytised juice, it stands apart from table wine entirely—a singular, immersive experience of sweetness and precision pushed to the limit.

Madeira (Boal or Malmsey)

Madeira delivers sweetness backed by volcanic acidity and oxidative depth—caramel, salt, coffee, burnt sugar, citrus peel. Sharper and more savoury than Tokaji, it channels sweetness through fire, stone, and slow evolution.

Rutherglen Muscat (Australia)

One of the world's richest sweet wines. They are thick, raisined, fortified, and intensely sticky. Against Tokaji's bright precision,

Rutherglen Muscat feels dense, dark, and syrupy, offering a form of sweetness that becomes dessert in its own right.

Myths or Misunderstandings

Many believe Tokaji is extremely heavy because of its sweetness. Its high acidity makes it feel lifted and balanced, often lighter on the palate than richer dessert wines. Another misconception is that Aszú wines must be extremely old to be good. While they age beautifully, young Tokaji Aszú can be dazzling, vibrant, juicy, and intensely aromatic.

Some also confuse Tokaji Aszú with simple late-harvest wines. Aszú relies on botrytised berries and a unique maceration process, giving it a complexity and intensity unmatched by standard sweet wines.

Closing Reflection

Tokaji Aszú is one of the world's most profound sweet wines, a harmony of sweetness, acidity, and botrytis-driven complexity that feels both ancient and alive. It carries the history of a region where volcanic soils meet cold wind and long autumns, and where noble rot transforms grapes into gold.

It teaches that sweetness can have structure, that luxury can have tension, and that the most memorable wines often balance opposing forces, richness and brightness, fruit and spice, intensity and elegance. For those who seek a sweet wine with soul, Tokaji Aszú is among the greatest experiences wine can offer.

Late-Harvest Riesling

Late-Harvest Riesling tastes like the moment autumn lingers before winter arrives, fruit at its ripest, sunlight at its warmest, and air at its crispest. Pour a glass and the aromas rise with a kind of gentle abundance: peach nectar, apricot, candied lemon peel, honeysuckle, ripe pear, and sometimes a glimmer of mango or pineapple. There is nothing heavy in the perfume, nothing sticky. It feels bright and golden at the same time, like warm light moving through cool air.

What makes late-harvest Riesling so distinctive is the way it gathers sweetness without losing its natural vitality. By waiting longer to pick the grapes, the winemaker captures richer aromas, deeper flavours, and higher natural sugar; yet Riesling keeps its acidity even at advanced ripeness, giving the finished wine a sense of motion rather than density. The result is a style that manages to feel both comforting and refreshing, indulgent and alive. It is sweetness illuminated from within.

Why People Love It

People love Late-Harvest Riesling because it offers pleasure without weight. The fruit feels pure, apricot, peach, citrus, lychee, and the sweetness glides across the palate rather than settling onto it. At the same time, the acidity keeps every sip alert and bright, the way a squeeze of lemon heightens the sweetness of summer fruit.

Emotionally, this is a wine for people who want sweetness that feels uplifting rather than decadent. It suits fruit desserts, pastries, soft cheeses, brunch dishes, and quiet evenings when something gentle and golden feels right. It is the kind of wine that brings warmth without heaviness, like a blanket light enough for early autumn.

How This Wine Feels

Late Harvest Riesling is sweet, smooth and medium in body, yet its core is always acidity. The first sip feels silky, concentrated with ripe stone fruit and citrus oils. Then the acidity rises, clean and crisp, and the sweetness feels lifted rather than heavy. The wine moves across the palate like honey brightened by light, its richness balanced by the natural freshness Riesling maintains even at full ripeness.

A swirl intensifies the aromatics, bringing forward peach nectar, apricot preserves, lime blossom, honeycomb and, at times, a soft mineral hint or a faint petrol tone in older bottles. After the wine leaves the palate, those flavours return in a gentle echo, settling into a finish that is sweet yet clear, with a lifted sense of brightness.

Understanding Late-Harvest Riesling, and How to Recognise It

Because Riesling is one of the most transparent grapes in the world, the idea of "late harvest" changes subtly depending on where the wine comes from. In Germany, the spiritual home of the style, the term appears directly on the label as *Spätlese*, a word that literally means "late picked." A bottle marked simply as Spätlese is usually sweet, though not always; German producers sometimes finish Spätlese wines dry or off-dry, and if they do, they'll say so. The ABV is also a helpful indicator. With Riesling a good rule of thing is the higher the ABV the lower the residual sugar. A Spätlese labelled *trocken* is dry, while one marked *feinherb* is gently off-dry. If no such term appears, you can trust you're holding a sweet late-harvest Riesling.

A step richer is *Auslese*, meaning "select harvest," a wine made from late-picked grapes chosen berry by berry. Auslese often includes fruit touched by noble rot, giving the wine more honey, spice, and depth. These wines are almost always sweet, with layers that unfold slowly across the palate.

Even sweeter, more concentrated tiers exist, *Beerenauslese* and *Trockenbeerenauslese*, but these move beyond the everyday idea of late harvest into rare, almost jewel-like dessert wines. They share the DNA of late harvest but amplify it dramatically.

Outside Germany, the language changes but the idea remains. In Alsace, the term is *Vendange Tardive*, and these wines tend to be rich, ripe, and occasionally kissed by botrytis. In Austria you'll see Spätlese and Auslese just as in Germany. In North America, where the language is simpler, labels often say "Late Harvest Riesling," with sweetness levels depending on the winemaker's intent, from lightly sweet to richly luxurious.

Wherever it's made, these wines share a core truth: sweetness shaped by ripeness, not fortification[2]; richness balanced by acidity, not masked by alcohol. The style is always defined by fruit that has been allowed to mature longer on the vine.

How Late-Harvest Riesling Differs from Dry Riesling

Tasting the two side by side feels like watching the same character in two different moods. Dry Riesling is taut and linear, lime zest, green apple, slate, cool wind, and hard-edged precision. Late-Harvest Riesling, by contrast, is relaxed, generous, peachy, honeyed, and warm, yet still brightly lit by acidity. Dry Riesling moves straight through the palate; late harvest moves outward, broadening as it goes.

The textures diverge too. Dry Riesling feels crisp and almost crystalline. Late harvest feels silky, sometimes faintly viscous, shaped by sugar but lifted by acidity. And then there is the emotional difference: dry Riesling sharpens the senses; late harvest softens them. One is the sound of a struck bell; the other is the glow after its final resonance.

If You Like This Wine... You May Also Like

German Spätlese (Mosel, Rheingau, Nahe)

You'll recognise the familiar interplay of sweetness and acidity, but Spätlese feels lighter and more airborne, shaped by cooler climates and intensely mineral soils. Where Late-Harvest Riesling leans toward ripe peach and soft honey, Spätlese moves toward lime, white blossom, and slate. For those who enjoy late-harvest styles but want gentler sweetness and sharper definition, Spätlese offers the same pleasure in a more ethereal register.

Alsace Vendange Tardive (Riesling or Pinot Gris)

Vendange Tardive shares late-harvest ripeness and concentration, but Alsace wines tend to be more structured and textural. Riesling adds brightness and savoury depth; Pinot Gris contributes warm orchard fruit, ginger, and supple spice. The result is fuller and more layered than typical Late-Harvest Riesling. For anyone drawn to late-harvest warmth who seeks a more intense, architectural style, Vendange Tardive is the natural progression.

Canadian Riesling Ice Wine

Ice Wine magnifies Riesling's purity, brighter acidity, heightened fruit concentration, and sweetness that feels crystalline rather than creamy. It differs in intensity but echoes Late-Harvest Riesling's clarity and orchard-fruit charm. For drinkers who love sweetness carried by acidity and want a more vivid, jewel-like expression, Ice Wine offers captivating precision.

Off-Dry Vouvray (Chenin Blanc)

Chenin mirrors the gentle sweetness and soft fruit but adds waxy texture, honeycomb, and quiet earth tones. Compared with Late-Harvest Riesling, it's rounder, more textural, and a touch less aromatic. For those who enjoy the comfort and balance of Late-Harvest Riesling but want deeper layers and a more grounded sensibility, Vouvray gives generosity with a subtle savoury undertone.

Gewürztraminer (Alsace, Medium-Sweet Styles)

Gewürztraminer matches Riesling's sweetness but shifts the aromatics toward rose, lychee, ginger, and warm spice. It's fuller in perfume, broader in texture, and lower in acidity. For those drawn to Late-Harvest Riesling's richness who want a more dramatic, exotic expression, Gewürztraminer offers sweetness with bold aromatic flair.

Stretch Wines

Sauternes (France)

Sauternes carries sweetness with greater warmth and luxurious breadth—honey, apricot, vanilla, saffron, and the creamy depth of noble rot. It trades Late-Harvest Riesling's clarity for opulence while maintaining balance. For anyone seeking richness delivered with deeper complexity, Sauternes speaks in a grander, more sumptuous voice.

Tokaji Aszú (Hungary)

Tokaji heightens everything: sweetness, acidity, aromatic detail. Citrus peel, apricot paste, tea, and spice create a wine that feels both radiant and profound. Compared to Late-Harvest Riesling, it is sharper, more vertical, and more dramatic. For those intrigued by sweetness carried on a beam of energy, Tokaji expands the style with striking intensity.

Beerenauslese (Germany or Austria)

BA resembles Late-Harvest Riesling but with greater concentration and botrytis influence. Textures become richer, flavours densify, sweetness deepens. It reads as Late-Harvest Riesling viewed through a more indulgent, luxurious lens. For drinkers wanting the same flavour family taken to a richer extreme, BA is the natural evolution.

Myths or Misunderstandings

Many assume that sweetness makes late-harvest Riesling heavy. Yet the opposite is true: the grape's acidity is so vibrant that even the sweetest versions remain energetic. Others believe Riesling must always be sweet; the grape spans a spectrum from bone-dry to lusciously sweet. Late harvest is simply one point on that continuum. And some worry that sweet wines must be dessert-only, when in truth late-harvest Riesling is one of the most versatile food wines in the world, brilliant with spice, salt, cheese, fruit, and even rich dishes that benefit from a touch of sweetness.

Closing Reflection

Late-Harvest Riesling is sweetness seen through the lens of light, a wine that gathers ripeness but refuses heaviness, that offers warmth without losing clarity. It moves with the grace of fruit at its perfect moment, supported by acidity that keeps everything shining. It is a reminder that sweetness can be refined, that richness can be gentle, and that some wines speak most beautifully when they balance indulgence with brightness.

For drinkers who want sweetness that feels alive, delicate, and expressive, Late-Harvest Riesling is one of the most captivating styles in the world. It invites slow enjoyment, thoughtful sipping, and a sense of gratitude for fruit that has lingered long enough to become something extraordinary.

Recioto della Valpolicella

Recioto della Valpolicella enters the glass with a quiet richness, a sweetness that doesn't shout, but glows. Its colour is a deep, warm ruby, almost velvety in the way it absorbs the light. Bring the glass close and the aromas rise in soft, concentrated layers: cherry liqueur, plum compote, cocoa, dried rose, gentle spice. Nothing feels heavy. Nothing feels overstated. Recioto carries its sweetness the way velvet carries warmth, with softness, texture, and an inviting depth.

Born from grapes dried slowly through winter, Recioto is the original style of the region, older than Amarone, and in many ways more tender. Where Amarone ferments to dryness, Recioto pauses early, leaving natural sweetness intact. The result is a wine that tastes both luxurious and comforting, like something meant to be savoured slowly rather than consumed quickly. It is sweet, but it is not simple.

Why People Love It

People love Recioto because it feels indulgent without excess. The sweetness is rich but balanced by acidity and a gentle, framing tannin. Each sip carries layers: dark cherry softened into jam, cocoa dust, dried violet, a touch of baking spice. Emotionally, it appeals to those who enjoy wines that feel intimate, wines that invite quiet conversation, warm light, and slow endings to long evenings.

It is a dessert in and of itself, but it is also a wine of reflection. It is sweetness shaped by patience.

How This Wine Feels

Recioto is sweet, full bodied and plush. The first sip feels round and smooth, with cherry, fig, plum and chocolate unfolding gently across the palate. The acidity lifts the sweetness and keeps it from feeling heavy, while soft tannins add enough structure to keep the wine from drifting into syrupiness. After the wine leaves the palate, the same dried fruit and soft spice rise again, creating a warm, lingering finish.

For all its richness, Recioto never feels sluggish. It moves slowly but with composure, holding its balance from beginning to end.

If You Like This Wine... You May Also Like

Port (Ruby or Late Bottle Vintage)

Port shares Recioto's dark fruit, chocolatey warmth, and rich generosity, but fortification sets it apart. The added spirit brings deeper sweetness, firmer alcohol, and a more powerful overall structure. For anyone who enjoys Recioto's indulgence but wants something more intense and fortified, Ruby Port forms an immediate bridge.

Banyuls (Southern France)

Banyuls mirrors Recioto's chocolate-friendly profile—dark fruit, spice, velvety sweetness—but leans more toward cocoa, caramel, and Mediterranean herbs. If Recioto appeals for its depth and softness, Banyuls offers that same comfort with a coastal, salt-kissed accent.

Malmsey Madeira

Malmsey captures Recioto's sweetness but expresses it with higher acidity and a more oxidative, caramelised tone. While Recioto is plush and fruit-driven, Madeira feels bright, nutty, and enduring on the palate. For those who appreciate sweetness balanced by freshness, Madeira provides a compelling contrast.

Sweet Lambrusco (Lambrusco Dolce)

Sweet Lambrusco reflects Recioto's dark-fruited generosity but adds gentle bubbles and a more playful frame. It lacks Recioto's depth but offers joyful, spirited sweetness—an easy-going red cousin for those who enjoy fruit-forward indulgence.

Recioto di Gambellara (Veneto, Garganega)

A white-wine relative in method rather than flavour. Made from dried Garganega grapes, it shares Recioto's slow concentration and luxurious sweetness but trades dark fruit for honey, apricot, and almond. For those who love Recioto's texture and richness but want a golden-hued expression, this is a graceful direction to explore.

Stretch Wines

Sauternes (France)

Sauternes diverges in flavour—honey, apricot, vanilla, saffron—yet mirrors Recioto's sumptuous texture. For drinkers drawn to Recioto's richness who would like something brighter, more aromatic, and shaped by noble rot rather than dried grapes, Sauternes broadens the horizon beautifully.

Tokaji Aszú (Hungary)

Tokaji blends sweetness with electric acidity, creating a profile that is both intense and lifted. Compared with Recioto's plush warmth, Tokaji feels sharper, more citrus-led, more layered. It shifts the experience toward tension and brilliance rather than softness.

Myths or Misunderstandings

One misconception is that all sweet red wines are simple or mass-produced. Recioto is the opposite, one of Italy's oldest and most artisanal dessert wines, requiring patience, precision, and careful drying of grapes. Another misunderstanding is that Recioto must be paired with dessert. It pairs beautifully, yes, but it is just as compelling on its own, especially at the end of an evening when conversation has slowed and warmth feels welcome.

Closing Reflection

Recioto della Valpolicella shows that sweetness can be deep, textured, and quietly elegant. It offers indulgence without excess and comfort without heaviness. It is a wine that encourages stillness, invites attention, and rewards slow sipping. It reminds us that dessert wines can be as profound as dry wines, capable of emotion, memory, and meaning.

It is sweetness with a voice.

---

1. Botrytis: A noble fungus that dehydrates grapes, concentrating sweetness and creating honeyed, apricot like flavours.

2. Fortification: adding a distilled spirit (usually grape) to wine to increase the ABV to approximately 16%-20%

Chapter 11
Fortified Wines

Wines shaped by spirit, time, and deepening concentration

Port

Port enters the glass with a sense of warmth, not just in flavour, but in mood. Its colour is deep and glowing, ruby to garnet to mahogany depending on style, and the aromas rise with a quiet richness: blackberries simmered slowly, dark cherries, plum liqueur, cocoa, cinnamon, toasted nuts, and the soft warmth of spirit woven gently through the fruit. It feels like stepping into a room lit by low lamps, the kind where conversation deepens and time slows. Port is a wine shaped by patience and sweetness held in balance, a wine that comforts even before the first sip.

Made in the Douro Valley, a landscape of steep schist terraces and sun-soaked slopes, Port is fortified while still fermenting, preserving natural grape sweetness and capturing fruit at its most vivid. Some Ports are bottled young to retain bright berry fruit; others age for decades in wood, slowly turning toward caramel, nuts, and warm spice. All share the same core: richness, depth, and an enveloping warmth that feels as much emotional as sensory.

Why People Love It

People love Port because it is one of the most generous wines in the world. The flavours feel abundant, dark fruit, chocolate, spice, yet the wine remains poised. The sweetness is full but never cloying. The texture is velvety. The warmth is gentle, not sharp. Port offers indulgence, but it also offers comfort. It is a wine that welcomes you in, invites you to settle, and asks you to take your time.

Emotionally, Port appeals to those who enjoy wines that create atmosphere, wines that feel cosy, reflective, celebratory, or intimate depending on the moment. It suits winter nights, long dinners, the last hour of an evening, or the quiet pleasure of a slow dessert. It is a wine for unwinding, for thinking, for sharing.

How This Wine Feels

Port is sweet, full bodied and warm, with a texture that can feel almost plush. The first sip shows concentrated black fruit such as cherry, blackberry and plum, followed by chocolate, spice and the gentle warmth of fortification. In young ruby and Late Bottle Vintage (LBV) Ports, the tannins provide firmness and structure, while tawny styles wrap the palate in caramel, roasted nuts and dried fruit.

A swirl reveals deeper layers: cocoa, fig, molasses, sweet tobacco, orange peel and toasted almond. After the wine leaves the palate, those flavours rise again in warm, spicy waves. The finish is long and unhurried, tapering gently rather than dropping away. Port is not a wine that moves quickly. It closes with the calm of a deep exhale.

The Main Styles of Port

Ruby Port

Ruby Port is the most youthful expression of the style, bottled to preserve the vivid fruit that comes from fortification early in fermentation. It tastes of dark cherries, blackberries, and plum, all carried by a gentle warmth that feels bright rather than heavy.

Ageing takes place mostly in large, neutral vessels, which protects colour and freshness. The result is a wine that feels lively and generous, a sweet red that offers comfort without complexity. Ruby Port suits drinkers who enjoy fruit-driven sweetness and a sense of immediacy, the feeling of wine captured at its most vibrant moment.

Late Bottled Vintage (LBV) Port

Late Bottled Vintage Port begins its life like a Vintage Port, made from grapes selected in a single harvest and fermented to retain natural sweetness. Instead of being bottled early for long cellaring, it rests for several years in wood where it gains structure and depth. LBV carries the concentrated fruit of Ruby Port but feels firmer, with tannins that provide a clear frame for the richness. Flavours of black cherry, cassis, cocoa and spice unfold slowly, supported by a warmth that feels measured rather than intense. It offers the presence of a Vintage Port in a more approachable form, ready to enjoy without long-term ageing.

Tawny Port

Tawny Port is shaped by time and air. It spends many years in smaller wooden barrels where slow oxidation transforms its character from bright fruit to warm, nutty softness. The colour drifts from ruby to amber to deep mahogany, and the flavours move toward toffee, roasted nuts, dried apricot and orange peel. The texture becomes silky and calm, gentle rather than firm. Older Tawnies carry layers of quiet complexity, each sip revealing warmth shaped by patience. They suit drinkers who enjoy sweetness expressed through depth rather than fruit, a style that feels autumnal and reflective.

Vintage Port

Vintage Port represents the style at its most powerful and long-lived. It is bottled after only a short time in barrel, capturing the concentrated fruit, tannin and spirit of a single exceptional year. In youth it can feel intense, marked by dense black fruit, firm structure and a broad warmth that suggests future longevity. With age, these elements soften and weave together, revealing notes of dried fruit, spice, cocoa and incense. Vintage Port is a wine built for decades, evolving slowly and rewarding patience. It stands at the peak of the Port family, a style for those who value richness balanced by structure and time.

White Port

White Port is made from white grape varieties and can range from dry to richly sweet. Fermentation is stopped early, as in red Port, but the flavours are entirely different. Expect citrus peel, honey, almond and soft stone fruit, carried by a gentle warmth. When aged in wood, White Port develops nutty, caramel notes that echo Tawny styles while remaining lighter on the palate. Served chilled, it becomes refreshing without losing depth, a sweet wine that feels bright and elegantly simple. White Port suits moments when sweetness is welcome but a lighter mood is preferred.

If You Like This Wine... You May Also Like

Tawny Port (Older Expressions)

If Ruby Port appeals with its dark fruit and warmth, older Tawnies offer a more introspective form of that comfort. You'll still find sweetness and richness, but the flavours shift toward toffee, roasted nuts, and dried orange peel. The tone becomes softer, nuttier, more autumnal. For anyone who enjoys Port's coziness but wants refinement and quiet complexity, Tawny Port is the natural progression.

Maury or Banyuls (Southern France)

These fortified reds echo Port's chocolate-friendly richness but speak with a Mediterranean accent—blackberry, fig paste, cocoa, and sun-warmed herbs. Compared with Port, they tend to feel slightly more savoury and lower in alcohol. If Port pairs beautifully with chocolate or strong cheeses for you, Banyuls and Maury offer the same pleasure with a gentler, more herbal frame.

Rutherglen Muscat (Australia)

Rutherglen Muscat shares Port's sweetness and depth but pushes everything further—intense raisin, toffee, caramel, coffee, and spice. It's heavier, richer, and almost syrup-like beside Port's fruit-driven warmth. For anyone drawn to Port's indulgence who wants to explore the extreme end of sweetness and viscosity, Rutherglen Muscat presents a daring, decadent parallel.

Madeira (Bual or Malmsey)

Madeira brings sweetness and warmth but builds them on acidity and oxidative depth, not fruit concentration. Expect burnt sugar, citrus peel, coffee, and a salty, lifted finish. Compared with Port's plushness, Madeira feels more vibrant, more fiery, more enduring. For those who enjoy Port but want sweetness delivered with tension and brightness, Madeira opens up a dramatically different experience.

Recioto della Valpolicella (Italy)

Recioto shares Port's velvety sweetness but expresses it through cherry liqueur, cocoa, and delicate florals. It's less powerful, less spirity, more tender. For drinkers who love Port's comfort but sometimes crave a gentler, more fruit-forward sweet red, Recioto offers a beautifully soft alternative.

Stretch Wines

Tokaji Aszú Dry (Hungary)

A dramatic jump in style. Tokaji is sweet yet electric—citrus peel, apricot paste, tea, and razor-edged acidity. It feels lighter, more vertical, more intricate than Port. For anyone curious about sweetness expressed with brilliance rather than warmth, Tokaji shifts the experience into an entirely different emotional range.

Sauternes (France)

Sauternes offers richness through honey, apricot, vanilla, and saffron rather than dark fruit. It is unfortified, creamy, and deeply luxurious. For lovers of Port who want a white wine delivering similar comfort and indulgence, Sauternes is the golden parallel.

Myths or Misunderstandings

Many assume Port is always extremely sweet. In truth, sweetness varies by style, and the best Ports balance it with acidity and tannin. Others believe Port is a "holiday wine," suited only for special occasions. Port shines in celebrations, but it is equally perfect for quiet evenings, cheese boards, chilled winter nights, or as a slow punctuation at the end of a long day.

Another misconception is that Port is heavy or overwhelming. While it is full-bodied, great Port is defined by balance, warmth supported by structure, sweetness lifted by acidity, richness shaped by depth rather than bulk.

Closing Reflection

Port is a wine that invites stillness, a wine that unfolds slowly, warms gently, and lingers with quiet generosity. It combines sweetness, depth, and warmth in a way few other wines do, offering comfort without losing elegance. It reminds us that richness can be harmonious, that sweetness can feel complex, and that some wines are meant not to rush, but to settle.

It is wine for firelight, for conversation, for endings that deserve something warm and kind.

Sherry

Sherry enters the glass with an air of quiet mystery, a wine shaped not only by grape and place, but by time, air, and the strange, beautiful life of flor. Its colours range from pale straw to deep amber depending on style, yet even the palest versions carry a depth of aroma that feels unexpected: sea breeze, green almond, fresh dough, chamomile, salted citrus, toasted nuts. Sherry does not rush to reveal itself. It opens slowly, like a story that deepens with every sip.

Born in the sunbaked triangle of Jerez in southern Spain, Sherry is a wine defined by atmosphere: dry winds, gleaming white albariza soils, and the unique microclimate that allows flor, a veil of yeast, to grow naturally on certain wines. Some Sherries age protected under flor, becoming saline and delicate; others age while exposed to air, becoming warm, nutty, and oxidative. Few wines carry such a wide emotional range.

Why People Love It

People love Sherry because it expands what wine can be. Dry styles feel savoury, complex, almost sculptural in their precision, wines shaped by umami more than fruit. Richer styles feel contemplative, carrying layers of nuts, caramel, and spice. Sweet styles unfold like dessert in liquid form.

Emotionally, Sherry appeals to those who seek wines with character, wines that feel grounded in place and transformed by time. It suits slow meals, thoughtful evenings, lively tapas tables, and moments when curiosity leads more than habit. Sherry offers not just flavour, but perspective.

How This Wine Feels

Dry Sherries such as Fino and Manzanilla are feather light yet profoundly savoury. They feel cool and saline, almost coastal, lifted by acidity and shaped by flor into something crisp and quietly intricate. The first sip is refreshing without leaning on fruit, showing almond, sea spray, fresh dough and chamomile.

Amontillado introduces warmth and depth. It begins life under flor, then shifts into oxidative ageing, gathering flavours of hazelnut, caramel and dried herbs. The impression is gentle heat settling over stone.

Oloroso forgoes flor entirely and ages in full oxygen contact, becoming a wine of walnut, spice, dried fruit and an aromatic softness that feels rounded and inviting.

The sweet styles move in a different direction. Pedro Ximénez is dense and velvety with raisin, molasses and coffee. Moscatel is fragrant, golden and honey toned. Each sip opens slowly, almost in layers.

Sherry never shows everything at once. It reveals itself gradually, moment by moment.

If You Like This Wine... You May Also Like

Fino → Manzanilla (Spain)

If Fino appeals with its dryness and savoury lift, Manzanilla offers the same core notes with added coastal salinity from its maritime ageing. It feels breezier, subtly briny, and more delicate in texture. For anyone who enjoys wines that are precise, refreshing, and essentially non-fruited, Manzanilla deepens that fascination with an even lighter touch.

Amontillado → Palo Cortado (Spain)

If Amontillado's interplay of flor character and oxidative depth resonates, Palo Cortado offers a more enigmatic evolution—combining the refinement of Amontillado with the warmth and richness of Oloroso. It carries greater weight and structure while keeping its elegance intact. For drinkers who savour nuance and savoury complexity, Palo Cortado genuinely feels like the next chapter.

Oloroso → Madeira (Sercial or Verdelho)

Oloroso shares much with Madeira's oxidative strength, but Madeira adds vivid acidity and a faint volcanic smokiness. It feels brighter, more lifted, more driven by tension. For anyone who loves Oloroso's caramel and nut tones but wants a style with more energy and coastal influence, Madeira offers that complexity shaped by fire and sea.

Pedro Ximénez (PX) → Rutherglen Muscat (Australia)

If PX captivates with velvety sweetness and raisin-chocolate depth, Rutherglen Muscat takes that indulgence and amplifies it. Expect caramel, toffee, roasted nuts, and immense concentration. For lovers of deeply rich, dessert-like wines, Muscat forms a natural, intensified parallel.

Dry Sherry → White Rioja (Aged Traditional Style)

Aged White Rioja delivers the savoury and nutty character found in Sherry but without fortification. Soft fruit—pear, quince—mingles with gentle oxidative notes. For those who admire Sherry's layered complexity but prefer an unfortified option, traditional White Rioja offers a graceful and expressive alternative.

Stretch Wines

Tokaji Szamorodni (Hungary)

Shaped by partial botrytis and oxidative ageing, Szamorodni echoes Sherry's savoury depth but brings higher acidity and a more aromatic, slightly untamed profile. For drinkers who appreciate Sherry for its structure and complexity, Szamorodni takes those qualities into a brighter, subtly wilder direction.

Orange or Skin-Contact White Wines

Skin-contact whites share Sherry's textural presence and savoury character, though they express it through tannin, grip, and herbal, tea-like aromatics rather than flor[1] or oxidation. For those drawn to the unconventional beauty of Sherry, orange wines open a parallel world built on texture and earth-driven detail.

Myths or Misunderstandings

One of the most persistent myths is that all Sherry is sweet. Most traditional Sherry is bone-dry, shaped by yeast, air, and time rather than sugar. Another misconception is that Sherry is old-fashioned, a dusty relic. Yet the styles that make Sherry unique are among the most vibrant and food-friendly wines in the world.

Some assume Sherry is difficult. It isn't. It's simply different, a wine whose flavours come not from fruitiness but from savouriness, atmosphere, and patience. Curiosity is all you need.

Closing Reflection

Sherry is a wine that reveals the beauty of transformation, grape to wine, wine to something shaped by air, yeast, and time. It offers complexity without pretence, savouriness without heaviness, and a sense of place that feels ancient yet alive. It reminds us that wine can be more than fruit and acidity; it can be texture, atmosphere, memory.

For those who want a wine that invites contemplation, Sherry offers some of the most fascinating and soulful experiences in the world.

Madeira

Madeira enters the glass with a brightness that feels paradoxical, a wine defined by heat, time, and deliberate oxidation, yet somehow more alive for it. Its colours range from topaz to deep mahogany, glowing like polished wood. Lift the glass and the aromas rise sharply, vividly: burnt orange peel, caramel, toasted nuts, sea spray, roasted coffee bean, dried fruit, and a fine thread of smoke. Madeira doesn't creep forward; it presents itself fully, with clarity and confidence.

This is a wine shaped not by avoidance of oxygen, but by an embrace of it. It is heated, exposed, tested, and emerges with greater energy, not less. The wines rest in warm lodges, sometimes for decades, slowly concentrating and developing flavours that feel simultaneously rich and electric. Few wines in the world carry acidity the way Madeira does. It gives the wine a spine like no other: straight, bright, unwavering.

Why People Love It

People love Madeira because it offers intensity without heaviness. The flavours are deep and layered, but the acidity keeps the wine dancing across the palate. Every sip feels like a wave folding over itself, caramel into citrus, spice into salt, richness into brightness. Emotionally, Madeira appeals to drinkers who enjoy wines that seem illuminated from within, wines that hold both power and precision.

Madeira suits moments of reflection, quiet evenings, strong cheeses, roasted nuts, rich desserts, or the final sips of a long meal. It is a wine that draws you in slowly yet holds your attention fully.

How This Wine Feels

Madeira ranges from dry to sweet depending on the grape and style. Sercial is dry and firm, Verdelho lightly sweet with a touch of smoke, Boal richer and darker, and Malmsey deeply sweet and velvety. Across all of them, the structure stays constant: high acidity that lifts even the richest sweetness, and oxidative depth that builds layers of caramel, spice and citrus.

The first sip feels sharp at the front and warm beneath, a meeting of brightness and richness. The flavours unfold gradually, orange peel, coffee, walnut, burnt sugar, dried fruit and at times a savoury hint of sea air. The finish lasts and lasts, glowing softly, like warm light settling into a dim room.

If You Like This Wine... You May Also Like

Sercial or Verdelho → Fino or Amontillado Sherry (Spain)

Sercial and Verdelho share Sherry's savoury, oxidative tone, but Madeira layers in unmistakable acidity and brightness. You still get salinity, nuts, and lifted savouriness, but carried on a more electric, high-tension frame. For drinkers who love Sherry's precision and want that same character expressed with greater drive and energy, dry Madeira continues the conversation in a sharper key.

Rutherglen Muscat (Australia)

Rutherglen Muscat mirrors Madeira's intensity but sends it in a different emotional direction—syrupy richness, raisin and caramel depth, and a warmth that feels enveloping rather than incisive. Where Madeira is shaped by acidity and fire, Muscat is shaped by viscosity and sweetness. For anyone who admires Madeira's concentration but wants a version defined by softness instead of voltage, Rutherglen Muscat provides that indulgent, plush counterpoint.

Vin Doux Naturel (Banyuls, Maury)

VDN wines echo Madeira's chocolate-friendly personality but express it through fruit richness instead of acidity. Expect warm cocoa, dried fruit, spice, and a fuller, plush texture. They feel gentler, rounder, and more comforting. For those who enjoy Madeira's depth but sometimes want something less sharp and more soothing, VDN offers warmth carried by fruit rather than tension.

Aged Tawny Port (Portugal)

Aged Tawny shares Madeira's oxidative, nutty complexity but presents it through rounder, silkier sweetness. Flavours lean toward toffee, almond, and dried apple instead of citrus peel and smoke. For drinkers who appreciate Madeira's sense of time and atmosphere but prefer a velvety, less piercing expression, Tawny aligns beautifully.

Stretch Wines

Tokaji Aszú (Hungary)

Tokaji matches Madeira's intensity but shifts the emphasis from oxidation to botrytis. Apricot paste, citrus marmalade, tea, and spice create a profile that is vivid and bright. Acidity soars, shaping sweetness through purity rather than caramelisation. For anyone intrigued by Madeira who wants to explore tension delivered in a different emotional register, Tokaji offers a captivating shift in style.

Sauternes (France)

Sauternes replaces Madeira's citrus-driven edge with honey, apricot, vanilla, and warm spice. It is rich, sumptuous, and golden, without Madeira's searing acidity. For those who admire Madeira's depth but prefer a softer, more opulent sweetness, Sauternes provides a gentler, warmly textured alternative.

Myths or Misunderstandings

Many assume Madeira must be sweet, but styles range from bone dry to deeply sweet. Another misconception is that Madeira is too intense for everyday enjoyment. In fact, its high acidity makes it more versatile than most sweet wines, pairing beautifully with savoury dishes as well as dessert. Some believe its oxidative character signals age or spoilage; in truth, oxidation is part of Madeira's identity and its greatest source of complexity.

Madeira is also famously long-lived; some bottles remain vibrant for a century or more. This is a feature, not a flaw.

Closing Reflection

Madeira is a testament to resilience, a wine that is heated, oxidised, and tested, yet emerges brighter and more expressive. It offers intensity without weight, sweetness without heaviness, depth without darkness. It is the rare wine that seems to glow, carrying flavours shaped by time and fire, and reminding us that beauty often comes from transformation.

It is a wine for contemplation, for slow evenings, and for those moments when you want to taste something that holds history, energy, and warmth all at once.

Rutherglen Muscat

Rutherglen Muscat enters the glass with a richness that feels almost otherworldly, dense, glowing amber, the colour of burnt sugar held to the light. Bring it closer and the aromas rise in deep, luxurious waves: raisin cake, toffee, caramel, dried apricot, cocoa, roasted nuts, coffee, warm spice. Nothing is subtle here, yet nothing feels crude. Rutherglen Muscat wears its intensity like velvet, weighty, smooth, utterly enveloping.

Made in the hot, dry region of Rutherglen in northeast Victoria, Australia, this wine begins with Muscat à Petits Grains Rouge grapes left to ripen until they are thick with sweetness. The fortified wine is then aged for years, sometimes decades, in warm, shallow cellars where evaporation concentrates everything. What emerges is a wine of astonishing depth and warmth, a liquid echo of sun-soaked fruit and slow ageing.

Why People Love It

People love Rutherglen Muscat because it is unapologetically indulgent. It offers sweetness in layers: caramel edged with citrus peel, raisin wrapped in cocoa, fruit deepened into richness. The flavours are bold, but the texture is impossibly smooth. Emotionally, it appeals to those who enjoy wines that feel comforting, decadent, and almost nostalgic, wines that wrap around the senses and fill the room with warmth.

It is a wine for winter nights, for chocolate desserts, for the quiet of late evening. It is also a wine for moments when you want something that feels like dessert on its own, rich enough to end a meal, gentle enough to sip slowly while the room settles.

How This Wine Feels

Rutherglen Muscat is sweet, full bodied and viscous, with a texture that moves across the palate like silk warmed in the hands. The first sip feels like a cascade of flavours: raisin, fig, caramel, burnt orange, toffee, spice and coffee. Acidity plays a quiet but essential role, lifting the sweetness just enough to keep the wine from feeling dense.

A swirl brings forward deeper tones such as dark chocolate, molasses, roasted nuts and occasional hints of smoke. After the wine leaves the palate, those dried fruit and caramel notes rise again in a slow, warm echo. The finish is long and gently persistent, fading gradually rather than ending with any abruptness.

If You Like This Wine... You May Also Like

Pedro Ximénez Sherry (Spain)

PX mirrors Muscat's velvety sweetness and raisin depth but shifts the profile toward molasses, coffee, and treacle. It's thicker, darker, and almost dessert-like in its intensity. For anyone drawn to Muscat's richness who wants an even denser, more liquid-dessert expression, PX takes that indulgence to a deeper shade.

Madeira Malmsey (Portugal)

Malmsey shares Muscat's sweetness and toffee-like warmth but counterbalances it with piercing acidity. The effect is entirely different: where Muscat envelopes, Madeira glows from within. If you love Muscat's flavour profile but crave greater lift and tension, Malmsey delivers sweetness illuminated by brightness.

Banyuls (Southern France)

Banyuls echoes Muscat's affinity for chocolate, offering dark fruit, cocoa, spice, and gentle warmth. It conveys richness through fruit rather than caramelisation, giving a Mediterranean tilt. For drinkers who enjoy Muscat with desserts but want something slightly drier and more herbal, Banyuls offers the same pleasure with a different accent.

Late-Bottled Vintage Port (Portugal)

LBV Port shares Muscat's intensity and warmth but channels them through structured tannin and concentrated dark-berry fruit rather than caramel and raisin. It feels firmer and more architectural. For those who appreciate Muscat's depth but prefer a wine with more backbone and a less overtly sweet impression, LBV Port offers familiar richness in a more disciplined frame.

Tokaji Szamorodni Sweet (Hungary)

Szamorodni sweet wines carry honeyed richness intertwined with oxidative notes that recall Madeira. Compared with Muscat, they are lighter, more aromatic, and more lifted. For anyone who enjoys Muscat's complexity but wants a sweeter wine with more fragrance and airiness, Szamorodni creates that bridge between sweetness and brightness.

Stretch Wines

Recioto della Valpolicella (Italy)

Recioto mirrors Muscat's depth but expresses it through dark cherry, plum, and cocoa rather than caramel and raisin. It is softer, less viscous, and more fruit-driven. For drinkers captivated by Muscat's richness who want a sweet red with more delicacy, Recioto offers an inviting shift.

Vin Santo (Italy)

Made from dried grapes, Vin Santo captures Muscat's warmth and nutty richness while adding dried apricot, almond, and gentle oxidative character. It is less dense, more contemplative, and shaped strongly by time. For those who love sweetness with depth but prefer a lighter, amber-toned profile, Vin Santo provides a graceful alternative.

Myths or Misunderstandings

One misconception is that Rutherglen Muscat must be overwhelming because it is sweet and viscous. In truth, the best examples balance richness with aromatic lift and acidity. Another misunderstanding is that it pairs only with dessert. While extraordinary with chocolate, nuts, and caramel desserts, Muscat is equally compelling on its own, when the evening has grown quiet and warmth feels welcome.

Some assume that all Muscat wines taste alike. Rutherglen Muscat is distinct, deeper, richer, more layered than most sweet wines bearing the Muscat name. It is a world unto itself.

Closing Reflection

Rutherglen Muscat is a wine of generosity, rich, unhurried, and full of warmth. It is sweetness with gravity, indulgence shaped by time, depth carried gently across the palate. It reminds us that dessert wines can be profound, that richness can be elegant, and that some wines are meant not to refresh, but to console.

It is a wine for endings, the soft glow at the close of a long night.

Vin Doux Naturel

Vin Doux Naturel feels like sunlight preserved, sweetness captured at the moment fruit reaches its warmest, most generous expression. Pour a glass and its colour shifts depending on the style and grape: pale gold for Muscat-based wines, ruby or garnet for Grenache-based versions from Rivesaltes, Banyuls, or Maury. Lift it to your nose and the aromas drift upward, gentle but abundant: peach and orange blossom in the pale styles; cherry compote, cocoa, and warm spice in the darker ones. Nothing feels exaggerated. These wines carry sweetness with a softness that feels effortlessly inviting.

The key to Vin Doux Naturel is timing. Fermentation is stopped early with a precise addition of grape spirit, preserving natural sugar while keeping the wine's fruit vivid and pure. The result is a wine that feels both sweet and bright, full and fresh, sweetness shaped by ripeness rather than concentration. In the Mediterranean heat of southern France, this technique creates wines that taste like summer held in place.

Why People Love It

People love Vin Doux Naturel because it offers sweetness that feels natural and easy, not heavy or elaborate. It's the kind of wine that slips comfortably into relaxed meals, fruit desserts, small bites, or quiet evenings. The fruit is generous, the warmth is gentle, and the texture is smooth. Emotionally, it appeals to those who want sweetness delivered with calm, something that feels indulgent but never demanding.

Muscat-based VDNs feel floral, light, almost aromatic in their sweetness. Grenache-based versions feel deeper, darker, shaped by Mediterranean sun and warm spice. Across the spectrum, Vin Doux Naturel feels like a soft step into fortified wines, warm, soothing, uncomplicated in the best way.

How This Wine Feels

VDN is sweet, medium to full in body, and gently warmed by fortification. The first sip depends on the style, yet the overall impression is always soft and welcoming. Muscat de Beaumes de Venise or Muscat de Rivesaltes shows peach, grape blossom, honey and citrus with a delicate, floating sweetness. Banyuls or Maury leans into red fruit shaped by cocoa, spice and a touch of tannin.

The sweetness spreads across the palate without sinking or feeling heavy. Acidity supports the structure and keeps the wine lifted, while the warmth remains soft and rounded. After the wine leaves the palate, the aromas drift back as fruit and blossom in the Muscat styles or cocoa and herb in the darker expressions. The finish lingers in a warm, glowing way, with sweetness that recedes slowly, like afternoon light settling at the end of the day.

If You Like This Wine... You May Also Like

Moscato d'Asti (Italy)

You'll recognise the gentle sweetness and bright fruit, but Moscato adds bubbles, lower alcohol, and a feather-light feel. It's more playful, more floral, almost weightless—a delicate, dancing expression of sweetness. For anyone who enjoys Muscat-based VDN but wants something breezier and lightly effervescent, Moscato brings sweetness with a refreshing sparkle.

Sauternes (France)

Sauternes shares VDN's generosity but expresses it through botrytis richness—honey, apricot, vanilla, saffron. The sweetness runs deeper; the texture becomes more opulent. Where VDN is about purity, Sauternes layers flavour on flavour. For drinkers who love sweet wines and want complexity shaped by noble rot, Sauternes opens the door to a richer, golden style.

Banyuls (for Muscat drinkers → red-fruit sweetness)

Though itself a VDN, Banyuls becomes a natural shift for Muscat drinkers—moving from peach and blossom into ripe cherry, cocoa, and gentle spice. It has the same softness but with deeper, darker fruit and a chocolate-ready profile. For those who love Muscat's charm but want a sweeter wine with more warmth and indulgence, Banyuls is a seamless next step.

Recioto della Valpolicella (Italy)

Recioto shares VDN's velvety sweetness but expresses it through dried cherry, plum, and cocoa rather than stone fruit or floral tones. It's richer and more textural than many VDNs. If you're drawn to VDN's softness but want a red sweet wine with greater depth and dark-fruited warmth, Recioto offers indulgence with a deeper, richer glow.

Port (Ruby or LBV)

Ruby Port holds onto VDN's sweet, fruit-forward appeal but adds firmer structure and the warmth of fortification. It's deeper, fuller, and more powerful, shaped by spirit and tannin. For drinkers who enjoy VDN's generosity but want to venture into a fortified style with more weight and backbone, Ruby or LBV Port provides the same comfort in a more robust form.

Stretch Wines

Madeira (Bual or Malmsey)

Madeira pushes sweetness toward brightness—caramel, citrus peel, roasted nuts—lifted by exhilarating acidity. It stands apart from VDN in intensity and architecture yet appeals to those who enjoy sweetness that feels both warm and vividly alive. Madeira turns that sensation into something electric and enduring.

Tokaji Aszú (Hungary)

Tokaji moves sweetness into a realm of tension and aromatic depth. Apricot paste, tea, citrus, and spice meet thrilling acidity, creating a profile that feels both rich and sharply defined. For those who appreciate VDN's warmth but want to explore sweetness in a more vertical, vibrant register, Tokaji offers a compelling and expressive leap.

Myths or Misunderstandings

One misconception is that all VDN wines taste alike. Muscat based styles feel bright and floral, while Grenache-based versions feel warm, spicy, and chocolate-friendly. Another myth is that VDNs are simple or unsophisticated. Their charm lies in purity, not complexity, sweetness shaped by fruit, not heavy ageing or oxidation.

Some assume VDN belongs only with dessert. It is lovely there, but just as compelling with cheese, salty snacks, or simply on its own as a gentle end to the day.

Closing Reflection

Vin Doux Naturel shows that sweetness can be light, natural, and quietly expressive. It offers warmth without density, fruit without heaviness, pleasure without effort. It reminds us that sweet wines do not always need grandeur, that there is beauty in wines that feel soft, sunny, and welcoming.

It is sweetness in its most relaxed form, a wine for afternoons that linger and evenings that ease slowly into night.

Marsala

Marsala enters the glass with a warmth that feels steeped in history, a deep amber glow, like sunlight filtered through old wood. Its aromas rise slowly, carrying notes of dried fig, toasted almond, orange peel, caramel, baking spice, and warm stone. Some versions lean toward savoury walnut and leather; others feel richer, rounder, almost honeyed. Marsala never feels hurried. It opens with the patience of a wine that has spent years evolving in casks, shaped by air, heat, and time.

Made on the western tip of Sicily, Marsala is a fortified wine with a character anchored in both place and tradition. Winds from the Mediterranean sweep across the vineyards; long, warm seasons ripen the grapes; and the wine undergoes oxidative ageing that draws out depth and complexity. Marsala can be dry or sweet, light or intense, youthful or decades old. But in every style, it carries a quiet, grounding warmth, a wine that feels lived-in, like a well-worn room with soft light and wooden floors.

Why People Love It

People love Marsala because it offers richness that feels grounded rather than extravagant. Its flavours move between sweet and savoury with ease, caramel next to spice, dried fruit beside earth. The wine feels warm and reflective, the kind that suits unhurried evenings and thoughtful conversations. Emotionally, Marsala appeals to those who enjoy wines shaped by time: wines that carry a sense of age, memory, and gentle oxidation.

It pairs beautifully with nuts, aged cheeses, roasted meats, pastries, and custards. But Marsala is equally compelling on its own, sipped slowly as the evening softens.

How This Wine Feels

Marsala's body ranges from medium to full depending on the style, yet its texture is consistently warm and enveloping. Dry versions show nutty, saline and savoury notes with dried citrus and warm earth. Semi dry and sweet styles move into richer territory, offering dried apricot, fig, caramel and spice wrapped in gentle sweetness. The first sip often feels like a blend of fruit and oxidation, something bright intertwined with something warm, followed by a soft glow of alcohol.

A swirl draws out deeper tones such as roasted nuts, pastry crust, vanilla bean, cocoa and at times a faint suggestion of smoke. Once the wine leaves the palate, those impressions return in a lingering mix of nutty sweetness or savoury depth, depending on the style. The finish is long, warm and quietly persistent, settling in slowly rather than fading quickly.

If You Like This Wine... You May Also Like

Amontillado Sherry (Spain)

You'll recognise the shared interplay of oxidation, nuts, dried fruit, and warm spice, but Amontillado is drier, more saline, and more tautly structured. It carries Marsala's savoury-sweet complexity into a brighter, more lifted expression. For anyone who enjoys Marsala's depth and wants a version with greater definition and coastal sharpness, Amontillado offers that refinement.

Oloroso Sherry (Spain)

Oloroso echoes Marsala's caramel, walnut, and spice, but does so through deeper oxidation and a firmer, decidedly drier frame. It feels broader, earthier, and more intense overall. For drinkers who love Marsala's warmth but want to explore a style with more heft and seriousness, Oloroso expands the profile in a powerful direction.

Madeira (Boal or Malmsey)

Madeira shares Marsala's oxidative depth yet adds piercing acidity and tension. Boal balances sweetness with lift; Malmsey leans toward caramel and richness. For those drawn to Marsala who want something brighter, longer, or more energetic on the palate, Madeira offers oxidative complexity delivered with vivid, electric drive.

Vin Santo (Italy)

Vin Santo mirrors Marsala's nutty, honeyed warmth but expresses it through dried-grape concentration instead of oxidative ageing. It is gentler, amber-toned, and more orchard-fruit centred. For anyone who appreciates Marsala's comforting sweetness but prefers a softer, more contemplative style, Vin Santo forms a beautiful parallel.

Rutherglen Muscat (Australia)

Rutherglen Muscat takes Marsala's warmth into a much richer, more decadent realm—raisin, caramel, toffee, chocolate, all woven into syrupy intensity. For drinkers who enjoy Marsala's darker dessert expressions and want to explore a wine with even greater richness and density, Muscat amplifies indulgence dramatically.

Stretch Wines

Tokaji Szamorodni (Dry or Sweet)

Szamorodni shares Marsala's oxidative signature but layers in botrytis-driven complexity and a level of tension Marsala rarely shows. Dry versions are nutty and structured; sweet versions glow with honey, spice, and citrus lift. For those fascinated by Marsala's savouriness, Szamorodni offers a stimulating, multifaceted extension of that character.

White Burgundy (Aged)

A surprising but compelling direction. Mature Chardonnay, especially from Meursault or Puligny, can develop nutty, oxidative nuances reminiscent of dry Marsala, yet carried on higher acidity and a different fruit palette. For anyone drawn to Marsala's emotional resonance but who prefers unfortified whites, aged White Burgundy delivers a similar depth through a completely different path.

Myths or Misunderstandings

Marsala is widely misunderstood because poor-quality "cooking Marsala" has overshadowed the authentic wine. True Marsala is complex, layered, and capable of elegance. Another misconception is that Marsala is always sweet when some of the finest are dry or semi-dry, expressing savoury depth rather than richness.

Some assume Marsala must taste heavy or thick. Good Marsala, even when sweet, has enough acidity and oxidative lift to stay balanced and engageing.

Closing Reflection

Marsala is a wine that feels both historic and intimate, shaped by time, warmed by sun, deepened by oxidation. It offers richness that comforts and savoury complexity that invites reflection. It reminds us that wines can evolve not through fruit intensity alone, but through the quiet magic of air and patience.

For those who enjoy depth without excess, sweetness without simplicity, and warmth that unfolds gently, Marsala is one of the most quietly compelling fortified wines in the world.

---

1. Flor is a thick, protective layer of yeast that forms on the surface of wine, particularly in the production of certain styles of sherry like Fino and Manzanilla. This biofilm prevents the wine from oxidising, which keeps it pale and contributes distinctive nutty, savoury, and slightly salty flavours to the wine.

Chapter 12
Fruity & Juicy Reds
Soft-tannin reds with open fruit and easy movement

Merlot

Merlot feels like sinking into a soft, comfortable chair, warm, inviting, familiar in the best possible way. Lift the glass and the aromas rise gently: ripe plum, black cherry, blackberry, cocoa, baking spice, and a faint herbal or earthy whisper depending on where the wine comes from. There is nothing sharp, nothing angular. Merlot's charm is its ease, its ability to feel plush and rounded, like fruit wrapped in velvet.

And yet, despite this quiet generosity, Merlot carries a strange cultural shadow, one that began with a single moment in pop culture. In the 2004 film *Sideways*, the character Miles famously declared, "I'm not drinking any f***ing Merlot," a line that reverberated across the wine world. It was meant as a joke, an expression of personal frustration, but it landed like a verdict. Merlot sales dropped. Pinot Noir surged. And for years afterward, people repeated the line as if Merlot were somehow unworthy.

But the truth is far more interesting. While the film temporarily damaged Merlot's reputation among casual drinkers, it also refocused attention on quality, pushing winemakers to craft better, more expressive versions. Meanwhile, Merlot remained the backbone of some of the most revered wines on earth: Pomerol, Saint-Émilion, Napa blends. The grape didn't change. Perception did. And now, with a new generation of drinkers rediscovering it, Merlot feels like a secret finally being remembered.

Why People Love It

People love Merlot because it is immediately pleasurable. The fruit is ripe and dark but never overwhelming. The tannins are soft, silky, and gentle on the palate, a contrast to the firm, angular grip of Cabernet Sauvignon. The acidity sits at a comfortable medium level, giving the wine freshness without tension. And the flavours linger with warmth: plum, mocha, cherry, chocolate, subtle herbs.

Emotionally, Merlot appeals to anyone who wants a red wine that comforts rather than challenges. It fits countless moments, a weeknight dinner, a slow afternoon, a relaxed gathering, and pairs easily with food. It is approachable without being simple, generous without being sweet, and structured without being stern.

How This Wine Feels

Merlot is dry, medium to full in body, with soft tannins and a smooth, almost cushiony texture. The first sip moves easily across the palate, showing juicy fruit supported by gentle structure. Plum, cherry, blackberry and a touch of cocoa create a rounded, velvety impression. Compared with more tannic reds, Merlot's mouthfeel feels distinctly plush.

Cooler climate versions lean into red fruit, herbs and earth, while warmer regions bring darker fruit, chocolate and spice to the forefront. A slow swirl deepens the aromas, revealing black cherry, mocha, cedar and baking spice. After the wine leaves the palate, those notes return in a soft rise of fruit and warmth, settling into a finish that feels smooth, rounded and quietly satisfying.

If You Like This Wine... You May Also Like

Malbec (Argentina)

You'll recognise the same plush fruit and smooth tannins, but Malbec pushes the profile darker—blackberry, blueberry, violets—and adds a little more intensity. It feels richer and more dramatic than Merlot. For anyone who loves Merlot's warmth and softness but wants deeper fruit and more colour, Malbec offers familiar comfort in a fuller, more expressive frame.

Zinfandel (California)

Zinfandel mirrors Merlot's generosity but channels it through brambly berry fruit and sweet spice. It's juicier, more exuberant, and often slightly higher in alcohol. If Merlot's friendliness appeals to you yet you're curious about a wine with more spice, energy, and boldness, Zinfandel brings that same warm-fruited charm with added verve.

Valpolicella Ripasso (Italy)

Ripasso shares Merlot's warm, rounded feel but adds depth through its dried-fruit character from the second fermentation. The texture stays smooth, while the flavours grow darker and more layered. If you enjoy Merlot's gentle richness and want something a touch more savoury or complex, Ripasso offers familiarity with extra dimension.

Côtes-du-Rhône (GSM Blends)

Grenache, Syrah, and Mourvèdre come together with the same easy, comforting appeal found in Merlot—ripe fruit, soft tannins, warm spice. These blends tend to feel sunnier, more herbal, more Mediterranean. If Merlot conveys comfort, Côtes-du-Rhône brings the same spirit with a southern accent.

Cabernet Franc (Loire Valley)

Cabernet Franc shares Merlot's moderate body and elegance but expresses its fruit in a redder, more aromatic register—redcurrant, graphite[1], herbs. It's less plush and more lifted. For drinkers who enjoy Merlot's smoothness but want greater freshness and a lightly savoury edge, Cabernet Franc reads as a refined cousin.

Right Bank Bordeaux (Merlot-Dominant Blends)

These blends show Merlot in its most structured, serious form. The familiar plum and cherry remain, but are framed by firmer tannins, subtle earth, and mineral nuance. For those who love Merlot's core identity and want to see it elevated through complexity and ageworthiness, Right Bank Bordeaux offers that deeper expression.

Stretch Wines

Syrah or Shiraz (Southern Rhône, USA, or Australia)

Syrah takes Merlot's warmth into richer, spicier territory. Firmer tannins, darker fruit, and more intensity create a bolder experience. If Merlot has built your comfort with fuller reds, Syrah extends the journey into a more structured and powerful style.

Sangiovese (Chianti Classico)

Sangiovese echoes Merlot's red-fruit profile but brings higher acidity and firmer, more savoury tannins. It feels brighter, earthier, more architectural. For anyone who enjoys Merlot's cherry-plum character but wants to explore something with more tension and Italian lift, Chianti reveals that next layer.

Barbera (Piedmont)

Barbera offers Merlot's warm fruit but replaces soft tannins with vivid acidity. It's juicier, brighter, and more energetic. If you want to move from smooth richness toward vibrancy while keeping a fruit-forward character, Barbera is an invigorating expansion.

Myths or Misunderstandings

One of the most persistent myths about Merlot is that it's bland—a reputation born from past overproduction, not from the grape's true nature. Well-made Merlot can be expressive, layered, and deeply characterful. Another misconception is that Merlot is always soft and easy-going. Whereas high-quality Merlot from places like Bordeaux, Washington State, or coastal Tuscany can be structured, serious, and remarkably age worthy.

Closing Reflection

Merlot reminds us that comfort and elegance can coexist. It offers warmth without weight, fruit without sweetness, texture without force. It is a wine that embraces rather than challenges, one that rewards attention yet never insists on it. In a world full of bold, declarative reds, Merlot offers a gentler path, a reminder that softness can be beautiful and deeply satisfying.

Pinot Noir (Fruit Driven)

Fruit-driven Pinot Noir enters the glass with a kind of quiet brightness, a pale, translucent ruby that catches the light like a gemstone. Bring it toward your face and the aromas rise softly: wild strawberry, red cherry, raspberry, rose petals, and a faint hint of warm spice or tea leaf. Nothing about it feels heavy or insistent. Its beauty lies in its lift, the way the fruit seems to hover rather than settle, the way the aromatics feel both delicate and inviting.

This style of Pinot Noir thrives in cooler New World regions where ripeness comes slowly and evenly. The fruit stays vibrant, the tannins remain gentle, and the acidity gives everything a sense of poise. Even at its most generous, fruit-driven Pinot Noir moves with a kind of graceful restraint. It doesn't overwhelm; it charms.

Why People Love It

People love fruit-driven Pinot Noir because it feels effortless. The flavours are vivid but never loud. The mouthfeel is smooth and silky, with just enough structure to feel complete. It is one of the few red wines that can feel refreshing, a wine suited to both summer lunches and autumn dinners.

Emotionally, this style appeals to those who seek nuance rather than power, red fruit rather than black, lightness rather than weight. It is a wine for relaxed evenings, gentle conversation, meals that don't require boldness from the glass. It feels like a companion rather than a statement.

How This Wine Feels

Fruit driven Pinot Noir is dry, light to medium in body, with bright acidity and very soft tannins. The first sip glides easily across the palate, showing strawberry, cherry, cranberry and a touch of floral sweetness. The fruit feels clear and pure. The tannins behave more like fine fabric brushing the palate, offering a gentle frame rather than any real grip.

A swirl brings subtle aromas to the surface, including rose petal, hibiscus, soft spice[2] and at times a hint of forest air. After the wine leaves the palate, those delicate red fruit and floral notes return in a light, lingering echo. The finish holds on through aroma rather than texture, staying present without adding weight.

If You Like This Wine... You May Also Like

Gamay (Beaujolais)

You'll notice the same light body, bright acidity, and charming red fruit, but Gamay leans juicier and a bit more playful. The tannins feel softer, the aromatics slightly more floral, the whole wine more exuberant. For anyone who enjoys Pinot Noir's delicacy yet wants something breezier and even easier to drink, Gamay is its closest, most natural companion.

Valpolicella Classico (Italy)

Valpolicella shares Pinot Noir's sense of lightness and red-fruit clarity but shifts toward tangy cherry and gentle herbal notes. It moves more briskly across the palate, trading silk for brightness. For those who love Pinot Noir's freshness and charm, Valpolicella offers that same appeal with an unmistakably Italian inflection.

Blaufränkisch (Austria)

Blaufränkisch carries the lift and brightness that Pinot Noir drinkers love, yet it introduces darker berries and a gentle spice that feels quietly distinctive. The acidity is lively, the fruit clear and focused, and the finish shaped by soft savoury notes that never overshadow its freshness. The wine moves lightly across the palate but leaves a confident impression. For those who enjoy the clarity and ease of fruit led Pinot Noir and wish to explore a style with a touch more depth and woodland spice, Blaufränkisch offers an inviting direction.

Grenache (Cool-Climate Expressions)

Cool-climate Grenache can mirror Pinot Noir's lifted strawberry and raspberry fruit, adding subtle spice and a slightly warmer tone. It shows a rounder mid-palate and often a touch more alcohol. If Pinot's fruit profile speaks to you but you'd welcome a little extra generosity, this style of Grenache feels familiar while offering a fuller embrace.

Cabernet Franc (Loire Valley)

Cabernet Franc offers red fruit and floral lift reminiscent of Pinot Noir, but with more aromatic herbs, graphite, and brightness. It tastes leaner and more overtly savoury. For drinkers who enjoy Pinot's lightness but want a wine with sharper herbal definition, Cabernet Franc extends that elegance into a more angular register.

Zweigelt (Austria)

Zweigelt echoes fruit-forward Pinot Noir with its cherry notes and light body but adds a bit more spice and slightly firmer texture. The difference lies in tone—Pinot whispers soft red fruit; Zweigelt leans darker and more vibrant. For those wanting something very close to Pinot yet with a touch more energy, Zweigelt bridges the gap effortlessly.

Stretch Wines

Sangiovese (Chianti)

Sangiovese shares Pinot Noir's red fruit but introduces firmer tannins and more savoury details of herbs, tea leaf, dried flowers. For anyone who loves Pinot's brightness but wants to explore wines with more tension and structure, Chianti extends the experience in a beautifully natural direction.

Aglianico (Entry-Level Expressions)

The lighter expressions of Aglianico offer red fruit framed by earthy tones and gentle tannin. The grape is inherently bold, yet in its softer forms you'll find an intriguing echo of Pinot Noir's aromatic lift. For drinkers curious about deeper reds who still want some delicacy preserved, Aglianico provides a confident outward step.

Syrah (Northern Rhône, Lighter Styles)

Cool-climate Syrah can share Pinot Noir's elegance and floral lift but layers in darker fruit and peppery spice. It carries more authority while maintaining freshness. For those wanting to move toward a more serious and savoury style without losing refinement, Northern Rhône Syrah creates a compelling contrast.

Myths or Misunderstandings

A common misconception is that Pinot Noir must be expensive to be good. While great Burgundy can be costly, fruit-driven New World Pinot Noir often offers exceptional delicacy and charm at approachable prices. Another misunderstanding is that Pinot Noir is too light to be "serious." In truth, lightness is its strength, the vessel through which it expresses nuance.

Some assume fruit-driven Pinot Noir should taste like sweet red berries because of its vivid fruit aromas. It is almost always dry; the sweetness lies in the scent, not the palate.

Closing Reflection

Fruit-driven Pinot Noir reminds us that subtlety can be captivating. It offers clarity without sharpness, fruit without weight, elegance without formality. It is a wine made for ease, for evenings when you want something beautiful but gentle, expressive but soft-spoken.

It teaches that delicacy has depth, that lightness can linger, and that some wines make their strongest impression by whispering rather than declaring.

Valpolicella Classico

Valpolicella Classico enters the glass with a kind of airy brightness, a red wine that greets you lightly, like sunlight glancing off red cherries. In the glass it is a clear, luminous ruby, never dense or brooding. Bring it closer and the aromas rise gently: fresh cherry, wild strawberry, a little rose petal, a faint herbal note carried from the breezy hills north of Verona. Nothing is dramatic. Nothing insists. The wine feels like ease, a kind of natural, unaffected charm that comes from grapes inclined toward purity rather than power.

What defines Valpolicella Classico is its sense of lift. The fruit is bright and red-toned; the tannins are soft and feather-light; the acidity gives the wine shape without edge. It feels like the red-wine equivalent of a cool linen shirt, simple, comfortable, refreshing in its clarity. It does not try to impress you; it tries to welcome you.

Why People Love It

People love Valpolicella Classico because it slips so easily into life. It is a wine you can pour without overthinking, one that feels as at home beside a casual lunch as it does beside relaxed conversation at the end of the day. The flavours are straightforward but satisfying. The texture is gentle. The mood is light.

Emotionally, it appeals to drinkers who prefer freshness over richness, who enjoy red wine but don't want heaviness, who look for a wine that supports a moment rather than shaping it. It is a red for warm weather, uncomplicated meals, and company where the wine is a companion rather than a focal point.

How This Wine Feels

Valpolicella Classico is dry, light in body, and driven by bright, mouth watering acidity. The first sip moves quickly across the palate, with red cherry and raspberry leading into a faint almond or herbal touch that reflects the region's native grapes. The tannins are soft and almost delicate, giving contour without any sense of grip. The finish is clean and lightly aromatic, more of a lift than a linger.

A gentle swirl brings up floral and red fruit notes. After the wine leaves the palate, those impressions return as a quiet trace of cherry skin and herbs. Nothing feels heavy. Everything remains clear, light and open.

If You Like This Wine... You May Also Like

Beaujolais (Fleurie, Chiroubles, Brouilly)

You'll recognise the same red-fruited brightness, soft tannins, and easy charm, but Beaujolais often brings more floral lift and a slightly juicier feel. Compared with Valpolicella, it comes across rounder, more perfumed, and a touch more expressive. For anyone who enjoys Valpolicella's freshness but wants a bit more aromatic colour, Beaujolais offers a seamless next step.

Fruit-Driven Pinot Noir (Oregon, California Coast, New Zealand)

The kinship lies in delicacy and red fruit. Pinot Noir feels smoother and more silken, with deeper tone and a gentle sense of warmth. It lingers longer on the palate, yet the emotional register stays similar—soft, expressive, approachable. For drinkers who love Valpolicella's lightness but want a little more tenderness, Pinot Noir fits beautifully.

Dolcetto (Piedmont)

Dolcetto mirrors Valpolicella's ease and everyday drinkability but moves into darker fruit and more savoury shading. The tannins are firmer while remaining friendly. It creates a feeling of familiarity with slightly more grounding—just as relaxed in spirit, yet capable of matching heartier dishes.

Bardolino (Lake Garda, Veneto)

A close relative in style, Bardolino offers even greater delicacy—more strawberry, more blossom, less structure. If you appreciate the gentle nature of Valpolicella Classico, Bardolino provides an even breezier, almost weightless expression of the same idea.

Dry Lambrusco (Emilia-Romagna)

Lambrusco shares Valpolicella's lightness and red-fruit charm but adds gentle bubbles and a burst of refreshing lift. It feels more playful and sprightly overall. For those who enjoy Valpolicella's ease but want a more lively, sparkling twist, Lambrusco brings that joy with its own personality.

Stretch Wines

Young Chianti (Sangiovese)

Chianti carries the same bright acidity and red fruit but introduces firmer tannins and a more savoury, architectural frame. It moves the experience toward structure while maintaining a similar sense of brightness and clarity.

Etna Rosso (Nerello Mascalese)

This Sicilian red echoes Valpolicella's delicacy but layers in volcanic minerality, gentle smoke, and a more serious profile. Still airy, still graceful, but shaped by altitude and earth. It stretches the style into a more subtle, terroir-driven direction.

Myths or Misunderstandings

Some assume Valpolicella Classico is simple because it is light when its charm lies in clarity, not complexity. Another misconception is that it belongs only with simple Italian dishes. Its brightness makes it one of the most versatile reds available, pairing beautifully with vegetables, seafood soups, lighter meats, and even as an aperitif.

Closing Reflection

Valpolicella Classico shows that red wine can be refreshing without being trivial, delicate without being empty. It offers fruit in its purest form, texture without weight, and pleasure without effort. It is a reminder that softness can be expressive and that some wines are meant not to command attention, but to brighten the moment they share.

Zinfandel

Zinfandel enters the glass with a kind of sun-warmed generosity, a deep ruby glow and a rush of ripe berry fruit rising toward you before you even swirl. The aromas feel expansive: blackberry jam, raspberry compote, sweet cherry, warm spice, a hint of vanilla or cocoa depending on where it's grown. There is an openness to Zinfandel, an immediacy, as though the wine has no interest in holding back. It feels like summer evenings, outdoor meals, easy laughter, a wine that greets you with warmth.

Part of Zinfandel's charm is the way it bridges juiciness and richness. It offers plenty of fruit, often with a little spice or sweetness of aroma, yet the tannins remain friendly and the texture broad but supple. It has depth without formality, structure without sternness. Even in its fuller styles, Zinfandel rarely feels intimidating. It keeps its sense of ease.

Why People Love It

People love Zinfandel because it feels abundant. The flavours are vivid and comforting, berries warmed by the sun, baking spices, gentle oak. The fruit is generous without heaviness, the tannins smooth, the mood relaxed. Emotionally, Zinfandel appeals to those who enjoy wines that feel celebratory and inviting, wines that lean into pleasure rather than restraint.

It suits barbecues, pizzas, slow-cooked dishes, casual gatherings, or evenings when you want a wine that feels friendly and full of life. Zinfandel rarely asks for attention; it simply adds warmth to whatever moment it enters.

How This Wine Feels

Zinfandel is dry, medium to full in body, with ripe fruit and moderate tannin. The first sip feels juicy and warm, showing blackberry, raspberry and plum, followed by spice that feels soft rather than sharp. The acidity stays gentle, giving the wine a round, comforting character.

A swirl brings up deeper layers of vanilla, cocoa, sweet spice and occasionally a touch of smoke. After the wine leaves the palate, berry compote and gentle warmth rise again in a lingering echo. The finish is smooth and slightly sweet in tone even when the wine itself is dry, always encourageing another sip.

If You Like This Wine... You May Also Like

Primitivo (Southern Italy)

You'll recognise the same exuberant fruit and warm-hearted richness which isno surprise given it is the same grape Zinfandel but with a different name. Primitivo tends to feel a touch earthier, with darker plum tones and more savoury spice. For those who enjoy Zinfandel's bold fruit and easy charm but want something with a rustic edge, Primitivo delivers that familiar energy with added grounding.

Valpolicella Ripasso (Italy)

Ripasso reflects Zinfandel's generous mid-palate and warm character but expresses it more quietly—red fruit instead of black, layered with a gentle dried-fruit note from the unique second fermentation. It's smoother, more restrained, more savoury. For drinkers who appreciate Zinfandel's warmth yet want something less exuberant and more nuanced, Ripasso feels like a natural progression.

Lodi Old-Vine Zinfandel (California)

A deeper exploration within the same family. Old-vine Zinfandel offers denser fruit, richer texture, and heightened spice compared with young-vine versions. It remains unmistakably Zin, just with more dimension and depth. For those who already love the grape and want a more complex interpretation, old vines reveal richness with added nuance.

Australian Grenache (McLaren Vale, Barossa)

Grenache shares Zinfandel's fruit-forward generosity and spice but presents it with more red-fruited brightness and a lighter, silkier touch. Sometimes herbal, always warm, it feels like Zinfandel viewed through a Mediterranean lens. For anyone who loves Zin's juiciness but wants something airier and sunnier, Australian Grenache offers that warmth in a gentler frame.

Carménère (Chile)

Carménère shares Zinfandel's generous fruit and easy warmth but carries it in a more aromatic and gently herbal direction. Black plum and dark berry mingle with soft green spice and a touch of cocoa, creating a wine that feels both familiar and intriguingly different. The tannins are smooth, the palate round, and the finish shaped by subtle savoury notes that add quiet complexity. For those who enjoy Zinfandel's openness and charm yet want to explore a style with a little more aromatic lift, Carménère offers a smooth and welcoming transition.

California Petite Sirah

Petite Sirah mirrors Zinfandel's density and dark fruit but leans deeper—blueberry, plum, baking chocolate—held together by firm tannins. It's richer and more powerful while still sharing Zin's signature warmth. For those who enjoy Zinfandel's bold side and want a wine with more structure and darkness, Petite Sirah brings intensity with familiar comfort.

Stretch Wines

Syrah or Shiraz (Warm-Climate Expressions)

Syrah matches Zinfandel's warmth but layers in pepper, smoked meat[3], and deeper, darker fruit. It's more structured and more serious. For drinkers who appreciate Zinfandel's richness and want to explore 'savourier,' more complex territory, warm-climate Syrah broadens the landscape.

Cabernet Sauvignon (California)

Cabernet shares Zinfandel's dark fruit and spice but tightens the frame—firmer tannins, more defined acidity, and a more pronounced oak imprint. For those who enjoy Zinfandel's power but want something more architectural and long-lined, Cabernet offers that next level of structure and depth.

Monastrell or Mourvèdre (Spain or Bandol)

Monastrell echoes Zinfandel's warmth but shifts towards black plum, wild herbs, and earthy spice. It has more grip, more savouriness, more brooding intensity. For anyone who loves Zinfandel but wants to step into something moodier and more complex, Monastrell provides a compelling, darker extension.

Myths or Misunderstandings

One common misconception is that Zinfandel is sweet. While some styles lean ripe, most quality Zinfandel is fully dry; the sweetness is a sensory illusion created by warm berry fruit and soft spice. Another misunderstanding is that Zinfandel is simple. In truth, old vines and careful winemaking produce deeply complex wines.

Some assume Zinfandel is too high in alcohol to be balanced. While warm-climate examples can be bold, the best versions integrate alcohol through fruit, spice, and texture.

Closing Reflection

Zinfandel shows that generosity can be graceful. It offers fruit without heaviness, warmth without heat, spice without sharpness. It is a wine that embraces pleasure and invites ease, a wine that fills a table with warmth, colour, and laughter. Its charm lies in its openness and in the way it turns even simple moments into something welcoming.

Gamay

Gamay enters the glass with a brightness that feels almost playful, a clear ruby glow, light enough that you can see straight through it. Lift it and the aromas rise in airy, joyful waves: strawberry, red cherry, raspberry, violets, and a soft suggestion of herbs or spice, depending on the village. Nothing is heavy. Nothing is dense. The fruit feels like it was gathered at dawn, cool and fragrant, still touched by morning air.

This is a grape that thrives on lightness. Even when it comes from serious crus of Beaujolais, Gamay retains an essential buoyancy, a sense that the wine moves rather than settles. It glides across the palate, carried by juicy fruit and a gentle floral lift. Gamay doesn't ask for analysis. It simply offers pleasure, delivered with charm.

Why People Love It

People love Gamay because it is unapologetically easy to drink, refreshing, lively, and softly expressive. It is one of the few red wines that feels suited to warm afternoons as well as cool evenings. Its tannins are low, its fruit is bright, and its mood is effortless.

Emotionally, Gamay appeals to drinkers who want red wine that feels cheerful, unpretentious, and versatile. It's perfect for picnics, simple meals, charcuterie, roast chicken, weekday dinners, any moment where you want wine to lift the atmosphere without taking centre stage.

How This Wine Feels

Gamay is dry, light in body, and driven by bright, mouth-watering acidity. The first sip carries vivid red fruit such as cherry, strawberry and pomegranate, moving quickly and cleanly across the palate. The tannins are soft and often barely noticeable in lighter styles, giving the wine a smooth, silky glide.

A swirl brings up floral tones like violets and roses, along with a faint herbal note or a quiet mineral thread in cru examples. After the wine leaves the palate, the fruit lingers in a delicate, fragrant echo. The finish is refreshing rather than long, leaving the palate clear and ready for another sip.

If You Like This Wine... You May Also Like

Fruit-Driven Pinot Noir (New World)

You'll recognise the same light body, bright red fruit, and gentle tannins, but Pinot Noir adds a silkier feel and slightly deeper aromatics—flowers, spice, and a touch of earth. It lingers a bit longer while keeping the same sense of ease. For those who enjoy Gamay's delicacy but want a wine with a little more nuance, New World Pinot Noir feels like a graceful extension.

Valpolicella Classico (Italy)

You'll find the same light-bodied, red-fruited charm, delivered with Italian brightness rather than floral lift. Valpolicella feels leaner, more herbal, and more cherry-driven compared with Gamay's berry tones. For drinkers who appreciate Gamay's ease and gentle acidity, Valpolicella offers a similar delicacy with a firmer, more linear shape—familiar softness with a different accent.

Bardolino (Italy)

Even softer than Valpolicella, Bardolino mirrors Gamay's brightness and light body almost exactly. The fruit leans strawberry-scented and gentle, the tannins feather-light. If Gamay feels like the perfect afternoon companion, Bardolino is the breezy lakeside version of that same mood.

Austrian Zweigelt

Zweigelt brings similar red fruit and light tannins but adds a subtle spiciness and a slightly darker tone. There's a bit more cherry-skin bite, a bit more vibrancy. For those who enjoy Gamay's liveliness but want an extra snap of energy, Zweigelt bridges that gap effortlessly.

Dry Lambrusco (Lambrusco Secco)

Lambrusco echoes Gamay's juicy red fruit but introduces bubbles, giving the wine a lifted, almost weightless feel. It's playful, refreshing, and full of spirit. If you love Gamay for its cheerfulness and drinkability, Lambrusco brings sparkle to the same bright personality.

Stretch Wines

Chianti (Basic Styles)

Chianti shares Gamay's red fruit and acidity but adds firmer tannins and savoury undertones. It stretches the style toward structure while keeping the brightness intact—an approachable step into more serious red wine.

Etna Rosso (Nerello Mascalese)

Etna Rosso preserves Gamay's airiness but adds smoky mineral nuance and subtle volcanic grip. It is more complex, more aromatic, more introspective. For those who adore light reds and want something with additional tension and landscape character, Etna Rosso offers elevated depth.

Cabernet Franc (Loire Valley)

Cabernet Franc retains red fruit and brightness but adds herbs, graphite, and a more pronounced savoury edge. It's sharper, more linear, more aromatic. For drinkers who enjoy Gamay's freshness yet want a step toward elegance with more definition, Cabernet Franc leads naturally onward.

Myths or Misunderstandings

Some think Gamay is simple because of Beaujolais Nouveau, a style meant for quick enjoyment, not for showcasing the grape's potential. In truth, Gamay from the Beaujolais crus (like Morgon, Fleurie, or Moulin-à-Vent) can be beautifully complex, floral, and mineral.

Another misconception is that Gamay lacks seriousness because it's easy to drink. But ease and depth are not opposites. Gamay's charm is intentional, a wine that proves lightness can be expressive.

Closing Reflection

Gamay shows that charm can be a virtue. It offers freshness without sharpness, fruit without heaviness, pleasure without pretence. It is a wine that brightens simple meals and full tables alike, that slips into moments gently and makes them feel more joyful. It teaches that not all reds need to speak loudly, some make their impression by being bright, delicate, and unmistakably alive.

Beaujolais

Beaujolais feels like a breath of fresh air in the world of red wine, a style that moves with brightness, charm and effortless pleasure. Pour a glass and the colour shines with a clear, ruby glow, light enough to catch the sun and vivid enough to promise fruit and energy. Lift it to your nose and a delicate world appears. You'll be dazzled with aromas of wild strawberry, raspberry, rose petal, fresh cherry and a faint hint of violet drifting over cool earth. The wine feels alive even before you taste it. This is Gamay at its most expressive, shaped by the southern edge of Burgundy, where rolling hills, granite soils and gentle sunlight create fruit that feels lifted, pure and quietly exuberant.

Beaujolais has a natural ease that few red wines achieve. It glides across the palate rather than marching across it, offering a combination of freshness and delicacy that feels both joyful and refined. Yet beneath the simplicity lies depth. The best examples, especially from the crus, carry floral nuance, subtle minerality and an inner tension that gives shape to the wine's playful fruit. Beaujolais bridges the gap between lightness and seriousness, a wine that can feel breezy one moment and quietly contemplative the next.

Part of its story is Beaujolais Nouveau, a wine released just weeks after harvest on the third Thursday of November, traditionally celebrated with festivals, midnight feasts and lively gatherings. Nouveau bursts with youthful fruit and bright colour, a glimpse of the vintage in its earliest stage. It is simple and joyful by nature, carrying a sense of celebration rather than complexity. Its immediacy is part of its charm, but it represents only one facet of the region. Beyond Nouveau lies the deeper heart of Beaujolais, where the crus reveal Gamay's true grace and nuance.

The contrast between Nouveau and cru Beaujolais highlights the grape's entire range, from exuberant fruit to elegant depth. Together they show that Beaujolais is not defined by one expression, but by a spectrum of possibilities, each shaped by place and time.

Why People Love It

People love Beaujolais because it feels open and welcoming. It offers the brightness of red fruit without heaviness, the charm of perfume without sweetness and the ease of a wine that suits almost any moment. Its gentle tannins make it comforting, its acidity keeps it refreshing and its floral lift brings a sense of lightness that lingers with each sip. Emotionally, Beaujolais feels spontaneous, a wine for picnics, shared meals, casual evenings, early lunches, late afternoons and conversations that drift easily from one subject to another.

Yet Beaujolais also appeals to those who appreciate nuance. The crus offer structure and depth while keeping the delicacy that defines the region. These wines reward attention without requiring it, which makes them perfect for drinkers who enjoy elegance but do not want formality. Beaujolais feels like a companion rather than a performance, a wine that joins the moment instead of shaping it.

How This Wine Feels

Beaujolais is dry, light to medium in body and carried by bright, mouthwatering acidity. The first sip glides across the palate, offering flavours of fresh strawberry, cherry and cranberry that rise gently into floral and earthy notes. The tannins are soft, almost silky, giving the wine shape without grip. In cru Beaujolais, the fruit deepens into raspberry and wild cherry, supported by gentle spice and mineral undertones from granite soils. The texture grows more layered, yet the sense of lift remains.

Beaujolais feels fluid rather than firm. It moves with grace, finishing with a soft, fragrant echo of red fruit and flowers. It leaves the palate refreshed and ready for more, a reminder that wine can be both light and complete.

If You Like This Wine... You May Also Like

Gamay from the Loire Valley (France)

Gamay in the Loire offers a slightly cooler expression, with redcurrant, cranberry and gentle herbal tones shaped by fresh acidity. The fruit feels tauter, the aromatics more subtle, creating a wine with a transparent, linear profile. It suits drinkers who love Beaujolais' delicacy but want more structure and brightness. Loire Gamay feels like a quieter, more restrained relative, delivering a calm and graceful expression of the same grape.

Cru Beaujolais (Morgon, Fleurie, Moulin à Vent, Brouilly)

These wines reveal the deeper soul of Beaujolais. Morgon brings dark cherry and gentle earthiness with firm, elegant structure. Fleurie speaks in flowers and soft red berries, tender and aromatic. Moulin à Vent feels more serious, more sculpted, showing how Gamay can gather weight without losing finesse. Each cru offers a distinctive voice while keeping the fruit and lift that define Beaujolais. For drinkers who enjoy the region's charm and want a step into greater complexity, the crus offer extraordinary depth.

Pinot Noir (Fruit Forward Expressions)

Fruit forward Pinot Noir shares Beaujolais' light body, soft tannin and red berry clarity, though it adds a gentle floral sweetness and subtle spice. Pinot Noir feels slightly more silken, with aromas that drift into rose petal, warm earth and delicate tea leaf. It moves with similar ease but carries a more aromatic and poetic shape. For those who love Beaujolais' elegance and want to explore something more refined without heaviness, Pinot Noir offers a beautiful continuation.

Valpolicella Classico (Italy)

Valpolicella Classico brings the same sense of ease and brightness, though with a tangy, cherry driven profile and a hint of Italian herbs. It feels breezy and lively, moving quickly across the palate with clear, refreshing fruit. Like Beaujolais, it pairs effortlessly with simple meals and relaxed gatherings. For drinkers who appreciate light red wines that refresh rather than weigh down, Valpolicella offers a charming and Mediterranean accented alternative.

Zweigelt (Austria)

Zweigelt echoes Beaujolais' playful fruit but adds a touch more spice, darker berries and a slightly firmer mid palate. The wine remains gentle and easy drinking, with soft tannins and a bright, aromatic profile. It suits those who enjoy Beaujolais' immediacy yet want a wine that feels a little more structured and a shade more vibrant. Zweigelt carries Gamay's spirit with an Austrian accent, offering warmth and clarity in equal measure.

Stretch Wines

Burgundy Pinot Noir (Village Level)

Burgundy Pinot Noir offers greater detail, earth and floral nuance, while retaining the delicacy that Beaujolais drinkers cherish. The fruit leans towards redcurrant and cherry, supported by fine tannins and a mineral thread that reflects limestone soils. These wines evolve slowly in the glass, revealing subtle layers of violet, forest floor and soft spice. For those who love Beaujolais' finesse and want to explore a more intricate expression with deeper tension, Burgundy provides a natural and rewarding progression.

Etna Rosso (Sicily)

Etna Rosso brings a volcanic dimension to light red wine, with bright red berries, dried herbs and smoky mineral notes that rise through a lifted, linear frame. The tannins are slightly firmer, the acidity higher and the aromatics more savoury, creating a wine that feels both delicate and haunting. It suits drinkers who enjoy Beaujolais' brightness but wish to venture into something with more tension and a sense of altitude. Etna Rosso offers lightness with an intensity that lingers.

Côte Roannaise (Loire)

Made from Gamay grown on granite in the upper Loire, Côte Roannaise feels like an echo of Beaujolais filtered through cooler air. The fruit is bright and red fruited, but accompanied by herbal notes, salt kissed minerality and gentle pepper that add lift and definition. The wine moves lightly, but with a more savoury inflection. For drinkers who enjoy Beaujolais' charm and want to explore its leaner, more angular cousin, Côte Roannaise offers a compelling and beautifully understated direction.

Myths or Misunderstandings

A common misunderstanding is that Beaujolais is light to the point of simplicity, yet the crus reveal extraordinary depth, tension and aromatic beauty. Another myth is that Beaujolais Nouveau represents the whole region, when in truth it is only its youthful, celebratory face. Some assume that Gamay lacks seriousness, but in the right soils it gains a quiet complexity that rivals far more famous grapes. There is also the belief that Beaujolais cannot age, yet many crus develop surprising elegance and savoury nuance over time. Beaujolais contains multitudes, far beyond its reputation.

Closing Reflection

Beaujolais shows that red wine can be both delicate and profound. It captures the feeling of early summer fruit, floral lightness and gentle movement, yet it also carries the structure and subtlety that reward thoughtful drinking. It is a wine that welcomes you in, offering generosity without weight and clarity without austerity. Beaujolais teaches that nuance does not always require intensity, and that charm can be every bit as meaningful as power. For those who love wines that feel bright, graceful and quietly expressive, Beaujolais remains one of the most enduring pleasures in the world of red wine.

---

1. Graphite: A mineral, pencil lead like aroma associated with certain structured reds.
2. Soft spice: A mild, subtle spice impression that enhances fruit without adding heat.
3. Smoked meat: A savoury, smoky character typical of cooler climate Syrah.

Chapter 13

Structured & Full Bodied Reds

Reds built on power, weight, and confident structure

Bordeaux (Red)

Bordeaux feels like the point where history, structure and quiet power meet. Pour a glass and the aromas rise in measured, confident waves: dark fruit, cedar, graphite, warm earth and subtle spice, all arranged with an elegance that never rushes. Bordeaux is not a single style, but a world contained within a name. Its wines are shaped by the rivers that divide the land, the gravel banks that warm the vines, the clay that holds moisture through long summers, and the traditions that have guided winemakers for centuries. This is a region where structure matters, where tannin and acid form the architecture on which flavour rests. Yet beneath the firmness lies beauty: blackcurrant unfolding into plum, violets merging with tobacco leaf, fruit carried by freshness rather than weight.

At the heart of Bordeaux is a gentle duality, two banks of land that look across the Gironde at one another while producing wines with distinctly different expressions. The *Left Bank* leans toward Cabernet Sauvignon, creating wines with firm lines, lifted aromatics and a sense of precision shaped by gravel soils. The *Right Bank* leans toward Merlot, producing deeper, softer wines that glow with plum, mulberry and warm spice, grounded by clay and limestone. Together they create a spectrum of red wine that feels complete, each side balancing the other, each revealing a different face of Bordeaux's character.

On the Left Bank, the wines come from communes that have shaped the identity of Cabernet Sauvignon for generations. Names such as *Médoc, Haut-Médoc, Saint Estèphe, Pauillac, Saint Julien* and *Margaux* often appear on labels. These places are known for their gravel soils that warm in the sun and help Cabernet Sauvignon ripen with poise. Farther south, *Pessac Léognan* and the wider *Graves* region offer a slightly softer expression, combining dark fruit with gentle smoke and earth. When you see these names, you can expect clarity, structure and a line of freshness that reflects the Left Bank style.

On the Right Bank, the wines come from vineyards shaped more by clay and limestone, places where Merlot finds depth and warmth. Labels from *Saint Émilion* and *Pomerol* dominate here, each with its own sense of elegance. Saint Émilion often feels lifted and aromatic, carrying red fruit, floral tones and fine tannins, while Pomerol leans darker and silkier, offering plum, violets and gentle spice. Surrounding villages such as *Lalande de Pomerol, Fronsac* and **Castillon** also share the Right Bank's generosity, giving wines that glow with warmth and supple fruit. When you see these names on a bottle, you are stepping into the Right Bank's softer, more embracing expression of Bordeaux.

Together these appellations form the map of Bordeaux that most drinkers encounter. They reflect the two halves of the region's identity, a landscape divided by rivers but united by a long history of thoughtful winemaking.

Bordeaux has been admired for centuries because it expresses both discipline and generosity. It feels like a wine built with intention yet shaped by nature. It asks for patience but rewards curiosity. It is a wine that invites contemplation without ever losing sight of pleasure. Bordeaux is a story of balance, of fruit held by structure, of warmth held by freshness, of strength delivered with grace.

Why People Love It

People love Bordeaux because it offers a sense of completeness. It is a wine where everything seems to be in its place: fruit, tannin, acid, spice, earth and time. There is a feeling of order, an inner calm beneath the surface, even in the most powerful examples. Bordeaux appeals to those who enjoy wines that evolve in the glass, wines that reveal themselves slowly, wines that match the rhythm of thoughtful meals and quiet evenings. The Left Bank brings confidence and clarity; the Right Bank brings warmth and depth. Between them lies something for nearly every palate.

Emotionally, Bordeaux gives a sense of grounding. It feels steady, structured, dependable. It carries the weight of tradition without ever becoming heavy handed. For many drinkers, Bordeaux represents arrival, the moment when one begins to understand how wine can age, how it can breathe, how it can gather complexity over time without losing its core. It feels both serious and comforting, a wine as suited to celebration as it is to reflection.

How This Wine Feels

Left Bank Bordeaux feels upright, clear edged and firm. The tannins are fine and confident, guiding flavours of blackcurrant, blackcurrant leaf, graphite, cedar and warm gravel across the palate. There is brightness in the acidity, a line that carries the wine forward with purpose. The finish lingers through earth, spice and refined length, leaving the impression of something sculpted and precise.

Right Bank Bordeaux feels rounder, deeper and more enveloping. Merlot leads with plum, mulberry, red cherry and soft florals. The tannins are plush but still structured, holding the wine in a gentle embrace rather than a firm grip. There is warmth in the mid palate, shaped by clay and limestone, and the finish carries a calm, savoury richness that rests quietly on the senses.

Both styles share a sense of composure. Bordeaux rarely feels hurried. It moves with intention, balancing fruit and structure with a natural grace that comes from generations of refinement. The texture grows with time in the glass, revealing layers of fruit, earth, spice, wood and gentle sweetness. Bordeaux feels like a wine that understands itself completely.

If You Like This Wine... You May Also Like

Rioja Reserva (Spain)

Rioja Reserva mirrors Bordeaux's balance of fruit and structure, yet it expresses it through a warmer, more leisurely frame. The fruit leans toward ripe cherry, plum and dried strawberry, wrapped in notes of vanilla, coconut, sweet spice and gentle tobacco from time in oak. The tannins feel polished and smooth, offering definition without intensity. Rioja Reserva suits drinkers who enjoy Bordeaux's savoury composure but want a wine with a softer glow and a slightly more expressive mid palate. It feels generous, familiar and quietly layered.

Chianti Classico Riserva (Italy)

Chianti Classico Riserva carries the brightness, savoury depth and structural clarity that Bordeaux drinkers appreciate, but shifts the fruit into red cherry, sour plum and dried herbs. The tannins are wiry and precise, giving the wine a vertical sense of movement, a lift that contrasts with Bordeaux's grounded warmth. There is a coolness to the acidity, a clarity to the aromatics, and a steady flow of earth and spice across the palate. For those who love Bordeaux's discipline but want more energy and herbal nuance, Chianti Classico Riserva offers a vibrant and compelling parallel.

Napa Valley Cabernet Sauvignon (USA)

Napa Valley Cabernet takes Bordeaux's core of blackcurrant, cedar and tobacco and expands it into a richer, more opulent register. The fruit becomes darker and more concentrated, the tannins broad yet velvety, and the oak more pronounced with notes of dark chocolate, vanilla and warm spice. The wine feels enveloping and confident, a fuller and more dramatic interpretation of Cabernet Sauvignon. For drinkers who appreciate Bordeaux's structure but want greater volume and plushness, Napa Cabernet offers a generous, vivid expression of the same architectural frame.

Super Tuscan (Italy)

Super Tuscans offer the same blend of structure and depth found in Bordeaux, yet they channel it through Italian warmth, Mediterranean herbs and riper, darker fruit. Expect black cherry, plum, sweet tobacco and savoury spice carried on firm tannins and bright acidity. These wines feel expansive yet controlled, combining the elegance of Bordeaux with the expressive richness of Italian reds. For those who desire a similar sense of scale but with a more sun drenched personality, Super Tuscans provide a captivating and resonant choice.

South African Cabernet Sauvignon and Merlot Blends

These wines share Bordeaux's structural foundation while offering fruit shaped by warmer days and coastal winds. Expect flavours of blackberry, blackcurrant, mint, cedar and gentle smoke carried on confident, polished tannins. The wines feel both familiar and distinct, combining Bordeaux's discipline with South Africa's clarity and freshness. For drinkers who enjoy the steadiness of Bordeaux but want a touch more sunlight and aromatic lift, these blends offer an inviting and thoughtful alternative.

Stretch Wines

Barolo (Italy)

Barolo takes the structural intensity found in Bordeaux and elevates it into something finer and more architectural. Nebbiolo brings high acidity and pronounced tannin, creating a wine that moves with tension and verticality. Aromas of dried roses, cherry, tar, anise and warm earth rise in delicate layers, offering complexity that unfolds slowly over time. For those who admire Bordeaux's seriousness but want something more ethereal, Barolo provides a profound and contemplative experience, one that rewards patience and reflection.

Ribera del Duero (Spain)

Ribera del Duero amplifies the depth of Right Bank Bordeaux while retaining a firm, upright structure. Tempranillo here feels dark and concentrated, with blackberry, plum and warm spice carried on powerful but refined tannins. The wines possess a quiet intensity, a sense of controlled force that mirrors Bordeaux's gravitas while leaning into darker flavours and a more muscular frame. For drinkers intrigued by Bordeaux's strength but seeking a deeper and more brooding style, Ribera del Duero provides an exhilarating path forward.

Cornas or Côte Rôtie (Northern Rhône)

These Syrah based wines echo Left Bank Bordeaux's savoury complexity while introducing black pepper, violets, smoked meat and mineral tension. The texture is firm, the aromatics lifted, and the fruit darker and more sinewy. Northern Rhône Syrah feels both rugged and elegant, a wine of contrasts that reveals its depths gradually. For those who enjoy Bordeaux's structure but want more aromatic intensity and a wilder sense of place, these wines offer a beautifully challenging and rewarding direction.

Myths or Misunderstandings

A common myth is that all Bordeaux tastes the same, yet the differences between Left Bank and Right Bank extend far beyond grape blends. Another misunderstanding is that Bordeaux must always be expensive, though many balanced and expressive wines are made at modest prices. Some believe Bordeaux requires decades of ageing, but modern winemaking often produces wines that are approachable in youth. There is also a notion that Bordeaux is overly formal or serious, yet its greatest strength lies in its versatility, its ability to accompany both simple meals and momentous occasions with equal grace.

Closing Reflection

Bordeaux stands as one of the most enduring expressions of red wine in the world, a region that marries structure with depth and tradition with quiet beauty. It reveals how soil, climate and time can shape not only flavour but emotion. A glass of Bordeaux carries history, yet it never feels distant. It feels calm, considered and complete, a wine that offers both direction and comfort. For those who appreciate balance, subtlety and the slow unfolding of complexity, Bordeaux remains a timeless companion, a wine that grows more eloquent with every moment spent in its company.

Cabernet Sauvignon

Cabernet Sauvignon enters the glass with a presence that feels unmistakable, a deep, opaque ruby that seems to hold its own gravity. Bring it close and the aromas rise with calm authority: blackcurrant, plum, cedar, graphite, tobacco leaf, a quiet thread of spice. Even before the first sip, the wine feels composed, grounded, confident. Cabernet does not rush forward. It unfolds.

Part of Cabernet's power comes from its structure. Thick grape skins give it firm tannins and deep colour; its natural acidity keeps the wine lifted; its flavour profile strikes a balance between dark fruit and savoury depth. Whether it comes from Bordeaux, Napa, Coonawarra, or Chile, Cabernet Sauvignon carries a sense of shape, an architectural quality that gives it spine, angle, and form.

Why People Love It

People love Cabernet Sauvignon because it feels complete. The fruit is dark and satisfying. The structure is firm but measured. The aromatics are deep, layered, and quietly expressive. Cabernet offers a sense of seriousness without austerity, a wine that can ground a meal, fill an evening, or mark a moment.

Emotionally, Cabernet appeals to those who enjoy wines that feel solid and enduring. It's a wine for contemplative dinners, for firesides, for dishes that ask for depth. It complements richness, strengthens quiet moments, and brings a sense of gravity to gatherings.

How This Wine Feels

Cabernet Sauvignon is dry, full bodied and firmly structured. The first sip brings blackcurrant and dark plum wrapped in tannins that feel like fine grained cloth, firm enough to give shape yet gentle enough to stay in balance. The acidity keeps the wine from settling into heaviness, while the oak contributes warmth, spice and a quiet touch of vanilla or cedar.

A swirl draws out deeper notes of graphite, tobacco, dried herbs and cocoa. After the wine leaves the palate, those darker fruit and savoury spice tones return in a lingering echo. The finish is long and steady, carried by tannin and depth rather than sweetness or softness. Cabernet speaks at its own pace, and its presence endures.

If You Like This Wine... You May Also Like

Syrah or Shiraz

You'll recognise the same depth and dark-fruited generosity, but Shiraz conveys its power through spice rather than structure. The fruit often feels sweeter-toned, the texture more open and plush. For those who love Cabernet's richness but want a wine with softer contours and more aromatic lift, Shiraz provides a seamless point of connection.

Colchagua Valley Carménère (Chile)

Colchagua Valley shows Carménère at its most composed. Black fruit and dark plum sit beside soft green spice and gentle cocoa, creating a generous yet quietly sophisticated profile. The tannins are smooth and full, the palate warm but not heavy, and the finish carries a subtle earthy echo. For those who enjoy the richness and structure of Cabernet Sauvignon and would like to explore a wine with a little more aromatic lift and a calmer, more supple frame, Carménère from Colchagua offers a deeply satisfying shift in tempo.

Malbec (Argentina)

Malbec reflects Cabernet's dark-fruit character but replaces its firm tannins with velvety smoothness. Blackberry, plum, violet, and a touch of cocoa shape a gentler, more sumptuous expression. If you appreciate Cabernet's depth but prefer something rounder and more immediately approachable, Malbec offers familiarity without the grip.

Rioja Reserva (Spain)

Rioja Reserva shares Cabernet's blend of fruit and structure but reveals it through redder fruit, warm spice, and polished oak tones. It's gentler, more aromatic, less driven by tannin. For anyone who values Cabernet's seriousness but wants a version with softer lines and an easier flow, Rioja Reserva provides depth with a relaxed elegance.

Bordeaux (Left Bank)

Left Bank Bordeaux presents Cabernet Sauvignon in its most classical form: structured, mineral, age worthy, with fruit that begins restrained and unfolds gradually. For those who appreciate Cabernet's architecture and want to explore it at its most refined and traditional, Bordeaux offers a more savoury, finely chiselled expression.

Napa Valley Cabernet (California)

Napa takes Cabernet's richness and elevates it—riper blackcurrent, broader tannins, more pronounced oak, deeper concentration. It is the grape at its most opulent and expansive. For drinkers drawn to Cabernet's plush power and looking to experience it in full amplitude, Napa is the natural direction.

Coonawarra Cabernet (Australia)

Coonawarra mirrors Cabernet's structure but infuses it with mint, eucalyptus, and graphite, giving a cooler, brighter tone. It feels refreshing yet unmistakably Cabernet. For anyone who enjoys the grape's classic shape but wants to taste how climate shifts the flavour profile, Coonawarra provides a clear, lifted interpretation.

Stretch Wines

Aglianico (Taurasi or Vulture)

Aglianico takes Cabernet's structural intensity and pushes it further—higher acidity, firmer tannins, deeper earth and smoke. It demands patience, but the complexity that emerges is profound. For those captivated by Cabernet's architecture and ready to explore a bolder, more brooding frontier, Aglianico stands as the next chapter.

Nebbiolo (Barolo or Barbaresco)

Nebbiolo parallels Cabernet's tannin and acidity but channels them into flavours of red fruit, rose, earth, and tar[1]. Lighter in colour yet often more structurally demanding, it offers an entirely different dimension of seriousness. For drinkers who enjoy Cabernet's gravitas and want to stretch toward something more ethereal yet equally firm, Nebbiolo opens that door.

Syrah or Côtes de Rhône (Northern Rhône)

Northern Rhône Syrah expands Cabernet's savoury spectrum—black pepper, olive, violets, smoked meat—woven into dark, precise fruit. The tannins are straighter, the mood more contemplative, the aromatics more intricate. For anyone intrigued by Cabernet's depth who wants increased detail and refinement, this style offers an elevated and deeply expressive contrast.

Myths or Misunderstandings

Many believe Cabernet Sauvignon must be tannic and assertive. While structure is part of its character, great Cabernet balances firmness with finesse. Another misconception is that it pairs only with steak. It shines with richer dishes, yes, but its acidity and savoury complexity can elevate many foods, mushrooms, roasted vegetables, aged cheeses, lamb, and braised dishes.

Some assume Cabernet must be aged to be enjoyable. While top examples improve with time, many modern Cabernets are beautiful young, offering fruit and depth without waiting.

Closing Reflection

Cabernet Sauvignon is a wine of structure, depth, and presence. It speaks in a steady voice, grounded, confident, enduring. It teaches that richness can be disciplined, that power can be elegant, and that some wines are meant not simply to accompany a moment, but to shape it.

For those who enjoy red wine with gravity and clarity, Cabernet offers one of the most complete expressions in the world.

Syrah or Shiraz

Syrah, or Shiraz, depending on where it is grown, feels like dusk settling over a warm landscape. It is a wine of shadows and spice, of dark berries and smouldering earth. Pour a glass and the colour is nearly opaque, the deepest shades of purple-black. Raise it to your nose and the aromas rise slowly but unmistakably: blackberry, blueberry compote, black plum, cracked pepper, violets, smoked meat, and the faint scent of warm earth after rain. Depending on origin, it can feel cool and savoury or bold and sun-drenched, but its identity never wavers. Syrah is a wine with a spine.

Why People Love It

People love Syrah or Shiraz because it marries richness with intrigue. The fruit is dark and powerful, yet wrapped in spice, herbs, and savoury undertones that keep it from ever feeling simple. It can be bold and plush, or taut and peppery; either way, it offers layers that reward both casual sipping and thoughtful attention.

Emotionally, Syrah or Shiraz appeals to those who enjoy wines with presence, wines that feel grounded and expressive, that seem to carry stories within them. It suits hearty food, smoky flavours, winter evenings, late-night conversations, and moments that call for depth rather than lightness. Whether from the Northern Rhône or the Barossa Valley, it carries intensity without chaos.

How This Wine Feels

Syrah and Shiraz are dry, full bodied and structured, with tannins that range from firm to velvety depending on climate and winemaking. The first sip brings a surge of dark fruit such as blackberry, blueberry and plum, followed quickly by pepper, herbs or smoky savoury tones.

Cooler climate Syrah, as in the Northern Rhône, feels taut and refined, showing black pepper, black olive, violet, smoked meat and graphite, all supported by acidity that sharpens the edges and tannins that feel sculpted. Warmer climate Shiraz from regions like Barossa or McLaren Vale leans into riper fruit, sweeter spice, chocolate, liquorice and a more generous, plush texture.

A swirl reveals deeper layers: violets, violet pastille, cedar, cured meat, cracked pepper, mocha and dark cocoa. After the wine leaves the palate, those notes return with pepper, spice and dark fruit that stay in the senses long after the sip has passed. Syrah and Shiraz often end with a finish that stretches out slowly, humming with warm spice and lingering depth.

If You Like This Wine… You May Also Like

Cabernet Sauvignon (Various Regions)

You'll recognise the same depth, dark fruit, and structural confidence, but Cabernet brings firmer tannins, a straighter, more disciplined architecture, and a cooler herbal edge. For those drawn to Syrah's richness who want more precision and backbone, Cabernet offers a more sculpted interpretation of power.

Malbec (Argentina)

Malbec echoes Syrah's dark fruit and warmth but softens the edges with velvety tannins and a fuller, more yielding texture. Blackberry, plum, and cocoa shape a generous, plush profile. If you enjoy Syrah's ripeness but prefer something smoother and more immediately approachable, Malbec provides a gentle and familiar shift.

Shiraz (Barossa, McLaren Vale)

Warm-climate Shiraz is simply Syrah in a richer, juicier, more opulent register. The dark fruit remains, but the spice turns sweeter and the texture grows fuller. For drinkers who appreciate Syrah's flavour palette but want greater volume and warmth, Australian Shiraz carries the style into a more indulgent realm.

Merlot (Warm-Climate Styles)

Merlot shares Syrah's comforting warmth but wraps it in softer tannins and a rounder, more forgiving frame. Plum, cocoa, and gentle spice stand in place of Syrah's savoury edges. For those who love Syrah's richness but sometimes want a smoother, more plush expression, Merlot offers a natural, relaxed alternative.

Valpolicella Ripasso (Italy)

Ripasso reflects Syrah's blend of warmth and savoury undercurrent but expresses it through cherry, dried fruit, and subtle spice rather than blackberry and pepper. It's smoother, less structured, and more quietly layered. If Syrah's warmth appeals to you yet you want something calmer and more meditative, Ripasso provides that softer perspective.

Washington State Syrah

Washington Syrah brings together the savoury depth of northern Rhône styles with the vibrant fruit of warmer climates. Blackberry and dark cherry mingle with hints of smoke, olive and cracked pepper, creating a wine that feels both generous and finely shaped. The texture is full without heaviness and the finish carries a gentle mineral line. For those who enjoy Syrah's broad spectrum of flavour and would like to explore a style that balances richness with poise, Washington offers a thoughtful middle ground.

Stretch Wines

Northern Rhône Syrah (Hermitage, Côte-Rôtie, Cornas)

Here Syrah reaches its most expressive form—deeply savoury, floral, mineral, and confidently structured. Compared with fruit-driven Syrah or Shiraz, these wines feel cooler, more sculpted, more serious. For anyone captivated by Syrah who wants to experience its most complex and resonant possibilities, the Northern Rhône stands at the peak.

Aglianico (Taurasi or Vulture)

Aglianico shares Syrah's depth and dark-fruit core but intensifies everything: higher acidity, firmer tannins, more earth, more tension. It demands patience but offers remarkable reward. If Syrah's structure appeals to you and you want to explore a more austere, powerful interpretation, Aglianico is the natural next ascent.

Monastrell or Mourvèdre (Spain, Bandol)

Monastrell delivers Syrah's darkness and warmth with a wilder, earthier edge—black fruit, herbs, game, and stony depth. It's moodier, more rugged, more elemental. For drinkers intrigued by Syrah's savoury side who want to venture into deeper, more primal territory, Monastrell stretches the style meaningfully.

Myths or Misunderstandings

One misunderstanding is that Syrah is always heavy or overpowering. In truth, some of the most elegant red wines in the world, especially from the Northern Rhône, are Syrah. Another misconception is that Shiraz and Syrah are different grapes; the name simply signals style and climate. Some believe Syrah is too savoury for broad appeal, but its blend of dark fruit and subtle spice makes it one of the most versatile full-bodied reds.

Closing Reflection

Syrah shows that power can be graceful. It offers depth without density, richness without excess, savouriness without austerity. It is a wine that brings warmth to the table and nuance to the glass, a wine that rewards attention, calms the evening, and speaks in a voice both strong and refined.

It reminds us that bold wines can still have poetry, and that intensity can be as elegant as it is expressive.

Valpolicella Ripasso

Valpolicella Ripasso feels like the moment late afternoon turns into evening, when something warm settles softly into the day. In the glass the colour deepens from the delicate ruby of Valpolicella Classico into a richer, more saturated hue. Bring it close and the aromas rise with an inviting warmth: ripe cherry, stewed plum, gentle spice, a touch of cocoa, and the faint dried-fruit note that hints at the technique behind it, a second fermentation on the skins of Amarone. Nothing feels forced. The wine simply seems fuller, broader, more assured.

Ripasso is Valpolicella with resonance. It carries the brightness of its lighter sibling but adds depth and quiet richness, as if the wine had deepened its voice. The fruit feels rounder, the texture smoother, the aromas slightly darker. It fills the senses not with intensity, but with a sense of comfort, like the way a room feels when the lights dim and conversation settles into a lower register.

Why People Love It

People love Ripasso because it offers warmth without heaviness. It feels richer than a light red but far more approachable than a powerful one. The flavours fan out gently before drawing together again in a soft, lingering finish. Emotionally, it appeals to those who enjoy wines that offer presence but not weight, wines suited to evenings when you want something comforting, generous, and quietly expressive.

Ripasso is a companion to cool weather, to slow-cooked meals, to evenings when depth is welcome but intensity would be too much.

How This Wine Feels

Ripasso is dry, medium to full in body, and marked by a rounded, velvety texture. The first sip shows ripe cherry and plum, followed by cocoa, spice and a gentle dried fruit richness. The tannins are soft but more noticeable than in Valpolicella Classico, giving light grip without any harshness. Acidity keeps the wine lifted and adds structure to the warmth.

A swirl draws out deeper notes of chocolate, soft herbs and faint touches of tobacco or dried orange peel. After the wine leaves the palate, its warmth and savoury detail return in a quiet echo. The finish is long, smooth and steadily persistent.

If You Like This Wine... You May Also Like

Merlot (Warm-Climate Expressions)

Merlot shares Ripasso's softness and ripe-plum generosity—rounded fruit, gentle tannins, and a welcoming warmth. The difference lies in flavour shading: Merlot leans toward chocolate and mocha, while Ripasso carries its small accent of dried fruit. For drinkers who enjoy Ripasso's smooth, comforting style, Merlot offers a similarly approachable, easy embrace.

Malbec (Argentina, Especially Uco Valley)

Malbec echoes Ripasso's fullness and dark-fruited richness but shifts toward deeper purple fruit and slightly firmer structure. Ripasso moves warmer and red-fruited; Malbec moves darker and more plush. It provides the same sense of generosity delivered with more colour, weight, and intensity.

Syrah or Shiraz (Moderate Warmth)

Syrah brings ripe fruit and spice that overlap with Ripasso's darker flavours. Cooler styles lean peppery and savoury; warmer ones emphasise plum, chocolate, and breadth. Compared with Ripasso, Syrah feels deeper, more structured, more commanding. It suits anyone drawn to Ripasso who wants to explore a wine with more spice and presence.

Rioja Reserva

Rioja Reserva offers similar mid-weight richness and gentle warmth, but adds layers of vanilla, coconut, and soft leather from its time in oak. The fruit feels more polished, the savoury tones more pronounced. For those who appreciate Ripasso's comfort and quiet complexity, Rioja Reserva gives that feeling through a distinctly Spanish lens.

Côtes-du-Rhône (GSM Blends)

Grenache, Syrah, and Mourvèdre combine to create warmth, red fruit, and spice that closely parallel Ripasso's spirit. Grenache adds softness, Syrah contributes spice, and Mourvèdre brings earth and depth. Compared with Ripasso, GSM blends feel a bit sunnier, more herbal, more Mediterranean in mood—familiar in warmth, but from a different climate.

Stretch Wines

Amarone della Valpolicella

The natural ascent from Ripasso. Amarone retains the same flavour family but expands everything—darker fruit, greater richness, more power, more concentration. It suits the moments when you want intensity rather than softness.

Aglianico (Taurasi or Vulture)

A more assertive leap. Aglianico carries Ripasso's seriousness but expresses it through firmer tannin, higher acidity, and volcanic depth. It offers a darker, more introspective style that rewards slow appreciation and invites deeper exploration.

Myths or Misunderstandings

Some believe Ripasso is sweet because of its dried-fruit tones. Ripasso is almost always dry; the impression of sweetness comes from ripe fruit and the influence of Amarone skins. Another misconception is that Ripasso is "baby Amarone." While related, Ripasso is its own style, fresher, gentler, and more versatile at the table.

Closing Reflection

Valpolicella Ripasso is a wine of quiet richness, one that deepens without darkening, warms without overwhelming. It offers a gentle evolution of Valpolicella's charm, adding fullness and depth while keeping its essential freshness. It is a wine that feels steady, welcoming, and deeply satisfying, the warmth of evening captured in a glass.

Malbec

Malbec feels like dusk settling into night, rich, velvety, and saturated with colour and warmth. Pour a glass and the wine settles into an inky, midnight purple, the kind of colour that seems to absorb light rather than reflect it. Bring it to your nose and the aromas rise vividly: blackberry, black plum, blueberry, violets, cocoa powder, warm spice, and a faint whisper of tobacco or earth. Malbec is not shy. It is a wine that greets you with open arms and a generous heart.

Though it has deep roots in France's Cahors region, Malbec found its modern voice in Argentina, where the high-altitude sun and cool nights of Mendoza shape it into something unmistakably bold yet surprisingly supple. The grape ripens easily, developing plush fruit and soft tannins, but the altitude preserves brightness, giving the wine both power and lift. It is this balance, richness without heaviness, depth without austerity, that has made Malbec beloved around the world.

Why People Love It

People love Malbec because it is both expressive and comforting. The fruit is ripe, dark, and abundant, offering immediate pleasure. The tannins are smooth and generous rather than strict or abrasive. The acidity is moderate and easy, making the wine feel full but not overwhelming. Whether sipped casually or paired with hearty food, Malbec feels satisfying.

Emotionally, Malbec appeals to those who want warmth in their glass, a wine that feels generous, flavourful, and grounded. It suits gatherings around a table, evenings that linger, grilled meats, winter stews, casual dinners, and moments when you want wine to feel expansive rather than reserved.

How This Wine Feels

Malbec is dry, full bodied and wrapped in broad, velvety tannins. The first sip usually brings a wave of dark fruit such as blackberry, plum and blueberry, followed by cocoa, spice or a touch of tobacco. The tannins feel plush and enveloping, giving structure without any sense of hardness.

In Argentina's high-altitude vineyards, Malbec shows an unexpected brightness: violet aromatics, lifted fruit, cool climate freshness and a long, smooth finish. In Cahors, its original home, the wine turns darker and more savoury, showing black tea, graphite and forest floor[2], with firmer tannins and a more brooding style.

A swirl brings out deeper layers of dark chocolate, espresso, clove, lavender or even mint. After the wine leaves the palate, warm fruit and spice return in a slow rise of aroma, settling into a lingering finish that feels both rich and comforting.

If You Like This Wine... You May Also Like

Merlot (Warm-Climate Expressions)

You'll find the same generous, plummy fruit and smooth texture, but Merlot softens the overall shape—gentler tannins, rounder curves, a quieter finish. For drinkers who enjoy Malbec's richness but sometimes want something less intense, Merlot offers familiarity in a more relaxed, plush form.

Syrah or Shiraz (Moderate Warmth)

Syrah shares Malbec's dark fruit and mid-palate weight but adds pepper, savoury accents, and a more aromatic lift. The structure is firmer, the flavours slightly deeper. If Malbec's warmth appeals to you yet you're curious about more spice and dimension, Syrah expands the style naturally.

Zinfandel (California)

Zinfandel echoes Malbec's boldness and fruit-driven generosity but channels it through brambly berries, sweet spice, and a juicier, more exuberant feel. For those who love Malbec's energy and want a wine that leans more playful and spiced, Zinfandel brings that warmth with a sunnier personality.

Valpolicella Ripasso (Italy)

Ripasso mirrors Malbec's richness and sense of comfort but shifts the flavour profile toward cherry, dried fruit, and soft spice. It's smoother, a bit more savoury, more layered. If you enjoy Malbec's weight but would welcome a touch more subtlety, Ripasso offers a gentler, more nuanced expression.

Cahors (Traditional French Malbec)

A natural sibling rather than a substitute. Cahors delivers the same grape in a firmer, earthier, more structured style—black fruit wrapped in tannin, minerals, and savoury tones. For anyone who loves Malbec and wants to explore its more serious, traditional side, Cahors reveals the grape's deeper roots.

Stretch Wines

Cabernet Sauvignon

Cabernet takes Malbec's depth and adds a stronger frame with firmer tannins, darker fruit, cooler herbal notes. For drinkers drawn to Malbec's intensity who want to move toward something more architectural, Cabernet provides a confident next step.

Aglianico (Taurasi or Vulture)

Aglianico mirrors Malbec's power but pushes it further with higher acidity, firmer tannin, and deeper earth-driven character. More demanding but profoundly rewarding. For those excited by Malbec's richness and ready for a wine with greater structure and ageworthiness, Aglianico stretches the palate upward.

Tempranillo (Ribera del Duero)

A shift into savoury depth. Ribera offers similar dark fruit and fullness but with more earth, spice, and tannic presence. If you love Malbec's body but want something more grounded and Old World in character, Ribera del Duero bridges that transition beautifully.

Myths or Misunderstandings

Many assume Malbec must always be heavy. Some of the finest versions, especially from high-altitude vineyards, are surprisingly lifted and aromatic. Another misconception is that Malbec lacks complexity; with proper vineyard work and restraint, it can show floral notes, minerality, and structure. Some believe Malbec belongs only beside steak, but its velvety texture and generous fruit make it versatile across cuisines.

Closing Reflection

Malbec offers warmth that feels generous rather than forceful, fruit that envelops, texture that comforts, depth that never becomes stern. It reminds us that boldness can be inviting, and that richness, when balanced by freshness, can feel both powerful and gentle. Malbec is a wine for evenings when you want fullness without formality, satisfaction without strain.

Rioja Crianza

Rioja Crianza feels like a deep breath taken in warm evening air, vivid fruit wrapped in soft spice, tradition meeting easy pleasure. Pour a glass and the colour settles into a luminous cherry red, bright at the rim, deeper at the core. Lift it to your nose and the aromas unfold gently but distinctly: red cherry, plum, strawberry compote, vanilla, warm cedar, sweet spice, and a faint earthy whisper that speaks of sun-baked soil. Rioja Crianza is not a loud wine. It is a balanced wine, a harmonious interplay of fruit, oak, and place.

This style comes from Spain's most famous region, Rioja where the grape Tempranillo forms the core of nearly every blend. By law, a Crianza must spend at least a year ageing in oak followed by time in bottle, enough to round the edges and add warmth without burying the fruit. It sits between youthful Rioja Joven, which is all fruit and freshness, and more serious Reserva and Gran Reserva, which lean into deeper spice and longer ageing. Crianza is the middle voice: approachable, structured, expressive, and quietly sophisticated.

Why People Love It

People love Rioja Crianza because it offers the perfect balance of fruit, spice, and smoothness. The red fruit is juicy and bright but never overwhelming. The oak adds gentle notes of vanilla, cedar, and warm spice without dominating. The tannins are firm enough to give shape, but soft enough to stay welcoming. It's a red wine you can pour for almost anyone, seasoned drinker or newcomer, and it will feel familiar in the best way.

Emotionally, Crianza appeals to those who enjoy warmth without heaviness, depth without density. It suits a wide range of moments: a tapas table, a cozy dinner, a grilled meal, a lingering conversation. There is something reassuring in its balance, a sense that nothing is out of place.

How This Wine Feels

Rioja Crianza is dry, medium to full in body, and built on a firm line of acidity with tannins that feel smooth rather than stern. On the palate you notice blackcurrant and dark plum from Tempranillo, often edged with red cherry or strawberry where

Garnacha plays a role. The fruit feels ripe but not heavy, framed by oak that adds vanilla, coconut or gentle baking spice rather than dominating. Everything sits in a measured, mid-weight frame: enough richness to feel satisfying, enough freshness to keep it moving.

Texture is one of the quiet pleasures of Crianza. The tannins feel like fine cloth along the gums, giving shape without roughness, while the acidity runs through the wine, lifting the fruit and stopping the warmth of alcohol from feeling thick. With air, subtler notes start to show: a touch of tobacco leaf, dried herbs, perhaps a hint of leather over the core of dark berry fruit. The finish is steady and savoury, carried more by tannin and spice than by sweetness, leaving behind a composed echo of oak, fruit and gentle earth.

If You Like This Wine... You May Also Like

Ribera del Duero (Spain)

You'll recognise the same Tempranillo core and warm red fruit, but Ribera del Duero presents it with greater force—darker fruit, firmer tannins, deeper structure. It feels fuller, more intense, more muscular. For those who enjoy Crianza's cherry-plum warmth yet want something richer and more powerful, Ribera offers a familiar profile in a more concentrated frame.

Chianti Classico (Italy)

Chianti mirrors Crianza's bright acidity and cherry-driven style but trades Rioja's oak spice for herbs, dried flowers, and firmer, more vertical tannins. It's earthier, more savoury, more lifted. If Crianza's balance appeals but you want more tension and a stronger sense of place, Chianti provides a refreshing shift.

Valpolicella Ripasso (Italy)

Ripasso shares Crianza's warm red fruit and gentle spice but delivers them with softer tannins and a dried-fruit nuance from its second fermentation. It feels smoother, rounder, more textural. For drinkers who appreciate Crianza's approachability but want added richness and depth, Ripasso feels instantly at home.

Côtes-du-Rhône (Southern Rhône)

Grenache-based blends echo Crianza's warmth and soft spice but weave in Mediterranean herbs and sweeter-toned fruit. Compared with Crianza's oak-shaped structure, Côtes-du-Rhône feels sunnier, looser, more relaxed. If you enjoy Crianza's friendliness, these blends offer the same comfort with a more playful, southern accent.

Australian Shiraz (Moderate Warmth)

Shiraz shares Crianza's generosity and spice but expands the fruit into darker, juicier territory. It's richer, fuller, more exuberant. For those who value Crianza's comfort but want something with more amplitude and expression, Shiraz widens the horizon.

Right Bank Bordeaux (Merlot-Driven Blends)

Here you'll find the same supple structure and red-fruit ease, but Bordeaux adds graphite, earth, and a cooler sense of restraint. It feels more classical, more composed. If you enjoy Crianza's balance and want to explore a deeper, more traditional interpretation of medium-bodied reds, Bordeaux creates a graceful connection.

Stretch Wines

Brunello di Montalcino (Italy)

Brunello takes Crianza's red fruit and subtle oak and stretches them into a more structured, more complex territory—greater tannin, deeper earth, more intensity. If Crianza feels like the perfect everyday red, Brunello reads as that same spirit elevated into richness and depth.

Barolo (Nebbiolo, Italy)

Barolo moves away from Crianza's warmth and into tension with high acidity, firm tannin, red fruit wrapped in earth and tar. It's lighter in colour but structurally more demanding. For those who enjoy Crianza's savoury elements and want to explore a more austere, profound side of Old World structure, Barolo offers a striking leap.

Cabernet Sauvignon (Various Regions)

Cabernet builds on Crianza's structure with darker fruit, firmer tannins, stronger oak presence, and greater intensity. For drinkers drawn to the seriousness within Rioja but wanting a more commanding, architectural profile, Cabernet forms a logical next step.

Myths or Misunderstandings

A frequent misconception is that Crianza is "simple" compared with Reserva or Gran Reserva. In truth, Crianza represents a stylistic choice as it is usually fresher, juicier, crafted for earlier enjoyment and versatility. Another myth is that Crianza is always oak-heavy; many contemporary styles use oak with finesse, letting fruit and brightness lead. Some assume Rioja must always taste traditional, yet Crianza often reflects modern winemaking: cleaner fruit, lifted edges, and a lighter touch.

Closing Reflection

Rioja Crianza shows how balance can feel welcoming, fruit that is neither loud nor shy, tannins that frame without gripping, oak that warms without overwhelming. It is a wine that feels grounded, steady, and quietly expressive. It teaches that red wine doesn't need grandeur to be deeply satisfying; sometimes, the most inviting wines are the ones that meet you gently and linger with warmth.

Châteauneuf-du-Pape

Châteauneuf-du-Pape feels like heat stored in stone, a red wine saturated with sunlight, spice, and the warm breath of the southern Rhône. Pour a glass and the colours glow in deep garnet and ruby, sometimes with a hint of amber at the rim. Lift it toward your face and the aromas gather not in a single thread but in a tapestry: ripe raspberry and strawberry, black cherry, fig, dried herbs, cracked pepper, warm stones, liquorice, and a whisper of smoke. This is a wine where fruit and earth speak simultaneously, a symphony shaped by sun and mistral wind.

Built on the infamous Grenache–Syrah–Mourvèdre (GSM) triad, Châteauneuf-du-Pape blends the generosity of Grenache, the structure of Syrah, and the depth of Mourvèdre into a wine that feels both powerful and expressive. Grenache is the beating heart, red-fruited, warm, and expansive. Syrah adds colour, spice, and shoulders. Mourvèdre contributes darkness, tannin, and a feral edge that gives the wine its grounding. The result is a wine that carries warmth with dignity, power with nuance, richness with a sense of origin.

Why People Love It

People love Châteauneuf-du-Pape because it offers richness wrapped in complexity. It feels generous, ripe fruit, warm alcohol, a broad mid-palate, yet it also carries herbal lift, savoury depth, and textural variety. It is a wine that delivers immediate pleasure while also rewarding reflection.

Emotionally, Châteauneuf moves people because it feels elemental. The stones of the region, the famous *galets roulés*, absorb heat by day and release it by night, and the wine seems to hold that warmth inside it. It suits robust meals, long evenings, celebrations, and chilly weather when you want a wine that fills space with presence.

How This Wine Feels

Châteauneuf-du-Pape is dry, full bodied and powerful, yet the tannins often feel soft thanks to Grenache's gentle structure. The first sip is broad and enveloping, with flavours that can range from strawberry and raspberry jam to cherry compote, plum or darker fruits depending on the blend. As the wine settles on the palate, layers of herbs and spice begin to unfold showing hints of rosemary, thyme, bay, lavender, pepper and warm earth.

The alcohol, which can be high, comes across as a steady warmth when the wine is in balance. Syrah contributes darker fruit, pepper and structure, while Mourvèdre adds depth, hints of game and a faint smoky tone. Together, the varieties give the mid palate breadth and the finish real persistence.

A slow swirl deepens the expression, bringing forward dried figs, cocoa, leather, incense and the dusty scent of sun warmed stones. After the wine leaves the palate, those fruit and herb notes rise again, creating a lingering savoury warmth that holds long after the sip has passed.

If You Like This Wine... You May Also Like

Gigondas (Southern Rhône)

You'll recognise the same sun-warmed fruit, herbal lift, and generous mid-palate that define Châteauneuf-du-Pape, but Gigondas carries a firmer, more structured shape. The fruit leans darker, the tannins are a touch more pronounced, and the garrigue notes show with greater clarity. For those who enjoy Châteauneuf's warmth yet want a bit more definition and tension, Gigondas offers the same Mediterranean soul in a more sculpted form.

Vacqueyras (Southern Rhône)

Vacqueyras mirrors Châteauneuf's red fruit, spice, and warmth, but conveys them with less weight and a more rustic, grounded charm. It's slightly earthier, slightly tighter, less expansive overall. If you appreciate Châteauneuf's flavours but sometimes want something humbler and more weeknight-friendly, Vacqueyras is the approachable sibling.

GSM Blends from Australia (McLaren Vale, Barossa)

These blends echo Châteauneuf's trio of Grenache, Syrah, and Mourvèdre, but present it through fuller fruit, sweeter spice, and a juicier, more plush texture. They feel sunnier, rounder, more fruit-driven. For drinkers who love the generosity of Châteauneuf and want something more exuberant and expressive, Australian GSM offers the same harmony with a brighter accent.

Bandol Rouge (Provence, France)

Bandol Rouge brings Mourvèdre to the forefront, creating a wine of quiet power and Mediterranean depth. Dark fruit sits beside wild herbs, warm stone and a gentle touch of game. The structure is firm yet composed, broadening slowly across the palate before settling into an earthy, lingering finish. There is a sense of sun and sea breeze folded into every sip. For drinkers who appreciate the richness and layered warmth of Châteauneuf du Pape and would like to explore a more contemplative, slightly wilder expression of southern French red wine, Bandol Rouge provides a captivating shift in perspective.

Rioja Reserva (Spain)

Rioja Reserva shares Châteauneuf's warmth and layered complexity but expresses it through redder fruit, savoury spice, and polished oak influence. It feels smoother, cooler in tone, and more refined. If Châteauneuf's depth appeals yet you prefer elegance over breadth, Rioja Reserva provides a graceful, composed parallel.

Zinfandel (California)

Zinfandel reflects Châteauneuf's generosity and spice but channels it through juicier fruit and a more playful, berry-forward personality. The herbal garrigue is absent, replaced by warmth and easy charm. For those who want Châteauneuf's spirit with a more relaxed, fruit-first expression, Zinfandel makes for a joyful sideways move.

Super Tuscan (Sangiovese + Bordeaux Blends, Tuscany)

Super Tuscans deliver similar depth and seriousness but frame them with firmer structure and cooler-toned fruit. Dark cherry, plum, herbs, and spice appear in a more focused, architectural style. If you enjoy Châteauneuf's complexity but want more tannin, tension, and savoury detail, Super Tuscans offer that contrast with precision.

Stretch Wines

Amarone della Valpolicella (Italy)

Amarone takes Châteauneuf's warmth and expands it into deeper, richer territory—dried cherry, fig, chocolate, and spice in concentrated form. Sweeter in tone, more enveloping, more opulent. For those who find Châteauneuf generous and want to explore full-tilt richness, Amarone is a luxurious evolution.

Bandol (Mourvèdre, France)

Bandol emphasises the brooding, earthy, muscular side of Mourvèdre. Darker fruit, firmer tannins, and a more serious, grounded mood define the style. If Châteauneuf's wild, savoury streak intrigues you, Bandol stretches that fascination into deeper, more elemental territory.

Northern Rhône Syrah (Côte-Rôtie, Hermitage)

This is a move toward structure, savouriness, and aromatic intensity—black pepper, violets, smoke, iron, dark fruit. It feels more vertical, more precise, more cerebral than Châteauneuf. For anyone who admires Châteauneuf's complexity but wants a cooler, more sculpted expression, Northern Rhône Syrah offers that elevated, focused experience.

Myths or Misunderstandings

A common misconception is that Châteauneuf-du-Pape is always heavy. While some styles are rich and powerful, many modern examples focus on freshness, lift, and elegance, Grenache in a graceful register rather than a dense one. Another misunderstanding is that all producers use the full list of permitted grapes; in practice, most rely heavily on Grenache, Syrah, and Mourvèdre. Some assume Châteauneuf must be oaky, but many of the best bottlings avoid new oak entirely, letting fruit and garrigue speak clearly.

Closing Reflection

Châteauneuf-du-Pape is a wine that carries warmth with dignity, expansive fruit, herbal lift, spice, and a sense of sunlit depth. It expresses generosity without losing balance, richness without losing grace. It reminds us that power need not be forceful, and that some wines feel like a landscape captured in flavour: stones, herbs, heat, wind, and time woven together. It is a wine for moments when you want fullness paired with harmony.

Amarone della Valpolicella

Amarone della Valpolicella enters the glass with a sense of gravity, not heaviness, but presence. Its colour is deep and saturated, a garnet that seems to hold warmth within it. Lift the glass and the aromas rise in slow, layered waves: black cherry, dried fig, dark chocolate, warm spice, a hint of balsamic depth, sometimes even a touch of tobacco or incense. Everything feels concentrated, as if the flavours have been carefully folded into one another. This is the result of the grapes being dried before fermentation, a process that intensifies every element of the wine. Amarone doesn't announce itself loudly; it simply fills the space with richness and calm.

Despite its power, Amarone is never chaotic. It moves across the palate with a kind of confident stillness, broad, full, and smooth, but held together by quiet structure. It is a wine shaped by time, warmth, and patience. It feels like stepping into a room lit by firelight: enveloping, soothing, and steady.

Why People Love It

People love Amarone because it feels complete. It offers depth without aggression, richness without sweetness, warmth without heat. The dried-grape process creates flavours that feel luxurious: fruit that leans toward the dark and dried, spice that feels warm rather than sharp, texture that feels velvety and continuous. Emotionally, Amarone appeals to those who want a wine that can anchor an evening, a wine that invites you to slow your pace, settle into conversation, and savour the moment.

It suits winter nights, hearty meals, and occasions that feel special simply because you've chosen to open a bottle of something profound.

How This Wine Feels

Amarone is dry or softly off dry, full bodied and intensely textural. The first sip feels expansive, with dried cherry, plum, fig, cocoa and spice spreading across the palate in broad, smooth layers. The tannins are firm but polished, wrapped into the richness rather than sitting apart from it. Acidity, often easy to miss in such a powerful wine, plays a quiet but essential role, lifting the weight and keeping the wine from feeling heavy.

As it opens, deeper tones begin to appear with subtle tones of bittersweet chocolate, dried herbs, warm cedar and dark earth. After the wine leaves the palate, those flavours rise again in slow, deep waves, resonant rather than sharp, lingering rather than fleeting. The finish is long and gently warming, the sort that seems to remain even after the flavours themselves have slipped away.

If You Like This Wine… You May Also Like

Châteauneuf-du-Pape (Southern Rhône)

You'll recognise the same generous warmth, layered fruit, and gentle spice, but Châteauneuf expresses these qualities through a more herbal, Mediterranean lens. Its richness is shaped by sun and garrigue rather than dried grapes. For anyone drawn to Amarone's fullness, Châteauneuf offers a similarly enveloping experience with a slightly lighter, more herbal step.

Australian Shiraz (Barossa or McLaren Vale)

Shiraz mirrors Amarone's depth and dark fruit but translates it into plush blackberry, sweet spice, and chocolate-edged richness. It's more extroverted, less introspective. If Amarone's power and texture resonate with you, Shiraz provides that same impact in a juicier, more outwardly expressive form.

Napa Cabernet Sauvignon

Napa Cabernet brings comparable weight and presence with dark fruit, velvety tannins, and a sense of fullness that echoes Amarone. The difference lies in structure: Cabernet rises vertically with firmer tannins, while Amarone spreads horizontally across the palate. For those who love Amarone's richness, Napa offers that same depth with clearer architectural lines.

Aglianico (Taurasi or Vulture)

Aglianico shares Amarone's gravity and depth but channels it through acidity, tannin, and volcanic earth. It feels more structured, less plush, yet equally profound. If Amarone's seriousness appeals to you and you're curious about a more austere interpretation, Aglianico makes a compelling next move.

Valpolicella Ripasso

Ripasso serves as Amarone's gentler sibling as it is usually softer, brighter, less intense. It remains within the same flavour family but offers a fresher, more approachable expression. If you love Amarone yet want something suitable for more frequent drinking, Ripasso carries the same imprint in a more relaxed frame.

Stretch Wines

Recioto della Valpolicella

Recioto carries Amarone's flavours—dried fruit, chocolate, spice—into the realm of sweetness, wrapping them in velvety, dessert-like richness. It's a move toward sweet wine, yet it preserves Amarone's emotional comfort and depth.

Madeira (Bual or Malmsey)

Madeira shares Amarone's warmth and resonance but adds acidity and oxidative character. It becomes more caramelised, more savoury, and astonishingly long-lived. For drinkers drawn to richness who want to explore a new tonal direction, Madeira shifts the experience into something brighter, deeper, and enduring.

Myths or Misunderstandings

A common misconception is that Amarone is sweet because of its dried-grape character. Most Amarone is dry; the richness of texture creates the impression of sweetness. Another misunderstanding is that Amarone must be overwhelming. While powerful, great Amarone is defined by balance, warmth held in structure, richness carried by acidity.

Closing Reflection

Amarone della Valpolicella shows that power can be gentle and intensity can be elegant. It offers warmth that wraps rather than overwhelms, depth that invites contemplation, and richness that feels more like a slow bloom than a surge. It is a wine for evenings when you want to settle in, unwind, and savour something that fills the senses completely, a reminder that fullness can be beautiful when it moves with grace.

---

1. Tar: A dark, smoky, resinous note characteristic of Nebbiolo.
2. Forest floor: An earthy aroma recalling damp leaves, soil, and underbrush.

Chapter 14

Earthy & Savoury Old-World Reds

Reds that emphasise soil, savouriness, and a grounded sense of place

Chianti (Sangiovese)

Chianti feels like a walk-through sun-warmed hillsides lined with olive trees, cypress, and herbs, a wine shaped by the landscapes of Tuscany, carrying both brightness and earth in every sip. Pour a glass and its colour glows like garnets in afternoon light: translucent ruby with flashes of brick at the edge. Bring it to your nose and the aromas rise with unmistakable Sangiovese clarity: sour cherry, red plum, dried herbs, tomato leaf, rose petal, leather, dusty earth, and the faintest echo of warm terracotta. Chianti doesn't try to seduce with plushness. It speaks in the language of place.

Although Chianti has many forms, from the everyday simplicity of Chianti DOCG to the more structured, terroir-driven Chianti Classico and the deeply expressive Gran Selezione, the heart of the region is Sangiovese. It is a grape that wears its transparency openly: it shows soil, sunlight, and season with almost no filter. And that transparency gives Chianti a kind of emotional honesty. It is a wine that feels grounded.

Why People Love It

People love Chianti because it offers both brightness and depth, both savouriness and fruit. The acidity is vivid, making the wine lively and food-loving. The tannins are firm but rarely harsh. The flavours feel authentic, cherry, herbs, earth, balanced with a rustic charm that suits everything from pizza and pasta to roasted meats and aged cheeses.

Emotionally, Chianti appeals to people who appreciate wines that taste like where they come from. It is a wine for shared tables, long meals, family recipes, and evenings that stretch without hurry. There is something reassuring in the way Chianti feels familiar even when you are tasting it for the first time.

How This Wine Feels

Chianti is dry, medium in body, and shaped by high acidity and firm, earthy tannins. The first sip lands with bright cherry that feels tangy rather than sweet, followed by dried herbs, a hint of leather and a warm, earthy undertone. The wine moves across the palate with a mix of brightness and gentle grip.

The acidity gives Chianti its distinct profile. It pushes the flavours upward, making the fruit feel lifted and sharpening the savoury tones. The tannins, often described as dusty, create texture without adding weight. A swirl brings more detail into view: red cherry, raspberry, dried flowers, tobacco leaf, cedar and a mineral note that recalls warm stones. After the wine leaves the palate, those herbal and cherry skin impressions return softly, settling into a clean, lingering finish.

Chianti Classico is usually more structured and layered; Chianti Classico Riserva adds depth and spice from ageing; Gran Selezione shows the greatest concentration and refinement. Through all these tiers, the core character stays consistent: bright fruit, earthy nuance and the sense of Tuscan sunlight running through it.

If You Like This Wine… You May Also Like

Brunello di Montalcino (Italy)

You'll recognise the same Sangiovese core of cherry, herbs, earth, but Brunello adds depth to every element. The fruit darkens, the structure firms, the texture broadens. It feels more contemplative, more layered, more commanding. If you enjoy Chianti's brightness and want a richer, more profound expression of those same flavours, Brunello is Sangiovese at its most elevated.

Barbera d'Alba (Italy)

Barbera reflects Chianti's acidity and food-friendly lift but replaces firm tannins with a juicier, more supple texture. The fruit turns darker strong flavours of plum and blackberry with the palate feeling rounder and more flexible. If you appreciate Chianti's energy but prefer something less structured and more playful, Barbera delivers Italian verve in a softer frame.

Valpolicella Ripasso (Italy)

Ripasso shares Chianti's warmth and red-fruit generosity but swaps acidity and herbs for a gently textured richness. It's smoother, rounder, slightly darker in tone. For those who enjoy Chianti's red fruit but want a bit more plushness and quiet depth, Ripasso offers an inviting sideways move.

Beaujolais Crus (Fleurie, Morgon, Moulin-à-Vent)

These crus echo Chianti's bright red fruit but lean into floral aromatics and softer tannins. They feel lighter, more perfumed, less earthy. If you enjoy Chianti's freshness but want a wine that speaks in a more delicate, flower-laden voice, Beaujolais crus deliver that lift without the savoury grip.

Rioja Crianza (Spain)

Rioja Crianza offers similar cherry fruit and gentle warmth from oak, but in a smoother, more polished frame. The acidity is softer, the spice sweeter, and the herbal tones give way to a rounder profile. If Chianti's balance appeals but you'd prefer something gentler and more softly spiced, Crianza fits effortlessly.

Cabernet Franc (Loire Valley)

Cabernet Franc reflects Chianti's savouriness and red fruit but presents it through herbs, graphite, and floral lift. It's cooler, leaner, and more aromatically etched. If Chianti's earthy side resonates and you'd like something more perfumed and precise, Cabernet Franc expands that spectrum beautifully.

Stretch Wines

Nebbiolo (Barolo or Barbaresco)

Nebbiolo takes Chianti's acidity and amplifies the structure with higher tannins, deeper earth, roses, tar, and red fruit wound tightly together. It is more demanding yet far more complex. For those who love Chianti's savoury tension and want to step into deeper, age worthy territory, Nebbiolo makes for a thrilling leap.

Aglianico (Taurasi or Vulture)

Aglianico echoes Chianti's acidity but adds darker fruit, volcanic earth, and firmer tannin. It feels more powerful, more structured, more introspective. If Chianti's combination of lift and seriousness appeals to you, Aglianico offers those same qualities in a deeper, more brooding register.

Tempranillo (Ribera del Duero)

Ribera retains Chianti's red fruit and savoury character but strengthens the body and tannin. It's darker, richer, more muscular. For anyone who enjoys Chianti and wants to explore a fuller, more intense style without sacrificing structure, Ribera del Duero provides a natural upward step.

Myths or Misunderstandings

One of the most common misconceptions is that Chianti is thin or rustic. That reputation comes from older, lesser examples; modern Chianti, especially Classico, is vibrant, structured, and beautifully expressive. Another myth is that Chianti must taste strongly of oak. In truth, the best versions rely more on acidity, fruit purity, and savouriness than on oak influence.

Some believe Chianti is only for Italian food, but its acidity and versatility make it one of the most adaptable reds for a wide range of dishes.

Closing Reflection

Chianti shows how clarity can be compelling, red fruit illuminated by acidity, savouriness balanced by freshness, structure carried with grace. It offers flavour and personality without heaviness, confidence without force. It is a wine that feels both grounded and bright, a reminder that elegance doesn't need volume and that some of the most satisfying reds speak in a voice shaped by earth, fruit, and heritage.

Tempranillo

Tempranillo, in its earth-driven form, feels like a walk-through sun-warmed Spanish soil, a wine shaped more by landscape than by fruit, carrying the scent of dry earth, cedar, tobacco leaf, and herbs alongside its quiet red and black berries. Pour a glass and the colour settles into deep cherry garnet, glowing at the rim with that classic brick hue that signals age, tradition, and savouriness. Lift it toward your nose and the aromas rise in gentle, layered tones: dried cherry, plum skin, leather, dusty earth, sweet tobacco, warm spice, and the faintest whisper of dried roses.

This is the Tempranillo found in its more traditional expressions, wines from places where oak and age are part of the identity, where time shapes the wine as much as terroir does. Think Rioja when it steps into Reserva and Gran Reserva territory; Ribera del Duero when it leans into earth, structure, and depth rather than overt fruit; Toro when it brings dark fruit wrapped in spice and minerality. These wines feel rooted. They feel like they have absorbed sun and soil and memory.

Why People Love It

People love earth-driven Tempranillo because it offers depth without weight, maturity without heaviness, and savouriness without austerity. The fruit is present but understated, dried cherry, red plum, a hint of blackcurrant, supported by layers of cedar, leather, spice, and earth. The tannins give firmness without aggression, and the acidity feels soft but steady, like a structure that holds the wine upright without drawing attention to itself.

Emotionally, these wines appeal to those who love stories inside their glass, wines that feel seasoned, wise, and quietly expressive. They belong on tables with roasted meats, aged cheeses, rich tapas, tomato-based dishes, mushrooms, lentils, and long evenings where conversation moves slowly and the wine deepens the mood.

How This Wine Feels

Earth driven Tempranillo is dry, medium to full in body, with moderate acidity and firm, dusty tannins. The first sip leans savoury, showing dried cherry, red plum and gentle redcurrant wrapped in cedar, leather and warm spice. Barrel influence, often from American oak, brings vanilla, coconut, dill and toasted wood, while many modern versions use French oak for a quieter, more restrained accent.

The texture sits in balance, with tannins that feel textured rather than thick and fruit that tastes mature rather than overtly ripe. The structure moves at a steady pace, giving the wine a calm, grounded feel. A swirl brings added depth: tobacco leaf, warm earth, dried herbs, clove, cinnamon and the faint sweetness of seasoned oak. After the wine leaves the palate, those earthy and spicy tones drift back in a gentle echo, creating a finish that feels savoury, composed and enduring.

Compared with fruit driven expressions of Tempranillo, this style feels more grounded and contemplative, a wine shaped as much by patience and ageing as by the grape itself.

If You Like This Wine... You May Also Like

Rioja Reserva (Spain)

You'll recognise the same Tempranillo depth. Notes osdried cherry, plum skin, tobacco, warm spice but Reserva extends every element. The fruit grows darker, the oak slightly sweeter, the texture smoother and more layered. If you enjoy the savoury calm of earth-driven Tempranillo yet want a wine with greater polish and quiet richness, Reserva expresses that familiar voice with added refinement.

Ribera del Duero (Spain)

Ribera del Duero carries Tempranillo's red fruit and savouriness into deeper, darker territory. The tannins firm up, the structure rises vertically, the fruit intensity increases. It feels like Tempranillo spoken with a bolder accent. For those who appreciate the grounded character of traditional Rioja or Toro but want something more concentrated and powerful, Ribera expands that path.

Cahors (Southwest France)

Cahors presents Malbec in a firmer, more traditional frame, shaped by cooler nights, limestone soils and a long history of rustic elegance. The fruit moves towards black plum and dark cherry, supported by earth, tobacco leaf and a savoury depth that sits easily beside matured Tempranillo. The tannins are confident yet measured, creating a calm, grounded structure. For drinkers who admire the composed seriousness of classic Rioja and wish to explore a darker and more quietly powerful expression of earth influenced reds, Cahors offers a natural continuation.

Chianti Classico (Italy)

Chianti shares Tempranillo's red fruit, acidity, and savouriness but translates them into brighter cherry, firmer tannins, and Italian herbal tones. It is more lifted, more energetic. If you value Tempranillo for its structure and earthiness, Chianti offers a more vibrant, more brisk interpretation of those same qualities.

Pinot Noir (Earth-Driven Styles: Burgundy or Oregon)

Pinot Noir echoes Tempranillo's earthy, savoury character but softens the structure and heightens the aromatics—forest floor, dried leaves, red fruit, gentle spice. It's lighter in body and tannin yet emotionally aligned. If Tempranillo's grounded calm speaks to you and you want something more delicate, more aromatic, earth-driven Pinot Noir provides that softer complexity.

Grenache (Southern Rhône)

Grenache reflects Tempranillo's warmth and spice but with rounder fruit—strawberry, raspberry, plum—and softer, more yielding tannins. It feels more open, sunnier, less structured. For anyone who enjoys Tempranillo's depth but wants a wine that leans more generous and relaxed, Grenache softens the savoury edges while keeping the warmth intact.

Stretch Wines

Barolo (Nebbiolo Italy)

Barolo amplifies Tempranillo's earthy core into something more intense—tar, roses, red fruit, piercing acidity, and assertive tannin. It is more demanding, more architectural, more ethereal. If you appreciate the savoury structure of Tempranillo and want to step toward profound complexity, Barolo leads in that upward direction.

Brunello di Montalcino (Italy)

Brunello shares Tempranillo's red fruit and herbal earthiness but renders them with greater weight, richness, and tension. The tannins are finer yet firmer, the flavours deeper, the finish longer. For those who enjoy Tempranillo's balanced seriousness and want something more monumental, Brunello is an elegant progression.

Aglianico (Taurasi or Vulture)

Aglianico echoes Tempranillo's savoury, earth-driven character but adds volcanic minerality, darker fruit, and a more commanding structure. It feels bolder, more intense, more elemental. If Tempranillo's depth resonates with you and you want to explore a more forceful, moody expression, Aglianico stretches the experience into richer terrain.

Myths or Misunderstandings

A common myth is that Tempranillo must always taste heavily of oak. While traditional styles showcase American oak's vanilla and coconut tones, many modern expressions favour subtle, integrated oak or neutral barrels that let fruit and earth speak more clearly. Another misconception is that Tempranillo is simple; in truth, it is one of Europe's most versatile grapes, producing wines that range from bright and juicy to deep, structured, and age worthy.

Closing Reflection

Tempranillo in its earth-driven form offers a quiet, grounded beauty, red fruit softened by age, savoury depth shaped by time, tannins that speak gently but firmly. It is a wine that reflects place and patience, a wine that does not rush. It reminds us that complexity can be found in restraint, and that age and earth can give wine a depth that feels both comforting and profound.

Pinot Noir (Savoury Burgundy-Inspired Expressions)

Savoury Pinot Noir feels like walking through a forest after rain, quiet, aromatic, and full of subtle detail. Pour a glass and the colour forms a translucent garnet, glowing with softness rather than saturation. Lift it toward your nose, and the aromas rise in slow, fine layers: red currant, wild strawberry, cherry skin, dried leaves, forest floor, truffle, violets, spice, and the faint mineral scent of damp stone. Nothing is loud. Nothing pushes. Instead, the wine speaks in a voice that invites you to lean closer.

This is Pinot Noir as Burgundy interprets it, a wine shaped by limestone, cool climates, and centuries of patient craftsmanship. While New World Pinot Noir often leans toward fruit and warmth, Burgundy-inspired expressions emphasize delicacy, earth, and nuance. They reveal not just the grape but the ground itself. The wine becomes a lens through which terroir is seen clearly.

Pinot Noir is famously sensitive, difficult to grow, and transparent to its environment. In the hands of careful winemakers from Burgundy, Germany, Oregon, Central Otago, or coastal Chile, it can become a red wine of profound subtlety: light in body, but deep in meaning.

Why People Love It

People love savoury, earthy-toned Pinot Noir because it offers complexity without weight. The fruit is present but restrained, tart cherry, red currant, cranberry, softened by floral tones and deepened by umami-like notes of mushroom, dried leaves, and earth. The acidity is bright but not sharp. The tannins are gentle but persistent, more like fine threads than heavy cords.

Emotionally, this style appeals to those who enjoy wines that unfold slowly, wines that reward attention and contemplation. It suits quiet dinners, thoughtful conversations, and moments when you want wine to deepen the atmosphere rather than dominate it. Earth-driven Pinot Noir doesn't shout. It murmurs in a way that draws you in.

How This Wine Feels

Earth driven Pinot Noir is dry, light to medium in body, with vivid acidity and finely knit tannins. The first sip feels lifted and precise, showing red fruit edged with earth and spice before it gently expands across the palate. The tannins act like soft fabric against the tongue, giving the wine definition without any force.

A swirl reveals further layers: crushed leaves, mushroom, dried herbs, cedar, black tea and the familiar forest floor character that blends earth, wood and dried plant matter. After the wine leaves the palate, cherry skin and earthy notes return in a quiet echo, creating a finish that feels long but understated, persistence without intensity.

Compared with fruit driven expressions, earth driven Pinot Noir has a firmer structure and a quieter fruit profile. Its restraint gives it depth, the kind that settles in slowly and resonates more deeply with each sip.

If You Like This Wine... You May Also Like

Red Burgundy (Village and Premier Cru)

You'll recognise the same forest-floor nuances, red-fruit subtlety, and fine, silken tannins, but Burgundy renders everything with greater detail. The minerality becomes sharper, the earth more articulate, the fruit more finely drawn. If you enjoy the grounded delicacy of earth-driven Pinot Noir and want to explore its most classic, intricate form, Burgundy speaks the same language with more nuance and quiet tension.

Gamay (Beaujolais Crus)

Gamay carries Pinot Noir's light body and red-fruited lift but channels earthiness through florals and gentle spice instead of forest tones. It feels juicier, brighter, a little more carefree. For those who love Pinot Noir's finesse but want something more cheerful and immediate, the crus of Beaujolais offer a lively, floral, earth-kissed alternative.

Cabernet Franc (Loire Valley)

Cabernet Franc mirrors Pinot Noir's savoury delicacy but frames it with herbs, graphite, and cooler red fruit. It feels more vertical, more aromatic, more angular. If you're drawn to Pinot Noir's subtlety and want a wine with firmer definition and herbal lift, Cabernet Franc extends those qualities into a slightly more structured style.

Nebbiolo (Langhe Nebbiolo or Entry-Level Barolo or Barbaresco)

Nebbiolo shares Pinot Noir's pale colour and soaring aromatics—rose, dried cherry, earth—but adds higher acidity and firmer tannins. It is more demanding, more architectural, yet emotionally similar in its transparency and lift. If Pinot Noir's perfume and earth draw you in and you want to explore a deeper, more structural expression, Nebbiolo offers a compelling next step.

Spätburgunder (Germany)

Spätburgunder offers the same quiet fragrance and gentle red fruit that define earth led Pinot Noir, yet it speaks with its own soft inflection. The fruit feels a touch cooler, the herbs a little fresher, the structure fine but certain. The best examples from regions such as the Ahr or Baden carry a subtle woodland clarity, a sense of air and light woven through cherry, wild strawberry and delicate spice. For drinkers who love Pinot Noir's whisper of earth yet want to discover a new expression shaped by northern sunlight and patient craftsmanship, Spätburgunder opens that path with grace.

Etna Rosso (Nerello Mascalese, Sicily)

Etna Rosso carries the same delicacy and mineral clarity but adds volcanic smoke, dried herbs, and altitude-shaped red fruit. It feels slightly more savoury, slightly more linear. For those who admire Pinot Noir's purity and earthiness, Etna Rosso presents those qualities through a landscape of ash, stone, and mountain air.

Stretch Wines

Sangiovese (Chianti Classico)

Sangiovese stretches Pinot Noir's red-fruit core into brighter acidity and firmer tannins. The flavours shift from berries and forest notes toward cherries, herbs, and dried flowers. If you enjoy Pinot Noir's savoury profile but want more grip and energy, Sangiovese offers a rewarding evolution.

Aglianico (Taurasi or Vulture)

Aglianico takes Pinot's earthy seriousness and renders it darker and more powerful. It usually has higher tannins, deeper fruit, volcanic minerality. It's a stretch toward intensity, suited to drinkers who want to explore a more commanding, more elemental version of savouriness.

Syrah (Northern Rhône, Lighter Styles)

Cool-climate Syrah captures Pinot Noir's perfume and elegance while deepening the spice and darkening the fruit. It remains lifted, floral, and savoury, but with more structure and tension. If Pinot Noir's aromatics appeal and you want something with greater depth and precision, Northern Rhône Syrah opens that path beautifully.

Myths or Misunderstandings

One misconception is that earth-driven Pinot Noir is too light to be complex. In truth, its lightness reveals rather than conceals earth, mineral, savoury spice, and delicate fruit become more vivid, not less. Another myth is that all earthy Pinot must be expensive; excellent expressions come from Oregon, Germany, New Zealand, and cool pockets of California.

Some assume Pinot Noir's earthiness indicates age or flaws. Those forest-floor tones are part of the grape's natural beauty, a sign of its sensitivity to place.

Closing Reflection

Earth-driven Pinot Noir shows that subtlety can carry immense depth. It speaks in soft tones, red fruit woven with earth, flowers drifting over stone, tannins fine as thread, yet leaves a lasting impression. It is a wine that encourages quiet attention, that rewards contemplation, that reminds us how eloquent delicacy can be.

Barolo

Barolo feels like a landscape carved into a wine, a wine of roses and earth, of quiet autumn light and long-forgotten stone. Pour a glass and the colour may surprise you: translucent garnet, almost fragile-looking at the rim, glowing like dried leaves. But don't be deceived by the pale robe, Barolo is one of the most powerful, structured, and emotionally resonant red wines in the world.

Lift it to your nose and the aromas rise in layers that feel both delicate and intense: dried roses, sour cherry, pomegranate, tar, tobacco, anise, truffle, tea leaves, warm earth, and sometimes a faint whisper of fennel or mint. Nebbiolo, the grape behind Barolo, is famously aromatic, and the scent alone feels like stepping into a forest at the edge of fall, leaves curling in the cold air, flowers still clinging to their memory of summer.

What makes Barolo so haunting is the way it balances this soft, floral perfume with a structure that can feel monumental. Nebbiolo tannins are firm, gripping, almost architectural; the acidity is high, bright, and linear; the flavours move with tension and drive. Barolo is a wine that doesn't rush. It unfurls.

Why People Love It

People love Barolo because it offers emotional depth. This is not simply a wine of fruit; it is a wine of sensation, of rose petals drying on stone, of red fruit sharpened by acidity, of earth warming under sunlight. It is demanding, in the sense that it asks for attention, but it rewards that attention with beauty that feels timeless.

Emotionally, Barolo appeals to people who seek wines with character and history. It suits meals slow enough to match its own pace, conversations with weight, moments of contemplation. It is a wine for cold nights, rich dishes, ageing cheeses, and occasions when you want a wine that speaks.

How This Wine Feels

Barolo is dry, full bodied in structure yet light in colour, with high acidity and very firm tannins. The first sip feels taut and gripping, showing sour cherry, redcurrant, rose and tar, all wrapped in tannins that stretch across the palate like fine grit. Beneath that tension sits a quiet elegance; the fruit feels delicate, the aromas floral, and the texture turns silky once you move past the initial grip.

With air and time in the glass, the wine begins to widen. Tobacco, truffle, dried flowers, cedar and anise weave into the red fruit, adding depth and nuance. The finish is long, savoury and calmly authoritative. Barolo does not drop away quickly; it lingers with the steady presence of a story still unfolding.

As the wine ages, whether five, ten or twenty years, the tannins soften, the fruit grows darker and the earth and floral tones deepen into something almost meditative: dried roses, forest floor, spice box, old leather and the scent of a wooden drawer that has stayed closed for decades.

If You Like This Wine... You May Also Like

Barbaresco (Italy)

You'll recognise Barolo's rose-petal perfume, red cherry, tar, and earth, but Barbaresco presents them in a gentler, more approachable frame. The tannins are finer, the fruit slightly softer, the overall impression more graceful. For those captivated by Barolo's depth who want something less demanding and more open in youth, Barbaresco stands as its closest, most elegant companion.

Brunello di Montalcino (Italy)

Brunello echoes Barolo's seriousness and its blend of red fruit and earth, but the structure feels broader and warmer with richer cherry, darker spice, firmer tannins, greater weight. For anyone who loves Barolo's complexity and seeks a wine with more warmth and richness while maintaining ageworthiness, Brunello offers power shaped by poise.

Etna Rosso (Sicily)

Etna Rosso carries Nebbiolo's pale colour and lifted perfume into a volcanic landscape that reshapes every detail. The red fruit feels tense and crystalline, the aromatics fine and smoky, the acidity alive with mountain freshness. Notes of dried herbs, mineral dust and faint embers give the wine a calm intensity that lingers. For those who love Barolo's combination of fragility and firmness yet want to explore a more vertical, high-altitude interpretation, Etna Rosso offers a compelling and quietly dramatic perspective.

Sangiovese (Chianti Classico Riserva or Gran Selezione)

These wines share Barolo's bright acidity, savouriness, and affinity for robust food pairings, but with redder fruit and gentler tannins, making them more accessible in youth. If Barolo's focus and structure appeal to you yet you want something less austere, the higher tiers of Chianti provide tension with added approachability.

Rioja Gran Reserva (Spain)

Rioja Gran Reserva mirrors Barolo's interplay of red fruit, earth, and long maturation. You'll find dried cherry, leather, spice, tobacco, and a serene, slow-building complexity. The structure is softer, the texture more polished. For those drawn to Barolo's aged character but seeking something smoother and less tannic, Gran Reserva offers a time-shaped depth that feels effortlessly composed.

Northern Rhône Syrah (Côte-Rôtie, Hermitage)

These wines share Barolo's aromatic spectrum with violets, earth, smoke, spice but express it through darker fruit and a leaner, more savoury structure. The tannins are more muscular, the mood similarly contemplative. For anyone who loves Barolo's aromatics and savouriness, Northern Rhône Syrah reveals a different yet equally profound path.

Stretch Wines

Aglianico (Taurasi or Vulture)

Aglianico is one of the few grapes capable of matching Nebbiolo's tannic stature. It brings darker fruit, volcanic earth, and immense ageing potential. For those drawn to Barolo's structure and ready to explore an even deeper, more brooding expression, Aglianico takes those qualities into a more elemental register.

Pinot Noir (Earth-Driven Burgundy)

This stretch moves toward finesse rather than force. Earth-driven Burgundy offers delicacy, earth, and perfume in a lighter, silkier frame, capturing Barolo's aromatic spirit through softness instead of structure. For drinkers enchanted by Barolo's fragrance who want an even more ethereal interpretation, Burgundy opens that door.

Cabernet Sauvignon (Old World Styles)

Old World Cabernet carries tannin, earth, and structure reminiscent of Nebbiolo but shifts the fruit darker and the frame more angular. It's less perfumed, more mineral and herbal. For those intrigued by Barolo's tension who want to see a similar discipline expressed through a different grape, Cabernet offers a grounded, rigorous perspective.

Myths or Misunderstandings

A common misconception is that all Barolo must be aged for decades before it is enjoyable. While many top examples improve with time, modern Barolo often shows earlier approachability thanks to careful vineyard work and gentler tannin management. Another myth is that Barolo is always austere; with adequate ripeness and thoughtful winemaking, it can be incredibly expressive even when young.

Some believe Barolo's pale colour signals weakness. Nebbiolo's light hue hides no lack of power, its tannins and acidity make it one of the most structurally formidable wines on earth.

Closing Reflection

Barolo is a wine that rewards patience and attention, red fruit and roses layered over earth, stone, spice, and time. It feels both fragile and powerful, transparent yet commanding. It teaches that beauty can arrive in whispers and that intensity can coexist with delicacy. Barolo is less a flavour than a journey, one that unfolds slowly and lingers long after the glass is empty.

Brunello di Montalcino

Brunello di Montalcino feels like standing at the edge of a hillside just before sunset, warm light stretching over stone and earth, everything glowing with a deep, steady intensity. Pour a glass and the colour is a radiant, dense garnet with a slight transparency at the rim, as if the wine holds both weight and luminosity at once. Bring it to your nose and the aromas rise slowly but unmistakably: dark cherry, red plum, dried fig, rosemary, tobacco, leather, warm terra cotta, dried flowers, and the subtle spice of seasoned wood. It is Sangiovese at its most profound, not louder, but deeper.

Brunello comes from Montalcino, a hilltop town in southern Tuscany where Sangiovese ripens more completely than anywhere else in Italy. More sun, more warmth, more wind, all of it allows the grape to express a darker, richer, more structured voice than its brighter, tangier expression in Chianti. The name "Brunello" simply means "little dark one," a reference to the Sangiovese clone that grows here, but the wines speak with a gravity far greater than their name suggests.

Why People Love It

People love Brunello because it offers gravity without heaviness, a wine with depth, power, and seriousness, yet never losing Sangiovese's essential brightness. The fruit is rich but not jammy[1]. The tannins are firm but not coarse. The oak adds warmth but not excess. Brunello balances everything: ripeness with tension, weight with levity, sun with stone.

Emotionally, Brunello appeals to those who seek wines that feel meditative, wines that carry the warmth of earth and time. It suits long dinners, winter evenings, deep conversations, and meals that unfold slowly. It is a wine that invites presence, the kind you sip deliberately, because each sip seems to reveal something new.

How This Wine Feels

Brunello is dry, full bodied and marked by firm, fine grained tannins supported by bright acidity. The first sip feels wide and generous, with dark cherry, plum and berry compote settling across the palate before Sangiovese's natural lift pulls everything upward, keeping the wine from feeling heavy.

The tannins wrap the mouth with calm authority, textured yet polished. As the wine opens, savoury tones begin to emerge: tobacco leaf, leather, rosemary, thyme, warm earth, cedar and dried flowers. Oak ageing, which must last at least two years and often stretches much longer, adds spice, structure and gentle warmth without ever overshadowing the grape.

A swirl deepens the expression, revealing forest floor, balsamic notes, blood orange peel and at times a mineral impression that recalls warm iron or stone. After the wine leaves the palate, fruit, spice and earth rise again in a quiet bloom of aroma, creating a finish that carries on softly but steadily, long, balanced and resonant.

Brunello is built to age. Over time the tannins soften, the fruit turns more savoury and the wine's core becomes a tapestry of dried flowers, spice, tobacco and earth. A mature Brunello often feels like memory held in liquid form.

If You Like This Wine... You May Also Like

Chianti Classico Riserva (Italy)

You'll recognise the same Sangiovese markers. Sour cherry, herbs, earth, lively acidity but Chianti Classico Riserva carries them in a leaner, brighter, more agile frame. The tannins feel firmer and straighter, the fruit slightly redder, the finish more lifted. For anyone who enjoys Brunello's flavour palette but wants something lighter, more refreshing, and easier to drink on a weeknight, Chianti Riserva offers that familiar voice in a sleeker expression.

Vino Nobile di Montepulciano (Italy)

Vino Nobile reflects Brunello's depth but presents it with softer tannins, gentler earthiness, and a rounder, more welcoming mid-palate. It is less intense, less brooding, more readily open. If Brunello's warmth and savouriness appeal to you but you prefer a wine that requires less ceremony and patience, Vino Nobile conveys the same Sangiovese soul in a more relaxed posture.

Rioja Reserva (Spain)

Rioja Reserva mirrors Brunello's balance of fruit, structure, and layered savouriness, yet expresses it through sweeter spice, smoother tannins, and a blend of American and French oak. The fruit is darker, more polished, the acidity softer, the texture silkier. If you admire Brunello's depth but want something gentler and more aromatically spiced, Rioja Reserva provides a graceful sideways exploration.

Bordeaux (Left Bank or Pessac-Léognan)

You'll find similar seriousness, tannic structure, and age worthy intent, but Bordeaux shifts the fruit toward blackcurrant and frames everything with graphite, cedar, and cool earth. It feels more mineral, more architectural. For those who appreciate Brunello's depth and want to see that gravitas expressed in a more restrained, structured idiom, Bordeaux offers a parallel with distinct flavours.

Aglianico del Vulture (Italy)

Aglianico captures Brunello's intensity, earthiness, and tannic presence, but channels them into darker fruit, volcanic minerality, and more dramatic structure. It is bolder, more elemental, more brooding. If Brunello's gravitas resonates with you and you want something that pushes further into power and tension, Aglianico takes those qualities into deeper terrain.

Stretch Wines

Barolo (Nebbiolo, Italy)

Barolo takes Brunello's savoury core and stretches it upward with higher acidity, firmer tannins, and more ethereal aromatics of rose, tar, dried cherry, and earth. It is more angular, more transparent, more demanding. For those captivated by Brunello who want a wine expressing similar seriousness through greater tension and lift, Barolo is a compelling step.

Syrah (Northern Rhône)

Northern Rhône Syrah shifts Brunello's mood toward darker fruit, pepper, violets, and smoke. The structure remains firm, the savouriness intact, but the tone becomes cooler and more aromatic. If Brunello's seriousness appeals and you're drawn to wines with greater spice, perfume, and linear precision, Côte-Rôtie or Hermitage expand the experience beautifully.

Amarone della Valpolicella (Italy)

Amarone takes Brunello's warmth and intensifies it. It brings deeper fruit, richer texture, more chocolate and spice. It is fuller, more opulent, less restrained. If you love Brunello but want a wine that leans further into richness and decadence, Amarone provides that amplified, luxurious expression.

Myths or Misunderstandings

Many believe Brunello must always be aged for years before drinking. While top bottles reward patience, many modern examples are crafted with gentler tannins and can show beautifully in their youth. Another misconception is that Brunello is heavy. In fact, its acidity keeps it surprisingly balanced, even refreshing, despite its depth.

Some assume that Brunello is simply "strong Chianti." While both wines share Sangiovese DNA, Brunello is shaped by the warmer climate of Montalcino, longer ageing, and a more structured expression, a cousin, not a duplicate.

Closing Reflection

Brunello di Montalcino feels like a wine made for slow evenings, deep, savoury, warm, and grounded. It carries the soul of Sangiovese in its most profound form: cherry and earth wrapped in a frame of tannin and time. Brunello speaks in a voice that is calm but resonant, powerful but poised. It reminds us that complexity grows from patience and that some wines offer not just flavour, but a sense of place and presence.

Pinotage

Pinotage carries a character that is both familiar and quietly distinctive, a wine shaped by the warmth and earthiness of its South African home. Pour a glass and the colour settles into deep ruby with hints of purple at the edge, a sign of its generous fruit. Lift it to your nose and a vivid mix appears: blackberry, plum, blueberry, soft smoke and a gentle floral note that drifts above the darker tones. Pinotage sits comfortably between brightness and depth, often revealing a smooth, supple texture that reflects both the sunlight and the coastal winds that shape South Africa's vineyards. At its best, it feels confident yet relaxed, a wine that carries its origins with clear, calm pride.

Pinotage has a unique story. Created in the early twentieth century as a crossing of Pinot Noir and Cinsault, it gathered the delicate aromatics of the former and the warm-hearted generosity of the latter. Over time it has become a defining grape of South Africa, a symbol of the country's ability to craft wines that are expressive, soulful and grounded in place. In the glass, this heritage shows in fruit that glows softly, joined by earthy tones and subtle spice. Pinotage ranges from bright and playful to deep and contemplative depending on the winemaker's intention. This versatility is part of its appeal.

The grape once carried a reputation for rustic, rubbery tones, the result of early winemaking challenges rather than anything inherent to the variety. Modern viticulture and careful cellar work have transformed the style. Today, well made Pinotage is generous, balanced and expressive, with none of the harshness once associated with it. It stands among South Africa's most distinctive and rewarding red wines, offering character, warmth and quiet complexity.

Why People Love It

People love Pinotage because it blends comfort with intrigue. The fruit feels ripe and welcoming, the texture smooth and the aromatics layered enough to hold attention without demanding it. Pinotage offers warmth without heaviness and depth without austerity. It suits relaxed evenings, slow cooked meals and conversations that unfold gently over time. The style appeals to drinkers who enjoy generous reds but still want freshness, gentle lift and a sense of place. There is a calm humanity to Pinotage, something approachable yet quietly thoughtful.

How This Wine Feels

Pinotage is typically dry and rounded, with medium body and a line of acidity that keeps the wine lively. The first sip brings blackberry, plum and blueberry, supported by subtle spice, soft earth and a gentle whisper of smoke. The tannins are smooth and pliant, giving shape without grip and allowing the fruit to glide across the palate with ease. In more structured expressions, the mid palate deepens, revealing savoury notes and a firmer sense of presence. The finish lingers with a warm, gentle impression of berry and spice. Pinotage feels grounded, expressive and quietly complete.

If You Like This Wine... You May Also Like

Cape Blends (South Africa)

Cape Blends share the soul of Pinotage while offering greater depth through the addition of Cabernet Sauvignon, Merlot and other Bordeaux varieties. These wines balance the warmth and generous fruit of Pinotage with firmer structure, gentle savoury tones and a more layered palate. They feel both familiar and expanded, a broader interpretation of the same landscape. For drinkers who appreciate Pinotage's sense of place and want a wine with a touch more architecture and complexity, Cape Blends provide a natural and rewarding progression.

Zinfandel (California)

Zinfandel offers a generous, fruit led personality that mirrors the warmth and friendliness of Pinotage. Expect flavours of bramble, blackberry and subtle spice carried on a smooth, inviting texture. The wine often moves with more exuberance and aromatic lift, yet it retains the same spirit of relaxed generosity. For those who enjoy Pinotage's richness but want a slightly brighter and more energetic expression, Zinfandel provides a lively and engageing alternative.

Shiraz from Western Cape (South Africa)

South African Shiraz echoes many of Pinotage's darker fruit notes while introducing pepper, violet and savoury earthiness. The wine feels slightly more structured, with firmer tannins and a more aromatic profile. It carries both warmth and tension, offering a step into greater detail while remaining firmly tied to South African flavour and light. For drinkers who appreciate the comfort of Pinotage but want something with added lift and complexity, Western Cape Shiraz offers a compelling path.

Cinsault (South Africa or France)

Cinsault reflects the bright, red fruited side of Pinotage's parentage, with cherry, raspberry and delicate floral tones carried on fine, gentle tannins. The wine feels light and buoyant, moving with ease and clarity across the palate. For those who enjoy Pinotage's easy charm but want something fresher and more delicate, Cinsault provides a graceful and refreshing alternative that still echoes the grape's heritage.

Stretch Wines

Cabernet Sauvignon Merlot Blends (South Africa)

These blends take the warmth and generosity of Pinotage and anchor them in firmer structure, cooler aromatics and a more classical frame. Expect blackcurrant, plum, cedar and gentle tobacco supported by confident tannins. The wines feel both familiar and more serious, offering greater depth while maintaining a sense of openness. They suit drinkers who want to explore a more architectural red without leaving behind the warmth and identity of South African wine.

Grenache from Spain (Garnacha)

Garnacha offers a broader, sun kissed style with ripe strawberry, cherry and herbal tones wrapped in a gentle, softly textured palate. It feels brighter and more expansive than Pinotage, with a lightness of touch that contrasts with Pinotage's darker, earthier notes. For drinkers who enjoy the comfort of Pinotage but want to explore a style with more openness and Mediterranean charm, Garnacha provides a smooth and inviting step.

Myths or Misunderstandings

A lingering myth is that Pinotage must taste smoky or reductive, yet these traits come from outdated winemaking, not the grape itself. Modern Pinotage is clean, vibrant and expressive. Another misunderstanding is that Pinotage lacks finesse, but thoughtful examples show subtle floral lift, balanced acidity and quiet depth. Some believe that Pinotage cannot age, yet well crafted wines develop savoury nuance, spice and gentle complexity over time. Pinotage offers far more grace and character than its early reputation suggests.

Closing Reflection

Pinotage is a wine that reflects South Africa's beauty and resilience. It carries the warmth of its climate, the texture of its soils and the generosity of its vineyards. It feels both familiar and distinct, shaped by heritage yet open to interpretation. Pinotage offers comfort, richness and a gentle complexity that rewards slow appreciation. For those who enjoy reds that feel warm, expressive and rooted in place, Pinotage stands as one of South Africa's most enduring gifts.

---

1. Jammy: A sweet, cooked fruit character suggesting ripe, concentrated berries.

Chapter 15

Grape Families & Clones

How small variations shape texture, tone, and style

Grapes, like people, belong to families. They share traits, temperaments, and tendencies. Some are aromatic; some are earthy; some are powerful; some are delicate. Understanding these relationships doesn't require memorisation, it simply helps you see patterns. Patterns reveal similarities, and similarities help you discover wines you'll love.

Clones, on the other hand, are like siblings within the same family: genetically similar but slightly different in personality. They shape nuance, not identity. You don't need to know their names to appreciate what they do.

The Families: personality over genetics

Wine grapes are often grouped into families based on sensory character rather than strict genetic lineage. These families help explain why certain wines feel related even when they come from different regions.

The Aromatics

This family is defined by fragrance, wines that lift from the glass in bright, perfumed waves. Grapes like Sauvignon Blanc, Riesling, Albariño, Viognier, Gewürztraminer, and Muscat show aromas of flowers, citrus, stone fruit, and herbs. Their personalities are expressive and energetic. If you enjoy one, chances are you'll enjoy others.

The Bright & Crisp Whites

These grapes create wines with freshness, tension, and clarity. Think Pinot Grigio (in its lean style), Soave, Muscadet, Grüner Veltliner, and dry Chenin Blanc. They share a structural similarity: light to medium body, clean texture, and acidity that feels like a breath of cold air.

The Rich Whites

Chardonnay, Marsanne, Roussanne, Viognier (in its fuller expression), Pinot Gris (Alsace), and mature Chenin Blanc form this textural family. Their wines feel broad and layered, shaped by ripeness, oak, lees, or time. They offer warmth and depth without losing elegance.

The Juicy, Fruit-Forward Reds

Pinot Noir (fruit-driven), Gamay, Zinfandel, and many Merlots belong here. They share soft tannins, bright fruit, and easy drinkability. If you love one of these wines, you'll often find the others feel like close cousins.

The Structured Reds

Cabernet Sauvignon, Syrah or Shiraz, Malbec, Rioja Crianza (Tempranillo), and Grenache-based blends. These grapes create wines with body, tannin, spice, and depth. Their personalities are confident, grounding, and bold.

The Earth-Driven Reds

Nebbiolo, Sangiovese, Tempranillo (aged or traditional styles), and Burgundy-style Pinot Noir form a family defined by savouriness and structure. These grapes express the soil, climate, and winemaking tradition fiercely. If you love earth, herbs, and quiet complexity, you'll feel at home here.

Sweet Grapes & Fortified Grapes

The aromatic sweetness of Muscat, the botrytised richness of Semillon and Furmint, and the dark power of fortified grapes like Touriga Nacional each form families of their own, but what unites them is intensity, of flavour, of texture, of emotional resonance.

Clones: the subtle variations

Clones are simply small genetic variations of the same grape. Think of them as personalities within the same family.

Pinot Noir has dozens of clones: some create delicate, floral wines; others produce darker, richer expressions. Chardonnay clones influence texture, weight, and ripeness. Sangiovese and Nebbiolo have famous clones that subtly shift fruit profile or structure.

You don't need to know clone numbers (though winemakers often do). What matters is that clones give diversity to wines made from the same grape. They allow a region to express itself with nuance.

Clones matter especially in grapes that are sensitive to place, Pinot Noir, Chardonnay, Nebbiolo, Sangiovese, where small differences in flavour or texture speak loudly.

Why all this matters for you

Understanding grape families helps you recognise patterns. If you love Albariño, you might also love Soave or dry Riesling because they share freshness. If you love Merlot, Zinfandel's juiciness might feel immediately comfortable. If you adore Barolo, Burgundy's earth-driven Pinot Noir might resonate with your palate.

The point is not to memorise anything.

It's to realise that grapes have relationships.

And once you sense those relationships, discovering new wines becomes intuitive.

The beauty of families and clones

Grape families show you your home base, the styles that naturally feel right.

Clones explain why wines from the same grape can feel slightly different from each other.

Together, they reveal that wine is not a collection of isolated bottles.

It is a living network of similarities, differences, and connections, a map you learn by feel, not facts.

Wine becomes easier when you see these patterns.

And once you recognise them, the world of wine stops feeling large and begins to feel familiar.

Chapter 16

How Wine Is Made: From Grape to Glass

A clear journey through the steps that shape a wine's character

Wine begins long before fermentation, long before tanks, barrels, or bottles. It begins with a landscape, a vine, and a season. Winemaking is simply the act of guiding fruit through a quiet transformation. The choices winemakers make along the way shape the way a wine feels: its brightness or richness, its texture or transparency, its depth or delicacy. You don't need to remember the steps. You only need to understand the movement.

Growing: Where Everything Begins

Vines spend an entire year preparing for the grapes that become wine. Sunlight, soil, rain, wind, and human care all shape the berries. Grapes do not need to be perfect; they need to be in balance, ripe enough to offer fruit, structured enough to hold their shape, fresh enough to stay alive in the glass. When harvest arrives, the decision of *when* to pick is the first and most important choice. Early picking creates brighter, more acidic wines; later picking gives richness, softness, and warmth.

At its heart, winemaking is farming. Everything that happens afterward, all the nuance of flavour and texture, is rooted in the vineyard.

Harvest: Choosing the Moment

Harvest can be done by hand or machine, quickly or gradually. Grapes picked early taste different from grapes picked late. In cool years grapes may hold more tension; in warm years they may carry more generosity. Winemakers walk rows tasting berries, feeling tannins, watching seeds and skins for subtle changes. The moment they choose to harvest is the moment they choose the wine's direction.

White Winemaking: Clarity and Light

White wines are usually made by pressing the juice off the skins early, before tannins or colour dissolve into it. The juice is allowed to settle, becoming clear and bright. Fermentation happens cool, preserving delicate aromatics: citrus, flowers, herbs, orchard fruit. The wine may rest in stainless steel for precision, in neutral barrels for softness, or on lees for texture.

White winemaking is about *preserving freshness*. Every step aims to keep the wine light on its feet, lifted, transparent, a translation of fruit and place into something luminous.

Red Winemaking: Colour, Structure, and Depth

Red wines are made with the skins. This simple choice, allowing skins to mingle with fermenting juice, gives red wine its colour, tannin, body, and shape. As fermentation warms, the skins rise to the surface and are punched down or pumped over, extracting flavour and structure. More extraction leads to fuller, darker wines. Less extraction gives lighter, more delicate ones.

Red winemaking is about *embracing texture*. The way tannins feel, gentle, gripping, silky, firm, comes from this dance between juice, skins, and time.

Rosé Winemaking: The Bridge Between Worlds

Rosé is made from red grapes treated with unusual gentleness. Winemakers press the grapes early or give only a brief moment of skin contact, just enough to pick up colour and a touch of structure. The juice is then treated like a white wine, fermented cool, kept fresh and crisp. Rosé lives in the space between red and white, carrying the brightness of one and the fruit of the other.

Different techniques create different styles:

- A direct press rosé is pale and delicate.

- A short maceration rosé is deeper and more expressive.

- A saignée rosé, drained off a red fermentation, tends to be richer and more vivid.

- Rosé is not a compromise. It is a deliberate choice.

Skin-Contact or Orange or Amber Wine: White Grapes, Red Approach

Skin-contact wines flip white winemaking on its head. Instead of pressing the juice off the skins immediately, winemakers allow the skins to ferment with the juice, just as they would for red wine. This gives the wine colour (ranging from pale copper to deep amber), tannin, grip, and savoury complexity.

These wines feel herbal, textured, sometimes tea-like, with flavours of dried citrus, apricot, and spice. They can be gentle or assertive, ancient or modern. Skin-contact wine is not about trend. It is about letting the grape speak in a deeper register.

Sparkling Wine: Capturing Light in Motion

Sparkling wine begins as still wine, then undergoes a second fermentation to create bubbles.

The *traditional method,* used in Champagne, Franciacorta, and many of the world's finest sparkling wines, creates bubbles inside the bottle itself. Yeast consumes sugar, produces carbon dioxide (the bubbles), and then breaks down slowly, giving the wine notes of brioche, pastry, and biscuit. This method creates the finest mousse and the deepest textures.

- The *tank method,* used for Prosecco, creates bubbles in a sealed tank before bottling. This preserves freshness, fruit, and floral aromatics, a gentler, more carefree expression.

- The *ancestral method* (pet-nat) allows the first fermentation to finish in the bottle, creating rustic, frothy wines full of spontaneity and charm.

Every sparkling method expresses a different type of joy: elegance, freshness, or playfulness.

Sweet Wines: The Art of Concentration

Sweet wine is not sugar added afterward; it is sweetness created through concentration of natural grape sugars:

- In *late-harvest wines,* grapes stay on the vine longer, ripening to honeyed intensity.

- In *botrytised wines* like Sauternes and Tokaji, noble rot pierces the berries, evaporating water and condensing sweetness, acidity, and flavour.

- In *ice wine,* grapes freeze naturally on the vine and are pressed while frozen, releasing only a few drops of intensely sweet juice.

- In *passito* styles, grapes are dried on straw mats, concentrating everything inside them.

- Sweet wines are meticulous, delicate, and extraordinary, always balanced by acidity so they feel bright rather than heavy.

Fortified Wines: Sweetness Held by Spirit

Fortified wines like Port, Madeira, Marsala, and Vin Doux Naturel are made by adding grape spirit during fermentation. This stops the yeast, preserves natural sweetness, and raises alcohol. These wines achieve a level of richness, structure, and longevity unmatched by unfortified wines.

Madeira undergoes deliberate heating and oxidation, becoming one of the most indestructible wines on earth. Port gains depth from blending, ageing, and tradition. Each fortified style expresses intensity in its own way, sweet, powerful, structured, and warm.

Traditional, Organic, Biodynamic, and Natural Approaches

Beyond technique lies philosophy.

Some winemakers follow *traditional* methods passed down over centuries.

Others work *organically*, avoiding synthetic chemicals.

Some adopt *biodynamics*, treating the vineyard as a living organism in rhythm with natural cycles.

And others pursue *natural winemaking*, intervening as little as possible and relying on native yeast, low sulphur, and minimal manipulation.

None of these approaches guarantees a certain taste; they simply reflect intention. The best wines from any philosophy are those in which the choices support clarity, balance, and expressiveness.

The Meaning Behind the Method

You don't need to memorise winemaking. All you need to understand is that every choice, from picking to pressing to fermenting to ageing, influences how a wine feels on your palate. Brightness or richness, softness or grip, delicacy or power: these sensations come from a series of small decisions guided by the winemaker's hand and the vineyard's voice.

Winemaking is the quiet craft behind the experience. It shapes the wine without ever needing to announce itself. And once you understand this simple movement, fruit becoming flavour, structure becoming texture, choices becoming emotion, wine feels not more complicated, but more alive.

Organic, Biodynamic & Natural Wines

Wine begins in the vineyard, and how that vineyard is tended shapes not only the flavours in the glass but the philosophy behind them. Organic, biodynamic, and natural wines aren't separate categories so much as different expressions of the same intention: to make wine with integrity, clarity, and respect for the land. These approaches ask a simple question, *how gently can we guide the vine, the soil, and the fermentation itself?*, and answer it in different ways.

Organic Wine: Reducing Intervention, Honouring the Vine

Organic viticulture avoids synthetic herbicides, pesticides, and fertilisers, relying instead on physical work, natural pest control, plant diversity, and soil health. The goal is not purity as a marketing idea; the goal is resilience. Healthy soils support healthier vines, which in turn can ripen fruit with more nuance and balance.

Organic certification varies by region, but the core principle is universal: remove the harshest chemicals, cultivate biodiversity, and let the vine find balance through natural cycles. In the winery, organic rules focus mostly on what is prohibited rather than what must be done, you can still use temperature control, cultured yeast, and sulphur. Organic winemaking does not reject modernity; it simply avoids synthetic shortcuts.

The emotional experience of organic wine is not that it tastes "cleaner," but that it feels grounded, a wine that mirrors the vineyard more closely because fewer layers stand between the vine and the glass.

Biodynamic Wine: The Vineyard as a Living Organism

Biodynamics goes further. Based on the ideas of Rudolf Steiner, it treats the vineyard as a self-sustaining ecosystem, a living organism connected to soil, plants, animals, microbes, seasons, and even lunar rhythms. Some aspects feel philosophical; others are deeply practical.

Biodynamic farming uses herbal preparations, composting, and strict attention to soil vitality. It seeks not just to grow grapes but to create harmony within the vineyard. The result is vines that often show striking health and consistency, producing grapes that ripen with balance rather than force.

Biodynamic wines are not defined by flavour but by *energy*, they often feel vivid, textural, and expressive in ways that are hard to describe scientifically. They carry a sense of presence, as if the vineyard's rhythms have become part of the wine's emotional signature.

Natural Wine: Minimal Intervention and Maximum Transparency

Natural wine is the least defined and most debated of the three. At its core, natural winemaking means fermenting with native yeasts, avoiding additives, keeping sulphur low or absent, and intervening as little as possible. The intention is simplicity: let the grapes and the place speak with as little interference as possible.

When natural wine is made with care, it feels alive, bright, savoury, textured, often slightly wild in its aromatics, with a transparency that makes you feel close to the vineyard. At its best, natural wine offers a sense of immediacy and intimacy: the grape and the landscape translated directly.

But minimal intervention is a delicate balance. Without the protective roles of sulphur or controlled fermentation, the wine becomes vulnerable to oxidation, microbial instability, and faults like mousiness or volatile acidity. Natural wine can be profound, or fragile. The best producers know when to step back and when to guide.

Sustainability: The Quiet Fourth Philosophy

Though often overshadowed, sustainability focuses on water use, carbon footprint, worker welfare, energy conservation, and long-term ecological health. It's less romantic than biodynamics and less headline-grabbing than natural wine, but it is one of the most impactful philosophies in the modern wine world. A sustainable winery may choose to use some chemicals sparingly rather than force the vineyard through stress, prioritising environmental balance over purity narratives.

What These Approaches Mean in the Glass

The flavour of organic, biodynamic, or natural wine does not come from certification, it comes from intention. Many of the world's greatest producers farm organically or biodynamically without mentioning it on the label. Others make low-sulphur natural wines with remarkable finesse. Some wines made with minimal intervention have tension and life that conventional wines cannot match; others tip into instability.

The key is not to idolise or dismiss any approach. Instead, recognise what they seek:

- Organic farming seeks resilience.
- Biodynamic farming seeks harmony.
- Natural winemaking seeks transparency.
- Sustainable winemaking seeks balance for the future.

What matters is *how* the wine feels: alive, stable, expressive, whole.

The Emotional Heart of the Matter

People are drawn to these wines not just for flavour but for ethos, the idea that the vineyard is a living place deserving of care, that wine can be made gently, that earth and craft can meet with respect. These wines invite you to taste not only the grape and the region but the philosophy behind them.

Organic, biodynamic, and natural wines remind us that wine is agriculture first, fermentation second, and philosophy third. They show that intention shapes experience, and that the choices made in the vineyard influence the wine's emotional resonance as deeply as its flavour.

How Wine Ages

Wine ages the way people do, not by becoming something else, but by becoming more deeply itself. Time reshapes wine's structure, softens its edges, deepens its layers, and reveals qualities that were once hidden. Not every wine is meant for this journey, but for the wines that are, ageing is a slow unfolding, a gradual shift from freshness to nuance, from brightness to depth, from immediacy to contemplation.

ageing begins the moment a wine is bottled. Inside that bottle, a small amount of oxygen interacts with tannins, colour molecules, acids, and aromatic compounds. This interaction is slow and quiet, happening in the dark, in stillness, at a gentle temperature. The wine evolves in a kind of suspended twilight, protected yet alive.

What Happens to Red Wine as It Ages

Young red wines often feel energetic: firm tannins, bright fruit, vivid colour. With time, tannins soften, knitting themselves into the wine until they feel less like edges and more like texture. Fruit flavours shift from fresh berries to dried or stewed ones, cherry becoming dried cherry, plum becoming prune, blackberry becoming black tea or forest floor. Earthy notes emerge such as leather, tobacco, dried herbs, cedar, spice, mushroom.

The colour fades from deep purple or ruby to garnet, then to brick at the rim. Red wines that age well aren't necessarily the heaviest; they are the ones with enough acidity, structure, and concentration to carry their flavours gracefully forward. Barolo, Brunello, Rioja Reserva, Bordeaux, and Northern Rhône Syrah are examples of reds whose architecture invites time.

Aged reds feel less like fruit and more like story, the narrative of the vineyard told slowly, with patience.

What Happens to White Wine as It Ages

White wines age differently. Young whites feel bright and floral, driven by freshness. Over time, acidity remains but becomes gentler. Aromas shift from citrus and green fruit toward honey, nuts, lanolin, dried flowers, and warm stone. Colours deepen from pale straw to gold, then to amber.

Certain whites age beautifully: Riesling (especially dry or off-dry), Chenin Blanc, White Burgundy, high-quality Chardonnay, and some oak-aged Spanish whites. These wines often gain more complexity with time, developing layers that feel almost architectural: wax, salt, spice, toasted grain, warm orchard fruit, sometimes even a hint of petrol in Riesling, which is natural and prized.

Aged whites feel like light filtered through amber glass, deeper, softer, more mysterious.

Sweet and Fortified Wines: Built for Time

Some wines seem almost immortal. Sauternes, Tokaji Aszú, Ice Wine, and other sweet wines combine high sugar with high acidity, a duo that protects them for decades. Their flavours move from honey and apricot to caramel, saffron, citrus oil, and candied nuts. They grow darker, richer, and more complex, but always balanced by their electric acidity.

Fortified wines, Port, Madeira, Marsala, Sherry, age with extraordinary grace. Madeira, especially, seems untouched by time, capable of lasting for generations. Because these wines begin with higher alcohol, concentrated flavours, and crafted stability, they evolve like slow-burning embers: deepening but never collapsing.

What Makes a Wine Age Worthy

ageing is not a reward for all wines; it is a path for the few meant to walk it. Most wines are crafted to be enjoyed young, when fruit is bright and energy is high. Age worthy wines share certain traits: firm tannins, substantial acidity, concentration of fruit, balance, and a core of flavour that can hold steady as other elements transform.

ageing does not "fix" a wine or make it inherently better. Instead, it reveals different facets, less fruit, more nuance, less immediacy, and more depth. Some drinkers love the complexity of age; others prefer youthful vibrancy. Both are valid. Choosing between them is simply choosing between two expressions of the same soul.

How to Age Wine Gracefully

Time's effect on wine depends entirely on conditions. Light, heat, and movement accelerate decay; cool, dark, stillness preserves grace. Ideal storage sits around cellar temperature (10–13°C or 50–55°F), but consistency matters more than perfection. Wine ages best when it is rarely disturbed, left to evolve in its quiet environment.

Bottles sealed with cork should lie on their sides to keep the cork from drying; screwcap wines can stand upright. As wine ages in bottle, it develops sediment, harmless but gritty, which is why older red wines benefit from decanting not to aerate them, but to separate the clear wine from the sediment.

The Emotional Truth of ageing

Aged wine is an acquired love, not because it is difficult, but because it asks for stillness and attention. Young wine sings brightly; aged wine hums deeply. Young wine is fruit; aged wine is memory. Young wine is moment; aged wine is time.

When you drink an aged wine, you are tasting not only the grape and the place but the years themselves, warm summers, cool nights, the patience of the cellar, the slow exchange of oxygen through cork and glass. ageing makes wine feel more human. It reminds us that transformation takes time and that beauty changes its form as it matures.

Wine does not get "better" as it ages. It becomes different. And that difference, when welcomed, offers some of the most profound experiences in the world of wine.

Chapter 17

Sulphites: Myths or Facts

What sulphites do, and why they matter less than many imagine

Many consumers believe that sulphites are the cause of headaches or allergic reactions after drinking wine, but this is largely a misconception. Sulphur dioxide is a preservative used in winemaking for antimicrobial and antioxidant protection, and the quantities permitted in wine are tightly regulated. Headaches are more commonly linked to alcohol itself, dehydration, biogenic amines, or histamines, rather than sulphites. Foods such as dried fruit and packaged snacks typically contain far higher sulphite levels than wine without provoking the same concerns.

Another persistent myth is that "natural" or "sulphite-free" wines contain no sulphur at all. All wines produce small amounts of sulphites naturally during fermentation, so a truly sulphite-free wine does not exist. Wines labelled as "no added sulphites" simply avoid additional sulphur dioxide during production but still contain naturally occurring levels and can be more fragile and prone to spoilage. The belief that sulphites equate to lower quality is also misguided: controlled sulphur dioxide use helps ensure freshness, stability, and longevity, and remains an essential tool for many high-quality producers.

Many people worry about sulphites in wine, but the concern is usually misplaced. Sulphites are a natural by-product of fermentation, and winemakers add small, carefully controlled amounts to protect wine from spoilage and oxidation. Despite the common belief that sulphites cause headaches, research shows that alcohol, dehydration, and compounds such as histamines or biogenic amines are far more likely culprits. The levels used in wine are low, strictly regulated, and- contrary to popular opinion- found in both high-end and everyday bottles. Using a modest dose of sulphur dioxide is often essential for keeping a wine stable, fresh, and true to style.

Where the myth really unravels is when you compare wine with the sulphite content of everyday foods. A typical glass of wine contains only a small amount in a standard serving. By contrast, many familiar snacks and ingredients contain far higher levels. Dried apricots, for example, have an average of 2,097 mg/kg of sulphites compared to 55mg/kg for a typical glass of red wine[1]. This means a small handful delivers many times more sulphites than a whole glass of wine. Fruit juices, soft drinks, pre-cut potatoes, and even some sausages routinely contain higher concentrations, yet they rarely attract the same scrutiny. Wine is a comparatively minor contributor to daily sulphite intake, and for most people these compounds are both safe and far less dramatic than the myths suggest.

Food / drink	Mean sulphites (mg/kg as SO_2)	Typical serving assumed	Approx. SO_2 per serving (mg)
Red wine	55 mg/kg	150 mL glass	≈ 8 mg
White wine	123 mg/kg	150 mL glass	≈ 18 mg
Beef sausages	275 mg/kg	75 g sausage	≈ 21 mg
Hamburger patty	129 mg/kg	100 g patty	≈ 13 mg
Frankfurt / hot-dog	55 mg/kg	60 g sausage	≈ 3 mg
Dried apples	1,252 mg/kg	30 g handful	≈ 38 mg
Dried apricots	2,097 mg/kg	30 g handful	≈ 63 mg
Sultanas (raisins)	76 mg/kg	30 g snack box	≈ 2.3 mg
Regular cordial (ready-to-drink)	10 mg/kg	250 mL glass	≈ 2.5 mg
Potato crisps/chips	3 mg/kg	30 g small pack	≈ 0.09 mg

Sulphites in Day to Day Foods

Where confusion arises is in the narrative that sulphites cause headaches or hangovers. Science tells another story: dehydration, alcohol, histamines, and other biogenic amines are far more likely culprits. In fact, sweet white wines, which often contain the most sulphites, are rarely blamed, while red wines with far fewer sulphites are. The myth persists because "sulphites" sounds chemical and therefore suspicious. But wine's reactions within the body are far more complex and rarely tied to sulphur alone

Sulphites are one of the most misunderstood parts of wine. They appear on almost every label, often with a sense of warning, yet they are among the gentlest and most necessary tools winemakers have. Sulphites are not a mysterious additive or a sign of industrial manipulation. They are simply compounds that keep wine stable, fresh, and expressive, protecting it from oxidation, bacteria, and premature ageing.

To understand sulphites, you only need to know what they *do*, how they *feel* in the glass, and why they are there at all.

Sulphites have been used in winemaking for centuries. Even homemade wines made without any added sulphur contain natural sulphites, byproducts of fermentation itself. What winemakers add is a small amount of sulphur dioxide to guard the wine from the forces that want to break it down: oxygen, heat, and microbes. Without sulphites, most wines would oxidise or spoil before they ever reached you. The protective role of sulphur is similar to how a squeeze of lemon slows the browning of cut fruit: it doesn't change the essence of what's there, it simply preserves it.

In the glass, sulphites are not something you taste as a distinct flavour. At normal levels, they are nearly invisible, felt only in the wine's clarity and freshness rather than sensed directly. When sulphur is imbalanced, however, it can briefly appear as burnt match, struck flint, or a faint acrid smokiness. These impressions usually fade as the wine receives air. Only when sulphur is mishandled does it linger in ways that feel intrusive.

Low-sulphur and sulphur-free wines can be beautiful, but they are not inherently purer or more natural, they simply rely on meticulous vineyard work and careful handling to remain stable. When done well, these wines taste energetic and alive. When mismanaged, they can drift into oxidation or microbial faults, losing the clarity that sulphites protect.

Sulphites themselves are not moral choices; they are technical ones. They help preserve freshness, stability, and the integrity of flavour. When used with intention and restraint, they disappear completely, leaving only the wine's true character.

Understanding sulphites is not about learning chemistry. It is about recognising that wine is fragile, and winemakers use every tool available, including sulphur, to ensure the wine reaches you as they intended: bright, balanced, and unspoiled.

Sulphites are not the enemy of authenticity. They are often its quiet guardians, keeping the wine alive long enough for you to taste its story.

---

1. Food Standards Australia New Zealand *The 21st Australian Total Diet Study* 2023 https://www.foodstandards.gov.au/sites/default/files/2023-11/21st-%20ATDS.pdf

Chapter 18

Wine Components

The elements of structure that define how a wine feels

Acidity

Acidity is the quiet architecture of wine, the structure you don't always see but always feel. It's the brightness that wakes the palate, the tension that gives wine shape, the invisible thread that keeps fruit flavours alive from the first sip to the last echo of the finish. Without acidity, wine would feel flat and warm; with it, wine feels vivid.

You've experienced acidity all your life. A squeeze of lemon over food, the snap of a tart apple, the refreshing bite of cold citrus, these sensations are simply acidity expressing itself. Wine behaves the same way. The sensation isn't sharpness for its own sake; it's energy. It's the thing that makes your mouth water, that makes flavours seem brighter, that makes wine feel clean rather than heavy.

You don't need to measure acidity or memorise terms to understand it. All you need is to notice what it does.

When a wine has *high acidity*, it feels bright, lifted, refreshing. It moves quickly across the palate, leaving a clean, mouthwatering trail behind it. Think of Sauvignon Blanc, Vinho Verde, dry Riesling, Txakoli, Muscadet, Champagne, wines that taste like cool air, like crisp light.

When a wine has *medium acidity*, it feels balanced, not sharp, not soft, simply harmonious. This is the territory of Chardonnay, Chenin Blanc, Merlot, Zinfandel, Pinot Noir. Wines that feel comfortable and welcoming.

When a wine has *low acidity*, it feels round, mellow, and warm. Its fruit feels ripe and soft; its textures feel smooth and gentle. This is where richer whites and fuller reds often reside, Viognier, oaked Chardonnay, warm-climate reds, some dessert wines.

Acidity is also the reason wine pairs so beautifully with food. A wine with good acidity behaves like a squeeze of lemon or a splash of vinegar in a dish, it brightens flavours, cuts through richness, and refreshes the palate. Without that acidity, food and wine can weigh each other down.

In red wines, acidity plays an even subtler role. It keeps fruit vibrant, prevents heaviness, and lifts savoury elements. This is why Sangiovese, Nebbiolo, and Pinot Noir, all high-acid grapes, feel energetic even when their flavours lean earthy or herbal.

And acidity is why some wines age gracefully. Over time, fruit may soften and tannins melt, but acidity remains as the spine, holding everything in place. A wine with insufficient acidity may taste generous in youth, but it rarely grows more interesting with age.

The beautiful thing about acidity is that you don't need to search for it. You simply notice how the wine behaves. Does your mouth water? Does the wine taste bright or energetic? Does it make you want another sip?

That is acidity speaking.

You might discover that you love wines with crispness and tension, or wines with gentler, rounder edges. Neither reflects knowledge; they reflect taste. Acidity isn't something to understand academically, it's something to recognise instinctively.

Wine reveals its brightness the same way light reveals itself: by how it changes what you see and feel. Notice that brightness, and you've already mastered acidity.

Tannins

Tannins are the texture of red wine, the subtle grip, the gentle dryness, the sensation that briefly brushes the sides of your tongue and gums. They are not flavours; they are feelings. They give red wine its structure, its shape, its quiet architecture. If acidity is light, tannin is touch.

You've felt tannins long before you ever tasted wine. Brew a cup of black tea and let the teabag steep too long, the drying, slightly puckering sensation on your tongue comes from tannins. Bite into the skin of a not-quite-ripe fruit or taste strong dark chocolate, that faint bitterness and grip is tannin, too. In wine, tannins behave the same way.

Tannins come mostly from the skins, seeds, and stems of grapes, and sometimes from the wood of barrels. Grapes with thicker skins, Cabernet Sauvignon, Nebbiolo, Syrah, Tannat, naturally have more tannin. Grapes with thin skins, Pinot Noir, Gamay, Grenache, have far less. The thickness of those skins, the amount of time the juice spends with them, and the winemaker's decisions all influence the final texture.

The beauty of tannins is that they give red wine its ability to feel three-dimensional. A wine without tannin would feel like juice; a wine with too much tannin would feel abrasive. The sweet spot is structure: tannins that frame the fruit, shape the mid-palate, and linger with a soft, drying finish.

When tannins are fine and integrated, they feel like a gentle brush across the palate, silky, smooth, almost powder-soft. Pinot Noir, mature Bordeaux, and well-aged Nebbiolo often show tannins of this kind.

When tannins are firmer, they feel like a handshake, confident, noticeable, but not aggressive. Many Cabernets, Tempranillos, and Syrahs fall into this territory, giving you substance without overwhelming force.

When tannins are young and bold, they can feel gripping, drying, or even a bit austere, the way a strong black tea feels when it first hits your tongue. Young Barolo, young Brunello, or certain structured reds from warm climates can feel this way until time softens their edges.

Tannins aren't simply about texture; they influence a wine's emotional character. Wines with soft tannins feel gentle and welcoming. Wines with moderate tannins feel balanced and dependable. Wines with firm tannins feel serious, grounded, and contemplative. This is why softer reds feel perfect for casual evenings, while structured reds feel suited to deeper moments or richer meals.

Food changes how tannins behave. Protein, meat, cheese, legumes, softens tannins, making them feel smoother. Fat does the same. This is why a tannic Cabernet Sauvignon becomes velvety with steak, and why Barolo sings with aged cheese: the food and wine complete one another's textures.

As red wines age, tannins evolve. They lose their rawness and become more delicate, moving from firmness into silkiness. This transformation is one of the great pleasures of cellaring wine: watching structure melt into elegance.

But you don't need to study tannins to understand them. Simply pay attention to how the wine feels. Does it grip? Does it glide? Does it brush past softly? Does it linger with texture? These sensations tell you more than any number or analysis ever could.

Tannins remind us that texture is as expressive as flavour, and that wine is a physical experience as much as a gustatory one. They give red wine its spine, its presence, its quiet strength.

Learn to feel tannins, and you begin to understand the heart of red wine.

Alcohol Body and Texture

Alcohol, body, and texture are the elements that shape how a wine *feels* more than how it tastes. They influence the wine's weight, its warmth, its presence, the way it moves across your palate and the way it settles in your memory. These traits often define whether a wine feels refreshing or rich, light or full, calm or powerful.

Alcohol: the quiet warmth beneath the flavour

Alcohol in wine isn't about strength; it's about sensation. A wine with higher alcohol doesn't necessarily taste "boozy", it simply feels warmer, broader, and more expansive. A wine with lower alcohol feels cooler, lighter, more delicate.

You've felt this instinctively:

- A crisp white at 11–12% alcohol feels clean, bright, almost cooling.
- A rich red at 14–15% feels warm, rounded, enveloping.

Alcohol gives wine its gentle glow. When balanced with acidity and fruit, this warmth feels inviting. When unbalanced, it can feel sharp or heavy. You don't need to pay attention to the number on the label, just notice the temperature of the finish. Does the wine feel warm? Does it feel cool? That sensation tells you almost everything.

Body: the wine's weight and presence

Body is simply the weight of the wine in your mouth, the difference between skim milk and cream. It has nothing to do with flavour complexity and everything to do with texture.

Light-bodied wines feel like water gliding over stones: crisp, swift, refreshing. Think Vinho Verde, Beaujolais, fruit-driven Pinot Noir, or Labrusco.

Medium-bodied wines feel balanced and smooth, neither light nor heavy. Sauvignon Blanc, Sancerre, Rioja Crianza, Chianti, Merlot, and many Chardonnays live here.

Full-bodied wines feel broad, rich, and rounded, wines that take their time across your palate. Oaked Chardonnay, Chenin Blanc, Cabernet Sauvignon, Malbec, Syrah, and many GSM blends express themselves fully, with a sense of depth.

Body affects emotion more than flavour. Light wines feel playful and uplifting; medium-bodied wines feel steady and comforting; full-bodied wines feel grounding and warm. Knowing which body style you enjoy is one of the easiest ways to find your wine family.

Texture: the sensation that defines character

Texture is where wine becomes physical, almost tactile. It's the silkiness of a well-aged Pinot Noir, the velvet of a ripe Merlot, the silk-and-bone combination of Barolo, the creamy glide of an oaked Chardonnay, the crisp snap of a bright Riesling.

Texture comes from tannin, alcohol, acidity, fruit weight, winemaking choices, and even the minerals in the soil. But you don't need to know the source. You only need to feel it, the way the wine touches your palate:

- Some wines feel linear, moving straight across the

tongue.

- Some feel broad, spreading outward.
- Some feel slippery.
- Some feel grainy.
- Some feel plush.
- Some feel delicate.

Texture is why two wines with similar flavours can feel completely different. It's also why you might love a wine one night and find it too heavy or too sharp on another. Texture is mood-driven, emotional, immediate.

Together they form the wine's "posture."

Alcohol, body, and texture are not separate ideas, they are parts of a single gesture. They create the wine's posture: how it stands, moves, and holds itself.

- A light, low-alcohol wine with bright acidity feels upright, quick, and refreshing.
- A full-bodied, high-alcohol wine with soft tannins feels reclining, rich, and enveloping.
- A medium-bodied wine with balanced elements feels calm, steady, versatile.

Once you understand posture, you stop thinking in categories and start thinking in sensations. You know whether you want something bright or something grounding, something soft or something structured, something that glides or something that presses gently into place.

Wine becomes less about type and more about feel. And when you choose wine by feel, you choose with confidence, because you're choosing what suits *you* in that moment.

Oak, Lees, and Winemaking Influence

The way a wine tastes is shaped not only by the grape and the place it comes from, but also by the choices a winemaker makes, choices that influence texture, flavour, and emotion in subtle but powerful ways. Oak ageing, lees contact, and fermentation decisions aren't technical details you need to memorise. They are simply tools that help create the sensations you feel in the glass.

Oak: the gentle frame around the wine

Oak does not exist to flavour wine; it exists to *shape* it.

Think of oak as a frame around a painting, it guides your attention, adds structure, and creates a sense of focus without stealing the spotlight. Used with restraint, oak adds warmth, spice, and texture. Used heavily, it can overwhelm the fruit.

New oak has the strongest voice: vanilla, baking spices, toast, caramel, smoke, coconut, cedar.

Older oak speaks more softly: gentle rounding, softened tannins, subtle warmth rather than overt flavour.

Large barrels give far less flavour than small ones, allowing the wine to breathe without absorbing too much wood.

In white wines, oak can add creaminess and subtle sweetness of aroma. In reds, it contributes polish, weight, and savoury spice. But the goal is always balance, to let the wine feel supported, not dressed up.

If a wine feels warm, smooth, and subtly spicy, oak is likely part of the story. If it tastes sharp, bright, and steel-like, it likely saw no oak at all.

Lees: the softening breath beneath the wine

Lees are the spent yeast cells left behind after fermentation. When wine rests on these lees, something quiet and transformative happens. The wine gains softness, creaminess, and savoury depth. It becomes rounder and more textured, like silk with a hint of weight.

Lees contact can create flavours of brioche, biscuit, dough, toasted grain, or nuttiness, especially in Champagne, where long ageing on lees gives the wine its signature complexity. In still wines, lees bring a gentle plushness, making whites like Chardonnay or Muscadet feel fuller and more harmonious.

Stirring lees (a technique called bâtonnage) amplifies the effect, adding richness without sweetness, body without heaviness. It is winemaking's way of creating texture from within rather than adding anything from outside.

Fermentation choices: the quiet decisions that change everything

Fermentation is where grape juice becomes wine, and the decisions made here influence aromatics and feel in profound ways.

A cool fermentation preserves delicate fruit and floral notes, perfect for aromatic whites.

A warm fermentation extracts deeper flavours, colour, and tannin, essential for structured reds.

Some winemakers use *whole clusters*, meaning stems and whole bunches ferment together. This can add spice, floral lift, and a subtle stemmy freshness to reds like Pinot Noir or Syrah.

Others choose *skin contact* for white wines, creating "orange wines" with deeper colour, tea-like tannin, and more savoury complexity. Here, texture becomes the focal point rather than fruit.

Even decisions like using stainless steel (bright, crisp, pure), concrete (textural, neutral), amphora (earthy, softly oxidative), or wood (warm, rounded) subtly influence the wine's posture.

Why these influences matter for you

You don't need to know any of these techniques by name. What matters is how they make the wine *feel*.

- If a wine tastes round, warm, or creamy, oak or lees may be part of its personality.
- If it tastes mineral, crisp, or linear, it likely avoided heavy winemaking influence.
- If it tastes spicy or floral in unexpected ways, whole-cluster fermentation may be quietly shaping its expression.

Winemaking choices are simply the artisan's touch, the way intention becomes emotion.

Wine shows you the craft, even if you don't know the terms

You don't need to study how the wine was made to understand what you're drinking. You just taste it. The sensations, richness, tension, softness, brightness, tell you far more than a technical sheet ever will.

Winemaking influence is the subtle shaping of texture and tone, the sculpting of fruit and structure. Notice how a wine feels, and you'll understand the choices behind it without trying.

Terroir

Terroir is a French word with no perfect English translation, not because it's complicated, but because it describes something we don't often name in everyday life: the character a place gives to what grows there.

It is the taste of landscape.

And although wine professionals often speak of terroir as if it were a mystical idea, you already understand it instinctively. Strawberries grown in your garden taste different from strawberries grown far away. Tomatoes from summer markets taste different from winter tomatoes. Water from different springs has different textures. Place matters.

Wine simply makes this idea visible.

What Terroir Really Means

Terroir includes everything that shapes the grapes:

- *Soil,* limestone giving tension, clay giving weight, granite giving energy, volcanic rock giving salt and smoke
- *Climate,* warmth ripening fruit, coolness preserving acidity
- *Light,* how the sun hits slopes, how heat radiates from stone
- *Elevation,* thinner air, cooler nights, more dramatic temperature swings
- *Wind,* drying grapes after rain, cooling vines in heat, shaping ripeness
- *Water availability,* the quiet stress that deepens flavour

- *The microbiology of the vineyard*, invisible life that influences fermentation

- *The human hand*, traditions, pruning, harvest timing, choices made over generations

But the value of terroir isn't in listing its components.

It's in *noticing what it creates*.

How Terroir Feels in the Glass

You can sense terroir before you ever name it.

A wine from limestone feels bright, taut, linear, like Chablis or Sancerre, where the earth seems to sharpen the edges.

A wine from volcanic soils tastes vivid, salty, or smoky, like Santorini, Etna, or parts of Sicily.

A wine from clay feels broader, richer, Chianti Classico's warmth, Rioja's depth, many great red Bordeaux.

A wine grown near the ocean often carries a faint salinity, a quiet echo of sea air.

This is why wines from the same grape can taste utterly different. Pinot Noir from Oregon is gentle and red-fruited; Pinot Noir from Burgundy feels more ethereal and earthy; Pinot Noir from Central Otago feels darker and more intense. The landscape writes its signature onto the wine.

Why Terroir Matters Emotionally

Terroir is not about geography; it's about identity.

Some wines taste like fruit. Others taste like fruit shaped by place. Those are the wines that feel the most alive, the ones that seem to carry memory, of sunlight, soil, and wind. They feel rooted. They feel specific.

Earthy red wines, Barolo, Brunello, Rioja, Chianti, Burgundy, are beloved not because of their grapes alone, but because they express the soil beneath them so clearly. The earthiness you taste is not a flavour added later; it is the landscape speaking directly.

Do You Need to Understand Terroir to Enjoy Wine?

No.

You only need to *notice* that different places create different sensations.

Terroir isn't homework. It's awareness.

It's the pleasure of recognising that the wine in your glass couldn't have come from anywhere else. That a Sauvignon Blanc from New Zealand tastes different from one from the Loire because one grows under cool, bright skies, and the other grows under intense sun and ocean winds.

As you taste more wines, you'll begin to sense the patterns without forcing them, brightness from limestone, power from heat, elegance from cool climates. These impressions become part of your internal map, helping you predict the wine's feel long before you take a sip.

The Heart of Terroir

Terroir teaches us that wine is not just a beverage; it is a place made drinkable. It's a story of landscape translated into flavour and texture. You don't need to decode terroir, you simply need to be open to the idea that the ground beneath the vines becomes part of the wine's voice.

In the end, terroir reminds us that wine is alive, shaped by the world around it, and that every bottle carries the quiet imprint of where it was born.

Old World vs New World

Terms like *Old World* and *New World* often get tossed around as if they're strict categories, but they're really just two broad ways of understanding how wine expresses itself. These ideas aren't about geography so much as *philosophy, climate, and style*, different approaches that shape the way wine feels in the glass.

Old World: wines shaped by place

Old World refers to Europe, regions like France, Italy, Spain, Germany, Austria, Portugal, and Greece. Here, winemaking traditions stretch back for centuries, and the emphasis has historically been on *place over grape*. Labels often name the region, not the grape: Chianti, Sancerre, Rioja, Burgundy, Barolo.

Old World wines tend to reflect their environment more transparently. They often feel:

- *earthy or savoury*, with flavours that lean toward herbs, spice, and soil
- *lighter in body*, especially in cooler regions
- *higher in acidity*, giving lift and brightness
- *less fruit-driven*, with more focus on nuance and texture
- *structured*, built for food and ageing
- *restrained*, letting layers unfold gradually

These wines feel like landscapes, shaped by history, soil, and tradition. They often carry a quiet confidence that rewards attention.

New World: wines shaped by fruit and climate

New World refers to countries where wine traditions are newer: the United States, Australia, New Zealand, Chile, Argentina, South Africa, and others. Here, grape names are typically the focus, Pinot Noir, Syrah, Cabernet Sauvignon, and winemaking often reflects a more modern, fruit-driven sensibility.

New World wines tend to feel:

- *riper and richer*, shaped by sunshine and warmth
- *more fruit-forward*, with flavours of berries, plum, peach, or tropical fruit
- *rounder in texture*, especially in warm climates
- *higher in alcohol*, due to riper grapes
- *less overtly earthy*, more about generosity than restraint
- *open and approachable*, delicious without years of ageing

These wines feel like brightness, vivid, expressive, immediately accessible.

Why this distinction helps you

You don't need to memorize which countries belong to which category. What matters is understanding the *sensations* these terms hint at.

If you enjoy wines that feel earthy, savoury, calm, and structured, you may gravitate toward Old World expressions.

If you enjoy wines that feel bold, fruity, smooth, and warm, New World wines might feel more like home.

Both worlds produce extraordinary wines. Both produce simple wines. Both offer personalities that suit different moods and different meals.

Where the lines blur

Modern winemaking has softened the boundaries.

You can find Old World wines made in a bolder style and New World wines made with restraint. Climate change also plays a role, warming traditional regions and reshaping their profiles. The world of wine is far more fluid than the old vocabulary suggests.

But the emotional distinction still holds:

Old World wines feel closer to earth.

New World wines feel closer to sun.

Old vs New World is not a hierarchy, it's a palette

Neither style is better. They simply offer different ways of experiencing the same grape.

Pinot Noir can taste like red cherries, flowers, and forest floor in Burgundy, or like ripe berries, baking spice, and sun-warmed fruit in California or New Zealand.

Chardonnay can taste like cool stone and green apple in Chablis, or like peach, vanilla, and soft cream in Sonoma or Margaret River.

Syrah can be peppery and lean in the Northern Rhône, or plush, dark, and velvety in Barossa.

These aren't contradictions. They are expressions.

The beauty of both worlds

Understanding Old vs New World isn't about dividing wine; it's about expanding your choices. It allows you to explore a grape you love from two different perspectives, like hearing the same song played on two different instruments.

Wine becomes richer, more interesting, more personal when you realise that style is a spectrum and geography is just one voice in the chorus.

Old World or New World, the question is the same:

Does this wine feel like the wine you want tonight?

If the answer is yes, then you've already chosen well.

Vintage Variation

Vintage variation is one of the quiet truths of wine, the idea that the same grape, grown in the same vineyard, made by the same people, can taste different from one year to the next. Not dramatically, not every time, but enough that wine retains a sense of being alive, shaped by seasons rather than formulas.

This isn't something to fear. Vintage variation is one of wine's greatest charms: the reminder that it comes from a place touched by weather, sunlight, rain, and wind. Wine is not manufactured; it is grown.

What vintage really means

The vintage on a label is simply the year the grapes were harvested. That year carries with it everything the vineyard experienced:

- A warm year yields riper fruit, fuller body, softer acidity.
- A cool year yields brighter fruit, higher acidity, lighter body.
- A dry year concentrates flavours.
- A rainy harvest can soften intensity.
- A storm can lower yields, concentrating what remains.
- A cool spring might shift ripeness later into the year.

Vintage is the story of a season captured in flavour.

How vintage affects what you taste

You don't need to memorise weather charts or vintage reports. What matters is the *feel* of the wine.

In cooler vintages, wines often feel brighter, tighter, more aromatic. Their flavours lean toward red fruit, citrus, and herbs. Their structure feels more energetic.

In warmer vintages, wines feel rounder, richer, darker in fruit. Their acidity softens, their textures broaden, and their flavours feel more immediate.

Neither is better. They simply express two moods of the same vineyard.

Why vintage matters more in some places than others

Vintage has the biggest impact in regions where the weather swings widely year to year:

- Burgundy
- Bordeaux

- Germany

- Northern Italy

- Northern Rhône

- Cool-climate regions of the U.S., Canada, and New Zealand

In consistently warm or stable climates, much of California, Argentina, Chile, Australia, vintage differences are more subtle. The sun smooths out variability.

For most wines under everyday pricing, the difference is small enough that you can choose freely by style rather than by vintage. It's only when you enter more age worthy wines, structured reds, top-tier whites, and classics like Barolo, Bordeaux, or Burgundy, that vintage becomes a richer part of the story.

Vintage and Ageing

Vintage also influences how a wine will age.

A warm year may produce wines that feel lush and open early but develop more slowly. A cooler year may produce wines that require time to unfold, but reward patience with deeper nuance.

But ageing isn't required to enjoy vintage variation. You can experience it simply by tasting two wines from different years, side by side. One may feel round and generous; the other bright and taut. You'll see how the vineyard's character remains constant while the season paints in different colours.

Why vintage variation matters emotionally

Vintage variation is a reminder that wine is never static. It's a living expression of its year, a kind of bottled weather. When you drink a wine, you're not just tasting a grape or a place; you're tasting a moment that will never repeat exactly the same way again.

This is why wine enthusiasts talk about vintages with affection. They aren't chasing perfection; they are appreciating personality. The small differences tell the story of a year, the climate, and the land, and that story deepens the experience.

You don't need to study vintages to enjoy wine

The purpose of this chapter is not to give you rules. It's to reassure you:

Vintage variation is real, but it is not a barrier.

You don't need to memorise good years. You don't need to avoid unfamiliar ones. Once you know your wine family and your preferred style, you can trust that most vintages will still feel like home, just painted in slightly different shades.

Wine that tastes a little different every year is part of the beauty of wine that is alive.

Wine Faults

Wine faults are simply moments when something interrupts the harmony a wine is meant to express. They can be dramatic or subtle, obvious or quiet, but they all have the same effect: they pull you out of the experience. Most faults are easy to recognise once you know what they feel like. A wine that should be bright becomes muted. A wine that should be generous becomes hollow. A wine that should feel alive seems disconnected from itself.

Faults don't require fear or expertise. They require attention, and a little understanding of how wine can go astray on its journey from vineyard to glass.

Cork Taint (TCA): When the Wine Falls Silent

Cork taint is one of the most common faults, yet also one of the quietest. A cork-tainted wine rarely smells aggressively wrong. Instead, it smells like *less*, less fruit, less sparkle, less life. You might sense damp cardboard, a mouldy cupboard, the smell of old newsprint, or the faint mustiness of a damp basement. But the defining feature is not the smell itself; it is the way the wine seems muted, as if someone dimmed all the colours.

This muted quality comes from a compound known as TCA (2,4,6-trichloroanisole), created when naturally occurring fungi in cork interact with chlorine-based cleaning agents once common in wineries. Even at parts-per-trillion, TCA suppresses aroma compounds, stealing the wine's voice. Nothing is harmed except pleasure: cork taint isn't toxic, but it is irreversible. No amount of swirling, warming, or patience will bring the wine back to life.

Cork taint is unpredictable and indiscriminate; it can affect the humblest bottle or the rarest. But once you recognise that sense of absence, you'll never miss it again. The wine feels like a song with the melody erased.

Oxidation: When the Wine Ages Before Its Time

Oxidation is the taste of a wine that has breathed too much, too soon. Instead of smelling fresh or alive, it smells like an apple left cut on the counter: bruised, brown, slightly stale. Whites turn deeper gold or brown; reds fade toward orange, losing their vibrancy. On the palate, oxidation tastes flat, tired, sometimes metallic, lacking the energy that acidity normally brings.

Wine always undergoes a graceful, slow oxidation as it ages, a controlled softening that creates complexity. But when oxygen rushes in too quickly, the wine ages prematurely. This can happen from a damaged cork, poor storage, or a flawed seal.

Phenolic compounds react with oxygen, creating aldehydes that add nutty, bruised aromas. In styles like Sherry, Madeira, or Vin Jaune, these oxidative notes are intentional and beautiful. But in a wine not meant for it, oxidation feels like a story told too early, before the wine had the chance to shape its own narrative.

Oxidised wine tastes like a memory of itself, faded at the edges, lacking tension, missing the spark that makes wine feel alive.

Heat Damage ("Cooked" Wine): When the Wine Loses Its Shape

Heat damage is the quiet thief of wine quality, often happening long before the bottle reaches your hands. A wine left in a hot car, sitting in direct sun, or shipped without temperature control can become "cooked." The fruit tastes stewed or jammy in an unnatural way, whites may taste caramelised, and reds can feel thick or blurry. The cork may bulge slightly, pushed up by expanding liquid.

Heat accelerates chemical reactions, effectively forcing the wine to age rapidly but poorly. Acids soften, aromatics break down, sugars brown, and tannins lose definition. It's as if the wine has melted inward, collapsing the structure that once gave it balance. Heat-damaged wine isn't dangerous, it's simply robbed of freshness. A crisp white becomes dull; a vibrant red becomes sludgy. No amount of air or patience can restore what heat has taken.

A cooked wine tastes like a photograph that sat too long in the sun, colours flattened, details lost.

Reduction: When the Wine Withdraws Into Itself

Reduction is the opposite of oxidation, not too much oxygen, but too little. When wine ferments or ages in oxygen-deprived environments, sulfur compounds can develop. These compounds create aromas of struck match, gunflint, rubber, cabbage, or even scorched hair. At first encounter these scents can feel jarring, like a curtain hiding the wine's true face.

But reduction is complex. A *hint* of reduction, flint, smoke, matchstick, can be part of a wine's character, especially in Chardonnay, Syrah, or high-acid whites. It can add tension, intrigue, and lift. It becomes a fault only when the aromas mask the fruit entirely. Hydrogen sulphide and mercaptans bind to form more stubborn compounds that swirling cannot easily dispel.

To recognise reduction, pay attention to its behaviour: if air softens it, it was simply a shy wine waking up. If air changes nothing, the wine remains trapped behind the fault, unable to open fully.

Reduction feels like the wine is whispering behind a closed door.

Volatile Acidity (VA): When the Wine Turns Sharp

Volatile acidity is the presence of acetic acid (vinegar) and ethyl acetate (nail-polish remover) in wine. It is caused by oxygen exposure or microbial activity during fermentation or storage. A touch of VA can make a wine feel lifted, a subtle brightness or aromatic tension. But when VA exceeds harmony, it overwhelms the fruit, leaving sharp edges and prickling fumes in the nose.

You'll recognise excessive VA immediately: it smells like vinegar, solvent, or fermenting apples. Wines with very high VA feel unstable, like they're vibrating at the wrong frequency. Some sweet and fortified wines tolerate slight VA because their richness absorbs it, but in dry wines, too much VA feels like static interrupting the flavour.

VA tastes like a wine that has lost its balance, leaning too far toward acidity without the fruit to support it.

Brettanomyces ("Brett"): When the Wine Goes Wild

Brettanomyces is a yeast that introduces savoury, animal-like aromas into wine: leather, barnyard, smoked meat, wet hay, medicinal notes, or an unmistakable "horse blanket" scent. In tiny amounts it can add a rustic, earthy complexity, a wild accent that once defined many traditional wines. But when Brett dominates, it blankets the fruit, obscuring clarity and freshness.

Brett produces compounds like 4-ethylphenol and 4-ethylguaiacol, which carry smoky, animal, or medicinal tones. These compounds do not fade with air; they are intrinsic to the wine once formed. Some regions and producers tolerate low levels for stylistic reasons, but excessive Brett makes a wine feel dirty, smothered, or monochromatic.

A Brett-heavy wine feels like a painting covered in dust, the outlines still visible, but the colours dulled beneath an unwanted layer.

Sulphur Faults: When Protection Becomes Interference

Sulphur is a natural part of winemaking, a guardian against oxidation and microbial spoilage. But when mismanaged, it creates aromas that feel chemical or off-putting: burnt match, rubber, rotten egg, onion, garlic, or struck flint without refinement.

These scents come from compounds like hydrogen sulfide, mercaptans, and disulfides. Some are easily corrected with air; others are stubborn and permanent. Because sulphur is both necessary and risky, its management requires balance. Good winemaking allows sulphur to protect the wine without ever announcing itself.

When sulphur faults appear, they make the wine feel obscured, as if bright fruit has been shrouded by a synthetic veil.

Microbial Faults: When Unwanted Life Takes Over

Wine is alive, and sometimes it hosts life that doesn't belong. Microbial faults create aromas of yoghurt, cheese rind, mouse cage, sour milk, or fermenting bread. These faults emerge when unwanted yeasts or bacteria take hold, often due to poor sanitation, low sulphur, or high-risk natural fermentations.

Mousiness, one of the most distinctive microbial faults, leaves a flavour that appears only after swallowing, like stale breadcrumbs, pet bedding, or a faintly sweet, unpleasant mustiness. It is a fault that thrives in low-sulphur wines and cannot be detected by smell alone.

Microbial faults make a wine feel unstable, wrong-footed, or chaotic. Instead of harmony, the wine tastes like competing voices none of which belong.

Why Understanding Faults Matters

Wine faults are not academic curiosities. They deepen your confidence, giving you the ability to recognise when a bottle is flawed rather than questioning your own palate. Faults are simply signs that something interfered with the wine's story.

When you recognise these interruptions, you can return the bottle without hesitation or simply set it aside knowing the issue is not you, it is the wine.

Faults remind us that wine is alive, vulnerable, and shaped by countless hands and conditions. And when you taste a bottle that is whole, expressive, and pure, its beauty feels even more vivid in contrast.

Chapter 19

The Future of Wine

How climate and culture are reshaping the wines we drink

The future of wine is already unfolding in vineyards, cellars, and climates around the world. It is a future shaped not only by tradition, but by change, by shifting weather patterns, evolving tastes, new technologies, and a growing awareness that wine exists in a living, fragile ecosystem. This is not a story of decline or doom; it is a story of adaptation, creativity, and resilience. Wine has always been shaped by the forces around it. Today, those forces are simply more visible.

A Changing Climate, A Changing Landscape

No factor influences wine's future more than climate. Regions that were once cool are now reliably warm; regions once too cold are becoming newly promising. Harvest dates creep earlier. Grapes ripen faster. Acidity falls more quickly in the heat. Alcohol rises. Classic flavour profiles shift.

Some winemakers respond by planting at higher altitudes, where nights are cooler and ripening slower. Others experiment with canopy management to shield grapes from heat. Some explore new grape varieties better suited to warmer conditions. Places long defined by traditional styles, Burgundy, Napa, Rioja, Chianti, are adapting quietly, adjusting harvest dates, fermentation strategies, and blending choices.

New regions are emerging as climate sweet spots: parts of England producing world-class sparkling wine; Scandinavia seeing experimental vineyards; Oregon and British Columbia gaining global attention. The wine map is expanding.

Wine has always been a conversation between vine and environment. Climate change simply changes the tone of that conversation.

Sustainability as Necessity, Not Trend

Sustainability is no longer a marketing term; it is a survival strategy. Water scarcity, soil degradation, energy use, and carbon emissions are real pressures on the wine world. Winemakers are reducing irrigation, adopting regenerative farming, installing solar arrays, preserving biodiversity, and reinventing packageing to reduce environmental impact.

Lighter bottles, recycled glass, renewable closures, and minimalist shipping methods are becoming the norm. Many wineries now measure their carbon footprint as seriously as their yields. Sustainability is not only about protecting the earth; it is about ensuring that vineyards remain viable for the next generation.

The Rise of New Voices

For centuries, wine culture was shaped by a narrow set of regions and traditions. That world is widening. Winemakers from diverse backgrounds are entering the field. Countries once peripheral to the wine conversation, Georgia, Greece, Uruguay, Mexico, Hungary, South Africa, are gaining recognition not as curiosities, but as peers.

Wine drinkers, too, are changing. Younger generations value authenticity, transparency, and story. They care as much about farming philosophy as about flavour. They are curious, open, and unafraid to taste outside established categories. This curiosity is reshaping the market, lifting once-obscure styles, pet-nat, skin-contact whites, amphora-aged reds, into the spotlight.

Technology With a Light Touch

Technology is entering the vineyard and cellar in ways that feel surprisingly gentle. Precision irrigation allows vines to thrive with far less water. Sensors track soil health. Canopy drones map sunlight exposure. Yeast biology is better understood. Temperature control is more refined. These tools are not replacing tradition, they are strengthening it, allowing winemakers to respond to the needs of the vine with greater nuance.

Meanwhile, advances in cork quality have dramatically reduced cork taint. Research in viticulture helps fight disease without harming ecosystems. The future of wine is not industrial; it is intentional.

Shifts in Style and Taste

Taste evolves. Today's wine drinkers lean toward freshness, balance, and authenticity, away from heavy oak, excessive sweetness, or overpowering ripeness. Wines with lower alcohol, higher acidity, and less manipulation are increasingly sought after. Rosé is no longer seasonal; sparkling wine is no longer reserved for celebration; lighter reds are enjoyed chilled.

This does not mean powerful wines are disappearing. It simply means the spectrum is broadening. Diversity of style is becoming the defining feature of the wine world.

The Emotional Heart of Wine's Future

Wine's future remains anchored in the same qualities that have defined it for millennia: connection, place, memory, emotion. No matter how vineyards adapt or philosophies shift, wine will always be a bridge, between people, between cultures, between land and time.

The greatest threat to wine is not climate or technology or shifting taste. It is the loss of attention, the failure to pause, to savour, to notice. And the greatest promise lies in curiosity: a generation willing to explore new styles, support sustainable growing, and value the stories behind the glass.

The future of wine is not a departure from its past. It is its continuation, shaped by new hands, new climates, new possibilities, but grounded in the same essential truth:

Wine is alive.

As the world changes, wine will change with it, evolving, adapting, and offering new beauty to anyone willing to taste with intention.

Chapter 20

Practical Wisdom

Simple guidance for choosing, enjoying, and understanding wine with confidence

How to Talk About Wine Without Jargon

Wine vocabulary often feels like a language invented to intimidate. But wine doesn't need rare words. It needs honest ones.

You never need to name every aroma. You don't need to identify obscure fruits or spices. You can simply say:

"It feels bright."

"It feels soft."

"It feels calm."

"It feels sharp."

"It feels warm."

"It feels full."

"It feels refreshing."

These words are enough. They describe not just flavour but emotion, the very heart of wine.

If you want to go deeper, speak in comparisons rather than notes: "I like this more than that," or "I wish this had more freshness," or "I enjoy wines that feel lighter or heavier." These statements reveal your palate clearly and naturally.

Your taste doesn't need to impress. It only needs to be true.

Reading Labels

Wine labels often look like small puzzles: regions instead of grapes, unfamiliar languages, numbers, symbols, and names that seem to hide more than they reveal. But once you know what matters, and what doesn't, labels become far simpler and far less intimidating.

A wine label tells you three basic things: what the wine is, where it comes from, and how it might feel. Everything else is ornament.

The most important piece of information is usually the grape or the place.

In many New World regions (like the U.S., Australia, Chile, South Africa), labels name the grape clearly: Chardonnay, Riesling, Pinot Noir, Syrah.

In much of Europe, the label names the place, not the grape. For example, Sancerre means Sauvignon Blanc, Chablis means Chardonnay, and Barolo means Nebbiolo. Once you learn a few of these, the map becomes intuitive.

The region itself often gives clues about style. Cool climates produce brighter, crisper wines with lighter bodies. Warm climates produce riper, fuller, richer wines. A wine from coastal California will feel different from one from northern Italy, even if they share the same grape.

Next is vintage, the year the grapes were harvested.

Vintage matters most in places where weather varies dramatically. In warm, stable climates, a difference of a year or two may not mean much. In cooler or more variable climates (like Burgundy, Bordeaux, or Germany), it can influence ripeness, acidity, and structure. But unless you're collecting wine or buying at high prices, vintage rarely needs deep study. Freshness matters more than the number.

Then there's the producer, the name of the winery. Some producers are classic and traditional; others are modern and fruit-forward. As you taste more, you'll notice that you like certain producers over others, even within the same region. Think of it like authors: two writers can explore the same topic and create completely different experiences.

Labels also show alcohol percentage, which gives a simple clue to weight.

Higher alcohol often means richer, fuller, riper wine; lower alcohol usually signals lighter, fresher styles. You don't need to memorise numbers; just notice how they make you feel. Over time, this becomes an easy shorthand.

Finally, there are the words that look intimidating but simply indicate style.

Terms like *Brut*[1], *Riserva*[2] or *Reserva*[3], *Sec*[4], *Trocken*[5], *Vendange Tardive*[6], *Kabinett*[7], or *Gran Selezione*[8] all tell you a little about what to expect. You'll learn these naturally as you encounter them, they don't need memorising now.

The real secret to reading labels is this: *You don't need to understand everything. You only need to recognize a few clues:*

Place. Grape. Producer[9]. Alcohol. Simple indicators of how the wine might feel.

Wine labels are not tests. They are invitations, small pieces of a story waiting to be opened. As you taste more wines and explore this book's style map, the labels that once felt cryptic will begin to feel familiar, even welcoming.

And soon enough, you'll find yourself scanning a bottle and thinking, "Yes, I *know what this wine will feel like.*"

Buying Wine

Buying wine shouldn't feel like a test. Yet for many people, standing in front of a wall of bottles or opening a restaurant wine list can feel like stepping into unfamiliar territory, too many options, too many terms, too much pressure to choose "correctly."

Here's the truth: there is no correct choice. There is only the wine that suits *you* in this moment.

The goal of buying wine is not to impress anyone. It is to find something that matches the mood, the meal, or the company. And once you understand how to make decisions based on feeling rather than fear, wine shopping becomes one of the simplest, most enjoyable parts of the experience.

The first question to ask yourself is not "What should I buy?" but "What do I want this wine to *do*?"

Do you want something refreshing for a warm afternoon? Something calm for a quiet night? Something bold to stand up to rich food? Something easy, something joyful, something contemplative, something celebratory? When you know the role the wine needs to play, the choices narrow naturally.

The second step is to trust broad categories rather than specific labels. If you want freshness, look to crisp[10] whites or chilled light reds. If you want warmth, choose fuller bodied reds or richer whites. If you want celebration, choose bubbles. If you want comfort, pick something soft and round. You don't need to know every grape; you just need to know the *feeling* you're aiming for.

The third step is to use whatever help is available. Good wine shops love guiding people. Tell them what you enjoy, what you're eating, and how much you want to spend. The same goes for restaurants: a sommelier[11]'s job is not to judge your taste but to understand it. A simple phrase like "I want something light and refreshing" or "I like juicy reds with soft tannins" is more useful than any list of grape names.

Price is often misunderstood. Higher prices don't guarantee better wine; they simply reflect scarcity, land, labour, or ageing. There is excellent wine at every price point. Choose what feels comfortable. A £15 bottle that suits your taste perfectly is far better than a £60 bottle that was chosen out of anxiety.

And finally, remember that buying wine is not a commitment. It's an exploration. Every bottle teaches you something about what you enjoy. Confidence doesn't come from choosing the perfect wine; it comes from realising that there is no penalty for choosing the "wrong" one. Every choice adds to your sense of direction.

If you know what you like, or even what you *think* you might like, then you already have everything you need to buy wine well.

Wine shopping becomes easy the moment you let your curiosity lead and allow this simple question to guide you:

"What do I feel like drinking tonight?"

How to Navigate a Wine List

A wine list can feel like a polite challenge, a page full of names, regions, grapes, and prices that rarely speak plainly. But a wine list is not a test. It's simply a table of possibilities. Once you understand how it's organised, everything becomes approachable.

Most wine lists follow a quiet logic. Whites lead to reds. Light leads to full. Local wines appear first; global classics appear next. Sparkling stands alone. Sweet and fortified wait at the end. Some lists add regions, placing France beside Italy beside California.

Others group by style, crisp whites, full whites, delicate reds, powerful reds. However it's arranged, the pattern is designed to guide your eye from simplicity to structure.

The key is to begin not with the list, but with your intention. What do you want the wine to *do*? Refresh? Comfort? Impress? Support? Brighten? Warm? Once you know the mood, ignore most of the list. Look where the wines that fit your intention naturally live: sparkling for celebration, crisp whites for energy, rich whites for texture, delicate reds for conversation, structured reds for depth.

If you feel lost, ask for help, not vague, intimidating help, but honest guidance. Tell the server or sommelier what you enjoy: "I like bright whites," or "I prefer juicy reds," or "I want something earthy but not too heavy." You don't need grape names. You don't need regions. A good sommelier will translate mood into wine instantly.

And don't be nervous about price. You never need to point at the cheapest or the most expensive. If you're comfortable, quietly indicate a price range by pointing to a bottle on the list and saying something like, "Something like this style and this range." It's discreet. It's normal. It works.

The most important thing is to let yourself choose, not out of fear or pressure, but out of curiosity and pleasure. A wine list is not a hurdle. It's an invitation.

Food Pairing

Food and wine pairing is often taught as a set of rules, but in truth it is simply a conversation between flavours and textures, one that anyone can understand intuitively. The goal isn't perfection. It's harmony: wine and food enhancing one another rather than competing for attention.

The simplest way to think about pairing is to *match the mood and the weight*:

- Light dishes feel best with lighter wines.

- Rich dishes feel best with fuller wines.

- Bright flavours like citrus, herbs, or tomatoes want wines with freshness.

- Earthy flavours want wines with savouriness.

- Sweet dishes want wines that are at least as sweet.

- Spicy dishes want wines that are gentle and soothing, not sharp or tannic.

This is pairing at its heart, not rigid rules, but natural instincts you already use every day. You wouldn't drink hot chocolate with oysters, or iced tea with lasagna. Wine works the same way.

Acidity is one of the most important elements to consider, because it acts like a squeeze of lemon in cooking. A bright white wine can lift seafood, salads, and richer dishes the way a small splash of acidity can transform a plate. Champagne and other sparkling wines work beautifully with salty or fried foods for the same reason: the acidity cuts through the richness while the bubbles scrub the palate clean.

Tannins, found in red wines, behave like texture. They need food with protein or fat, something to soften them and make them feel supple. This is why Cabernet Sauvignon loves steak, and why Chianti thrives with tomato sauce and olive oil. Without something to balance the tannin, a wine can feel sharper than intended.

Sweetness matters too. If a dish is sweeter than the wine, the wine will taste flat and sour. But when a wine's sweetness matches or slightly exceeds the sweetness in the food, fruit desserts, pastries, blue cheese with honey, both elements feel more complete. Sweetness also works as an excellent counterpoint to spice. It is a surprisingly effective combination.

And then there's flavour:

- Earthy dishes, mushrooms, lentils, roasted vegetables, sing with wines that have the same earthy undertone: Pinot Noir, Nebbiolo, Sangiovese.

- Herbal dishes, basil, parsley, rosemary, come alive with wines that naturally have herbaceous lift, like Sancerre or Sauvignon Blanc.

- Spice loves contrast: Off-dry whites can soften chilli heat, but many spicy dishes pair equally well with high-acid dry whites such as Riesling, Grüner Veltliner, or Sauvignon Blanc depending on cuisine.

But even these ideas are just starting points.

The most powerful pairing principle is this: *What grows together goes together.*

Mediterranean wines with Mediterranean food. Alpine wines with Alpine dishes. Coastal wines with seafood. These are not formal rules, just the quiet logic of place.

And if you forget everything else, remember the most forgiving pairings of all: sparkling wine with almost anything, and rosé with nearly everything. Both bridge the gap between styles, adapting with ease.

Food and wine pairing isn't about impressing anyone or chasing perfect matches. It's about enhancing pleasure, noticing when a sip makes a bite more delicious, or when a bite unlocks something new in the wine. You don't need to master pairing. You just need to observe how food and wine behave together and follow the combinations that feel right.

When in doubt, trust your taste.

The best pairings are the ones you want to experience again.

Wine for Occasions

Choosing wine for an occasion is less about matching rules and more about matching energy. Every gathering, whether intimate or lively, celebratory or quiet, carries a certain rhythm. The right wine simply supports that rhythm, the way lighting or music does. It doesn't need to be perfect; it just needs to feel right in the moment.

Think first about the *mood* rather than the menu.

Is the occasion relaxed? Elegant? Joyful? Reflective? Energetic?

Wine responds to mood more naturally than it responds to rules.

For celebrations

Moments of joy feel brighter with bubbles. Champagne brings elegance and lift; Prosecco brings charm and approachability; sparkling rosé brings colour and delight. Sparkling wine is emotional shorthand for celebration, the sound, the lightness, the shared anticipation as the bottle opens.

For quiet evenings

Soft, contemplative moments ask for wines with calm depth: a silky Merlot, an earthy Pinot Noir, a savoury Tempranillo, or a gentle Chenin Blanc. These wines don't compete for attention; they fill the room with warmth.

For gatherings with friends

Choose wines that are friendly, easy going, and versatile. Fruity reds like Valpolicella Classico or Gamay, crisp whites like Soave or Vinho Verde, and generous rosés all carry a sense of openness and ease. These wines make conversation flow without asking for interpretation.

For dinners that feel special

Occasions with intention, a thoughtful meal, an anniversary, or a carefully planned evening, are enhanced by wines with shape and presence. A structured Cabernet, a Syrah with spice and depth, a rich Chardonnay, or a layered sparkling wine can turn a meal into a memory. Chocolate-based dishes pair best with sweet or fortified wines (e.g., Port, Banyuls, sweet Sherry).

For food that takes centre stage

When the meal is the star, a holiday feast, a slow-cooked roast, a complex pasta, let the wine support rather than overshadow. Chianti with tomato dishes, Malbec or Cabernet with grilled meats, Off Dry Riesling with spice, Champagne with anything fried or salty. Let the food lead; let the wine enhance.

For spontaneity

Some nights call for wine with no purpose other than pleasure. Reach for something juicy, refreshing, or familiar, whatever feels good. A chilled Pinot Noir, a crisp rosé, a simple bubbly, a Sauvignon Blanc. These are wines for living, not planning.

For gifting

The most memorable wine gifts are not the most expensive; they are the most thoughtful. Choose something with a story, a wine you love, a bottle from a place meaningful to you or the recipient, or a style they've never tried but might enjoy. A short note about why you chose it makes the gift personal and lasting.

The real secret

The best wine for any occasion is the one that supports the moment rather than steals it. You don't need the "perfect pairing." You need a wine that feels emotionally aligned with the atmosphere, something that raises the temperature of the room in the right direction.

Wine does not create the occasion.

It enhances what is already there.

Choose the bottle that matches the feeling, and you will always choose well.

Wine and Seasonality

Wine has seasons in the same way landscapes do. Not because certain wines are forbidden at certain times of year, but because our bodies respond differently to flavour, weight, and texture depending on the weather, the light, and the mood around us. Seasonality is not a rule, it is a feeling. Once you start paying attention to it, choosing wine becomes effortless.

In *spring*, when the world feels fresh and the air begins to soften, we gravitate toward wines with brightness and lift. Crisp whites, floral rosés, and aromatic wines pair naturally with the season's energy. Albariño tastes like the first warm breeze. Sauvignon Blanc mirrors the sharpness of new herbs and green shoots. Rosé captures that gentle glow between cool mornings and warm afternoons.

In *summer*, warmth calls for refreshment. Wines that feel cool, zesty, or lightly chilled become irresistible. Vinho Verde, Soave,

Picpoul, Muscadet, and pale rosé fit the season as naturally as cold water and open windows. Sparkling wine becomes even more joyful in the heat, its bubbles cutting through salt, grilled food, and sunshine with ease. Light reds like Gamay and Pinot Noir, served slightly chilled, offer fruit without heaviness.

In *autumn*, our palates shift as the air cools. We reach for wines with more body, more depth, more savoury detail. Earthy Pinot Noir, Sangiovese, and Tempranillo echo the season's flavours: mushrooms, roasted vegetables, smoke, dried herbs. Chenin Blanc, oaked Chardonnay, and Alsace whites bring richness that matches the warmth of autumn meals. These wines feel like soft light on turning leaves.

In *winter*, we want comfort and intensity, wines with weight, warmth, and presence. This is the season for Cabernet Sauvignon, Syrah, Malbec, Brunello, and GSM blends. Wines that feel generous and grounding, suited to stews, roasts, spice, and longer evenings. It is also the natural home for fortified and sweet wines: Port, Madeira, Sauternes, Tokaji, Rutherglen Muscat. These wines feel like blankets, like firelight, like the warmth we seek during the coldest months.

Of course, wine is not bound by the calendar. You can drink Champagne in July or August; you can enjoy crisp whites in December. But seasonality offers a gentle guide, a way to choose wines that feel aligned with the world outside and with your own inner tempo.

Ultimately, seasonality is emotional:

- In warm months, we crave freshness and light.
- In cool months, we crave warmth and depth.
- In transitional months, we crave something in between.

When you choose wine by season, you're really choosing wine by state of mind. And that is one of the most intuitive, liberating ways to explore.

Serving Wine

Serving wine isn't about ritual or formality, it's about helping the wine show its best self. A few small choices can completely change how a wine feels in the glass, not because the wine changes, but because *your senses do*. Temperature[12], air, and the shape of the glass influence how aromas rise and how texture unfolds.

This chapter isn't a rulebook. It's a short guide to making wine more enjoyable with almost no effort.

Temperature: the quiet key

Temperature shapes wine more than most people realise.

- A wine served too warm feels heavier, flatter, and more alcoholic.

- A wine served too cold feels muted, tight, and thin.

- The sweet spot depends on style, but you don't need numbers, just the sensation:

- Crisp whites and rosés should feel cool and refreshing, not icy.

- Rich whites feel best just below room temperature, where their texture can open.

- Sparkling wines should feel cold enough to sharpen the bubbles and brighten the acidity.

- Light reds benefit from a slight chill as it tightens the fruit and lifts the aromatics.

- Full-bodied reds taste better slightly cool, not warm as heat makes tannins feel harsher.

If a wine tastes sharp or simple, let it warm slightly. If it tastes heavy or alcoholic, give it a minute in the refrigerator. Temperature is not science here, it's comfort.

Air: when a wine needs space

Some wines taste better once they've had a moment to breathe[13]. Oxygen softens tannins, opens aromatics, and helps rich wines become more graceful in the glass.

You do not need a decanter unless you enjoy using one. Pouring wine into a glass and giving it a swirl accomplishes most of the same effect.

Let wines breathe when:

- They feel tight or closed
- Aromas seem faint
- The flavours feel compressed
- Tannins are firm and need softening

Young Cabernet, Syrah, or structured Italian reds often benefit from air. So do some full-bodied whites with oak or lees[14] ageing.

But if a wine tastes wonderful right away, don't wait for it to open. Let the wine tell you what it wants.

Glassware: use what works, not what impresses

Wine marketing often makes glassware seem essential and complicated, but you truly only need two shapes:

A tulip-shaped glass for most white, rosé, and sparkling wines, something that keeps aromas focused and the wine cool.

A slightly larger bowl for reds, enough room to swirl, but not so wide it flattens the aromatics.

Everything else is optional.

The perfect glass is simply the one you enjoy using.

Pouring & pacing

A smaller pour, just an inch or two, helps the wine stay cool, gives you room to swirl, and lets the aromas rise with clarity. Refill when you want more. This small habit makes every wine taste better.

And if you're tasting different wines, move from *lighter to fuller, crisper to richer, dry to sweet*. This order keeps your palate awake.

Opening bottles with confidence

Corkscrews don't need to be fancy. The simple waiter's corkscrew is still the best: balanced, compact, and reliable. Cut the foil below the lip, insert the worm (the curly part) straight and slightly off centre then pull steadily. Confidence makes everything easier.

For sparkling wine, hold the cork firmly, twist the *bottle* instead of the cork, and let it sigh open rather than pop. The quieter the sound, the finer the bubbles remain. Always keep your thumb on the cork until the pressure is released. They can be surprisingly harmful projectiles.

Serving is just part of the pleasure

Serving wine isn't about rules or appearances. It's about making small adjustments that let the wine shine and make your experience more enjoyable.

Think of it the way you'd think about lighting a room: soft light makes a dinner feel warmer; harsh light makes it feel colder. Serving wine well is simply setting the right light.

Pour gently.

Taste slowly.

Let the wine breathe if it needs to.

And enjoy the moment, because serving wine is at its heart, an act of hospitality; whether the guest is someone else or it is just for yourself.

Glassware

Glassware is one of the most misunderstood parts of wine. The industry often makes it sound like you need a cupboard full of specialised shapes, a different glass for Burgundy, Bordeaux, Champagne, Riesling, Nebbiolo, Pinot Noir, and so on. But the truth is far simpler, and far kinder: *a wine doesn't need the perfect glass. It just needs the right environment to express itself.*

You can enjoy great wine from almost any glass. But certain shapes make it a little easier to appreciate what's already there.

A SIMPLE RULE: SHAPE AFFECTS AROMA, NOT FLAVOUR

The purpose of a wine glass is to help aromas gather and rise. That's it. The way a glass concentrates or disperses scent changes how the wine *feels*, its clarity, its openness, its intensity.

All the complex science breaks down into something beautifully simple:

- A smaller, tulip-shaped glass focuses fresh, delicate aromatics.

- A slightly larger, rounder bowl gives reds more space to open and soften.

These two shapes cover nearly everything you'll ever want to drink.

The Tulip Glass: your everyday companion

A tulip-shaped glass, narrower at the top, wider at the bottom, works beautifully for:

- white wines

- rosé

- sparkling wine

- light and aromatic reds

- dessert wines

The narrower rim guides aromas gently upward. The slightly wider bowl gives the wine enough air to release its perfume. And the shape keeps the temperature stable longer.

This one glass could serve you for almost all categories if you wanted to simplify completely. If you can only choose one, this is the one to choose.

The Universal Red Glass: when you want a little more space

A slightly larger glass, not huge, not heavy, allows reds to stretch out. Reds often benefit from extra oxygen to soften tannins and reveal deeper notes.

This glass works for:

- Merlot
- Pinot Noir
- Gamay
- Syrah or Shiraz
- Cabernet Sauvignon
- Malbec
- Nebbiolo
- Sangiovese

The goal is not a giant globe that swallows your face, but a bowl roomy enough for a swirl and a rim narrow enough to hold aromatics. Think of it as a breathing space for the wine.

Specialised Glassware (and why you probably don't need it)

There are beautiful glasses designed for individual grapes, Burgundy balloons[15], Champagne flutes[16], Bordeaux stems[17], Montrachet bowls[18], and they do offer subtle effects. A Burgundy glass enhances the gentle aromatics of Pinot Noir; a flute keeps bubbles tight and lively.

But these refinements matter only if you *want* them to. They are not prerequisites for enjoyment. Great wine does not demand ceremony. It simply wants to be noticed.

If you love collecting glassware, enjoy it, the beauty is part of the pleasure. If you don't, two shapes are enough for a lifetime of delicious wine.

The most important glass? A clean one.

Residue from soap or cabinets can mute aromas. A quick rinse with hot water, then a swirl of wine before the first sip, is all you need.

Holding the Glass

Hold the stem if the wine is chilled. Hold the bowl if the wine is too cool and needs your hand's warmth. Neither is right or wrong; it's simply a way to help the wine find the temperature where it feels alive. Holding the stem, while it might feel awkward at first, helps minimise unwanted temperature changes of your wine and maximise your enjoyment.

What Matters Most

Glassware should never feel like a barrier. It should feel like a small kindness that helps the wine express itself. The right glass doesn't improve the wine, it simply helps reveal what was always there.

Two shapes, a gentle swirl, and a clean surface are more than enough.

Wine doesn't ask for perfection.

Just attention.

When to Open a Bottle

Some bottles ask for a special moment. Most bottles ask simply to be enjoyed.

You don't need to wait for anniversaries, holidays, or rituals. Instead, notice your mood. Notice the weather. Notice who's with you. Wine opens best when you feel curious, relaxed, or generous, not when you feel obligated.

If you're saving a bottle for "someday," consider this: someday is rarely scheduled. It's the evening you didn't expect, the conversation that lasted longer, the moment you felt grateful. Wine is for those moments.

A bottle unopened is potential. A bottle opened is presence.

Storage

Storing wine well isn't about cellars, special equipment, or elaborate systems. It's about keeping wine comfortable, sheltered from the things that cause it to fade before its time. Most wines are meant to be enjoyed within a year or two of purchase, so storage is less about ageing and more about caring. A few simple habits make all the difference.

Keep it cool, but not cold

Wine prefers cool, steady temperatures. It doesn't need a cellar carved into stone; it simply needs a place that avoids heat. Warmth ages wine too quickly, flattening its freshness and softening its shape. If the bottle feels warm to the touch, it has probably lost some of its brightness.

Ideal storage sits somewhere around the cool side of room temperature. A closet, a shady shelf, or a cupboard away from appliances is often perfect. Refrigerators are too cold for long-term storage, but ideal for chilling a bottle before serving.

Protect it from light

Wine and sunlight have never been friends. Too much light, especially direct sun, can degrade aromatics and create flavours that feel hollow or strange. A dark corner, a cabinet, or even the back of a pantry protects wine far better than an open display shelf.

Avoid motion and vibration

Wine prefers stillness. Constant vibration from appliances or loudspeakers can disturb sediment in bottles meant for ageing and can subtly disrupt the quiet settling that keeps wine stable. You don't need absolute silence; just avoid the top of the refrigerator or the corner of a noisy laundry room.

Lay down bottles with corks, stand up bottles with screwcaps

Cork needs contact with the wine to stay hydrated. If it dries out, air slips inside and dulls the wine long before you open it. Bottles sealed with cork should rest on their side.

Screw-capped wines may be stored upright or on their side; orientation does not materially affect ageing because the seal does not require moisture.

Open bottles: keep them fresh, not perfect

Once a bottle is open, exposure to oxygen is inevitable. Some wines fold gracefully over a day or two; others fade faster. To keep wine fresh a bit longer, recork it tightly or use a simple wine stopper and refrigerate it, even if it's red. Cooler temperatures slow oxidation.

Richer reds may hold for a couple of days. Delicate whites and rosé often last one to three. Sparkling wine can keep its bubbles for a day with a proper Champagne stopper, though most of its charm lives in the first few hours.

Most of the gadgets on the market don't really do much and aren't work your hard-earned money. The ones that remove air or replace air with other inert gases tend to be more effective, with the latter being very expensive.

Ageing Wine: only if you want to

95% of wines don't improve with age and are designed to be consumed in the first few years. they simply hold steady until they're ready to be enjoyed. ageing them will only result in a reduction of fruit flavours and aromas, freshness, and the elements that made that wine delicious. Only a tiny portion of the world's wines are made for long-term evolution, and this book will point out those that truly benefit from cellaring.

Wines need high tannins, sugars, alcohol, and / or acidity to be worth ageing. Less than 5% of wines are suitable. If in doubt, ask your local wine shop.

Wines that are not made for ageing aren't *lesser wines* – they are just made to be consumed young and wonderful wines in their own right.

If you decide to age wine intentionally, the requirements are simple: consistent cool temperature, darkness, stillness, and time. But ageing is an elective joy, not a requirement. Don't wait for wine to become perfect; open it when you're ready for pleasure.

Storage is not about complexity, it's about kindness

Wine doesn't ask for a castle. It simply asks for comfort: cool, dark, quiet, and sideways if it has a cork. These small considerations keep a bottle tasting the way the winemaker intended, vibrant, expressive, and alive.

The goal of wine storage isn't preservation for its own sake. It's ensuring that when you open a bottle, it greets you the way it meant to.

Building Your Wine Collection

A wine collection doesn't need a cellar or a budget. It simply needs intention, a handful of bottles chosen because you want to reach for them at the right moment. The best collections fit your life, not someone else's.

Start small. Choose six to twelve bottles that represent different moods:

- A crisp white for afternoons.
- A richer white for dinners.
- A rosé for effortless moments.
- A sparkling wine for celebration.
- A juicy red for casual meals.
- A structured red for deeper evenings.
- A sweet wine for dessert or reflection.
- A fortified wine for winter nights.

A collection like this is not about quantity. It's about readiness, having something that suits the moment without needing to think.

If you decide to grow your collection, buy two bottles at a time: one for now, one for later. This is how you learn what age does to wine, not by reading, but by tasting. Keep notes if you want; trust memory if you don't.

Store your bottles cool, dark, and undisturbed. Don't save everything for a perfect day in the future. Perfect days rarely announce themselves. Open bottles when curiosity calls.

A wine collection is not a display. It is a set of possibilities, a quiet comfort waiting in the corner of a room.

Hosting With Wine

Hosting isn't about impressing people; it's about making them feel at ease. Wine helps when it feels like part of the room rather than the star of it.

Begin with something welcoming, a sparkling wine or a crisp white that feels bright and easy. Move into rosé or juicy reds if the evening is light and conversational. Open fuller reds if the dinner is rich or structured. Always have water nearby. If someone wants a small pour, give them one. If someone doesn't want wine at all, celebrate that too.

Pour slowly. Notice when glasses are empty but don't rush to refill them. Wine should follow the conversation, not drive it.

The best wine for hosting is the wine that loosens shoulders and lifts the room by a few degrees, not the rarest, or the most expensive, or the most talked about.

Travelling With Wine

Bringing wine home from a trip is like bringing home a piece of landscape. It's also easier than most people imagine.

Wrap each bottle in clothing or bubble wrap. Place them in the centre of your luggage, cushioned on all sides. Most airlines allow wine in checked baggage with no fuss as long as it's well-protected.

If you want to ship wine directly, check local regulations, some regions make this simple; others restrict it. But a surprising number of wine shops and wineries can arrange shipping to many parts of the world.

The one thing to avoid is leaving wine in a hot car or sunny window. Heat is wine's quiet enemy.

Wine & Health

Wine and health live in a delicate intersection, a space shaped by science, culture, emotion, and personal experience. The relationship is neither simple nor universal, and any honest understanding begins with a quiet truth: *wine has alcohol, and alcohol must be approached with care*. But wine is also more than alcohol alone. It is a fermented food, a cultural ritual, a sensory pleasure, and, when enjoyed thoughtfully, a companion that can fit into a balanced life.

This chapter is not here to moralise or advise. It is here to offer clarity, to dissolve myths, and to help you make choices that align with your body, your mind, and your well-being.

Moderation: The Heart of the Conversation

Most scientific discussions about wine and health return to the same principle: *quantity matters*. Small amounts of wine, often described as "moderate drinking", have been associated with potential cardiovascular benefits, though recent research questions whether wine is the cause or whether lifestyle plays a greater role. Larger amounts, however, offer risk without benefit. The line between "a glass" and "too much" is narrower than many people realise.

Wine is best enjoyed slowly, with food, in the company of others, or in a context where the experience matters more than the sensation of alcohol. The more mindful the drinking, the lower the risk of harm and the higher the chance of pleasure.

Alcohol's Effect on the Body

Alcohol touches nearly every organ. Its effects are dose-dependent: minimal at low doses, increasingly harmful at high ones. It can disrupt sleep, raise blood pressure, irritate the digestive system, and strain the liver when consumed excessively. It dehydrates, contributing to headaches, which are far more often caused by alcohol and histamines than by sulphites.

Red wine contains antioxidants like resveratrol, but these compounds appear in quantities too small to serve as meaningful "medicine." Wine is nourishment for the spirit, not the body. Its benefits come not from chemistry but from *context*, shared meals, relaxation, rituals of connection.

Individual Sensitivity and Histamines

People differ remarkably in how they respond to wine. Some feel flushed or headache-prone from red wines but not white. Others struggle with tannins, histamines, or certain fermentation byproducts. Natural wines, with their elevated levels of biogenic amines, can affect sensitive drinkers differently than conventionally produced wines.

None of these reactions reflect quality. They simply reflect biology. Listening to your body is the most reliable guide. If a certain style or grape consistently leaves you uncomfortable, drink something else. Wine should enhance life, not burden it.

Health and Emotion

Wine offers something that is more difficult to quantify: it slows us down. A small glass at day's end can soften the transition between noise and quiet. A shared bottle can mark celebration, intimacy, connection. These emotional benefits are real, but they depend entirely on intention. Wine used for comfort can be nourishing; wine used for escape can be destructive.

Like any pleasure, it becomes dangerous when it replaces the very things it is meant to support, rest, joy, community, delight. Wine is not a solution; it is an accompaniment.

The Mindful Glass

The healthiest way to drink wine is with curiosity and awareness. Notice how much you pour. Notice how fast you sip. Notice how your body feels not only in the moment but the next morning. Notice whether a second glass adds or subtracts from the experience. Notice whether wine enhances your life or complicates it.

Mindfulness makes every glass more satisfying, because it reconnects you with the reason you drink wine in the first place: pleasure, not numbness.

Wine Can Be Part of a Balanced Life, But Never Its Centre

If wine enriches your meals, your relationships, your rituals, your sense of connection, it is serving you well. If wine overshadows those things, even subtly, it deserves reflection. Balance is not static; it is something we navigate continuously.

Wine has no health "halo," but it also need not be feared. It fits gracefully into a life where joy, caution, and self-knowledge coexist. And when it is approached that way, wine becomes what it was always meant to be: a companion to experience, not a substitute for it.

Wine and health share the same principle as wine and pleasure; the right amount turns everything toward harmony.

A Final Note on Practical Wisdom

Practical wine wisdom isn't about rules or expertise. It's about removing friction, making wine a gentle companion to daily life. Once you can choose with intuition, order with confidence, and open bottles without hesitation, wine stops being a subject to study and becomes a part of the world you move through.

Wine is not about performance. It is about ease, connection, and pleasure.

The rest is simply technique, and technique, once learned, fades quietly into instinct.

---

1. Brut: A dry style of sparkling wine with very little sugar remaining.
2. Riserva: An Italian ageing term indicating longer maturation before release.
3. Reserva: A Spanish ageing term indicating regulated periods in barrel and bottle.
4. Sec: A French term for dry, though in Champagne it refers to a sweeter off-dry style.
5. Trocken: A German term for dry wine.
6. Vendange Tardive: A late-harvest style that often produces richer, sometimes sweeter wines.
7. Kabinett: A light dry German Riesling style made from early harvested grapes.
8. Gran Selezione: The highest classification of Chianti Classico, made from the estate's best fruit with extended ageing.

9. Producer: The winery or estate responsible for growing the grapes or making the wine, often shaping the wine's style.

10. Crisp: A wine that feels brisk and refreshing because of its acidity.

11. Sommelier: A trained wine professional in a restaurant who helps guests choose wines that suit their preferences and their meal.

12. Temperature: The warmth or coolness at which wine is served, affecting aroma, texture, and balance.

13. Breathe: The brief exposure of wine to air that softens structure and opens aromas.

14. Lees ageing is the maturation of wine in contact with its dead yeast cells (lees), which enhances texture, complexity, and stability.

15. Burgundy Glass: A large bowl-shaped glass that enhances delicate aromatics in Pinot Noir and similar wines.

16. Champagne Flute: A tall narrow glass that preserves bubbles in sparkling wine.

17. Bordeaux Glass: A taller glass with a straighter bowl designed for structured reds with firm tannin.

18. Montrachet Bowl: A wide bowl glass used for rich, aromatic white wines to release complex aromas.

Chapter 21
References

Burton, J. (2021) *The Concise Guide to Wine and Blind Tasting*. Infinite Ideas.

Button, Roddy & Oliver, Mike (2011) *Wine – 101 Truths, Myths and Legends*.

Easton, M. (2018) *Vines and Vinification*. The Crowood Press.

Edwards, Jamie B. (2018) *A Beginner's Guide to Drinking Wine*. Lulu Press.

Goode, J. (2014) *Wine Science: The Application of Science in Winemaking*. Infinite Ideas.

Goode, J. (2023) *The New Viticulture*. University of California Press.

Goode, J. (2024) *Faultless*. University of California Press.

Grainger, K. (2021) *Wine Faults and Flaws: A Practical Guide*. John Wiley & Sons.

Harding, J., Robinson, J. & Thomas, T.Q. (eds.) (2023) *The Oxford Companion to Wine* (5th ed.). Oxford University Press.

Johnson, H. & Robinson, J. (2019) *The World Atlas of Wine* (8th ed.). Mitchell Beazley.

Lepeltier, P. (2024) *One Thousand Vines: A New Way to Understand Wine*. Mitchell Beazley.

Nunes, F.M., Cosme, F. & Filipe-Ribeiro, L. (eds.) (2022) *Wine Sensory Faults: Origin, Prevention and Removal*. MDPI.

Patterson, T. & Buechsenstein, J. (2018) *Wine and Place: A Terroir Reader*. University of California Press.

Puckette, M. & Hammack, J. (2015) *Wine Folly: A Visual Guide to the World of Wine*. Avery.

Puckette, M. & Hammack, J. (2018) *Wine Folly: Magnum Edition: The Master Guide*. Avery.

Ribéreau-Gayon, P., Dubourdieu, D., Donèche, B. & Lonvaud, A. (2021) *Handbook of Enology. Volume 1: The Microbiology of Wine and Vinifications* (3rd ed.). John Wiley & Sons.

Ribéreau-Gayon, P., Dubourdieu, D., Donèche, B. & Lonvaud, A. (2021) *Handbook of Enology. Volume 2: The Chemistry of Wine Stabilization and Treatments* (3rd ed.). John Wiley & Sons.

Robinson, J. (2000) *How to Taste: A Guide to Enjoying Wine*. Simon & Schuster.

Robinson, J. (2016) *The 24-Hour Wine Expert*. Penguin Books.

Robinson, J., Harding, J. & Vouillamoz, J. (2012) *Wine Grapes: A Complete Guide to 1,368 Vine Varieties, Including Their Origins and Flavours*. Allen Lane.

Shepherd, G.M. (2017) *Neuroenology: How the Brain Creates the Taste of Wine*. Columbia University Press.

Skelton, S. (2019) *Viticulture: An Introduction to Commercial Grape Growing for Wine Production* (3rd ed.). Stephen Skelton MW.

Smith, B.C. (ed.) (2007) *Questions of Taste: The Philosophy of Wine*. Oxford University Press.

Smith, C. (2013) *Postmodern Winemaking: Rethinking the Modern Science of an Ancient Craft*. University of California Press.

Schneider, E. (2012) *Wine for Normal People*. Chronicle Books.

Stevenson, T. (2020) *The New Sotheby's Wine Encyclopaedia* (6th ed.). National Geographic.

Thomas, S. (ed.) (2016) *Grapes: Polyphenolic Composition, Antioxidant Characteristics and Health Benefits*. Nova Science Publishers.

Wine & Spirit Education Trust (2025) *WSET Level 4 Diploma in Wines: D1 Wine Production*. WSET.

Wine & Spirit Education Trust (2025) *WSET Level 4 Diploma in Wines: D3 Wines of the World*. WSET.

Wine & Spirit Education Trust (2025) *WSET Level 4 Diploma in Wines: D4 Sparkling Wines*. WSET.

Wine & Spirit Education Trust (2025) *WSET Level 4 Diploma in Wines: D5 Fortified Wines*. WSET.

Chapter 22
Glossary

A

ABV (Alcohol by Volume)

The percentage of a wine's liquid that is pure alcohol. It's printed on the label and gives a sense of how strong and full-bodied the wine will feel. Higher ABV usually means more warmth and weight; lower ABV wines tend to feel lighter and fresher.

Acetic Acid

An acid naturally produced in wine. At low levels it can add lift; at high levels it smells and tastes like vinegar and is considered a fault.

Acidity

The aspect of wine that makes your mouth water and the wine taste fresh and bright. High-acid wines feel crisp and lively; low-acid wines can seem soft, round, or "flabby." Acidity balances sweetness and alcohol and helps wines age well.

Aeration or Letting Wine Breathe

Allowing wine to mix with air, by opening the bottle, swirling in the glass, or decanting, so aromas can open up and youthful wines can soften.

Ageing (Bottle Ageing or Barrel Ageing)

How a wine develops over time:

- **Bottle ageing** happens in a sealed bottle, slowly adding complexity and softening tannins.

- **Barrel (or oak) ageing** happens in wooden barrels and adds gentle oxygen exposure and flavours such as vanilla, spice, toast, or smoke. Only a minority of wines improve with age; most are meant to be enjoyed within a few years of release.

Alcohol

The result of yeast converting sugar into alcohol during fermentation. Alcohol contributes to body and warmth. When well balanced, it feels integrated; when too high for the wine's fruit and acidity, it can make the wine taste hot or harsh.

Amphora

A clay vessel (often egg-shaped) used to ferment or age wine. Amphorae allow gentle oxygen exchange and can create wines with earthy, textural characters. Common in some traditional and "natural" winemaking.

Ancestral Method / Pétillant Naturel (Pét-Nat)

A way of making sparkling wine by bottling a wine before it finishes fermenting. The remaining sugar ferments in the sealed bottle, creating natural bubbles. These wines are often lightly fizzy, sometimes cloudy, and feel fresh and unpretentious.

Appassimento / Passito

A technique, especially in Italy, where grapes are partially dried after harvest (on straw mats or in airy lofts) before pressing. This concentrates sugar, acidity, and flavour. Used for rich dry wines such as Amarone and for sweet wines such as Recioto.

Appellation (AOC / DOC / DOCG / DO / AVA, etc.)

A legally defined winegrowing area with rules about where grapes are grown and often how the wine is made. Examples include **AOC** (France), **DOC** and **DOCG** (Italy), **DO** (Spain), and **AVA** (American Viticultural Area in the US). Appellations signal origin and typical style, but not automatically quality.

Aromatic Variety / Aromatic Wine

A grape (or the wine made from it) that naturally gives very pronounced aromas, often floral, citrus, stone fruit, or spicy notes. Examples include Riesling, Gewürztraminer, Muscat/Moscato, and many New World Sauvignon Blancs.

Aroma

The smells you pick up when you sniff a wine. Aromas can suggest fruit, flowers, herbs, spices, earth, nuts, and more.

Astringency

The drying, puckering sensation on your gums and tongue, similar to strong black tea. Caused mostly by tannins from grape skins, seeds, stems, and sometimes oak.

Autolysis

The slow breakdown of dead yeast cells (lees) after fermentation, especially in wines aged "on the lees" or in traditional-method sparkling wines. This process can add creamy texture and flavours like brioche, toast, biscuit, or nut, particularly in Champagne and similar styles.

B

Bâtonnage (Lees Stirring)

The practice of stirring the lees (dead yeast and sediment) in a barrel or tank to increase texture, richness, and complexity. Often used for Chardonnay and other top-quality whites.

Balance

How well a wine's components, fruit, acidity, tannin, sweetness, and alcohol, work together. A well-balanced wine feels harmonious, with nothing sticking out.

Barrel Fermentation

Fermenting grape juice directly in barrels rather than in stainless steel. This can give a rounder texture and subtle oak-derived flavours.

Barrique

A small oak barrel (traditionally 225 litres in Bordeaux). Often used for ageing quality wines to add complexity and gentle oak flavour.

Biodynamic Viticulture

A holistic farming approach that treats the vineyard as a living system, using organic practices plus specific herbal preparations and timing tasks with lunar and seasonal cycles. Aims for healthy soils and expressive, site-driven wines.

Body

The weight or richness of a wine in your mouth.

- **Light-bodied** wines feel delicate, like skim milk.
- **Medium-bodied** wines feel comfortable and rounded.
- **Full-bodied** wines feel rich, dense, and mouth-filling.

Botrytis Cinerea (Noble Rot)

A fungus that can either spoil grapes (grey rot) or, under the right conditions, gently dry them on the vine. In its "noble" form it concentrates sugar and flavour, allowing the creation of great sweet wines such as Sauternes and Tokaji, with honeyed, apricot, and marmalade notes.

Brettanomyces ("Brett")

A wild yeast that can grow in wine. At low levels it may add complexity (leather, spice); at higher levels it can smell like stables, sticking plasters, or farmyard, and is then considered a fault.

Brightness

The sensory impression of a wine's acidity and energy, often perceived as freshness or lift on the palate.

Brut / Extra Brut / Demi-Sec (Sparkling Wine Sweetness Levels)

Terms indicating how dry or sweet a sparkling wine is:

- **Brut Nature / Zero Dosage** – bone dry
- **Extra Brut** – very dry
- **Brut** – dry (most common style)
- **Extra Dry / Extra-Sec** – just off-dry
- **Demi-Sec** – clearly sweet

C

Cap / Cap Management

In red and some rosé fermentations, grape skins float to the top and form a thick "cap." Cap management, by **punching down** (pushing the cap into the juice) or **pumping over** (pumping juice over the cap), controls how much colour, flavour, and tannin are extracted.

Carbonic Maceration / Semi-Carbonic Fermentation

A winemaking method where whole bunches of grapes ferment in a closed tank full of carbon dioxide. This creates bright, juicy, low-tannin wines with intense fruit and often a hint of bubblegum or candied fruit. Classic in Beaujolais Nouveau and some light, "glou-glou" reds.

Cascading Aromas

The experience of aromas unfolding in layers: first fresh fruit, then flowers, then spice or earth as you swirl and taste the wine.

Chaptalisation

Adding sugar to unfermented grape juice (must) before or during fermentation to raise the final alcohol level when grapes are less ripe. Legal in some cooler regions; not allowed in many warmer ones.

Charmat / Tank Method

A method of making sparkling wine in pressurised tanks rather than in individual bottles. It preserves fresh, fruity, floral aromas and produces soft, open bubbles. Used for Prosecco and many easy-drinking sparkling wines.

Clone

A genetically identical version of a vine, selected and propagated from a single "mother" vine for specific qualities (yield, ripeness, flavour, disease resistance).

Corked / Cork Taint (TCA)

A musty, mouldy aroma (damp cardboard, wet dog, dusty cellar) caused by a compound called TCA, usually from contaminated cork or winery equipment. It dulls the fruit and is a wine fault.

Creamy

A texture descriptor, often used for wines that feel smooth and rich, sometimes due to lees ageing or malolactic fermentation.

Crianza / Reserva / Gran Reserva / Riserva / Gran Selezione

Ageing terms used mainly in Spain and Italy:

- **Crianza (Spain)** – moderate ageing, often including some time in oak and bottle.

- **Reserva / Riserva** – longer ageing, more complexity and integration.

- **Gran Reserva / Gran Selezione** – the longest ageing, often from top sites or best grapes, with more developed flavours and structure.

Cru

French word meaning "growth" or "vineyard." In Burgundy a cru is a recognised vineyard (Premier Cru, Grand Cru). In Champagne and Beaujolais it can refer to top villages or specific high-quality sites.

Cuvée

A specific blend or lot of wine. In sparkling wine, "cuvée" can also refer to the base wine that undergoes second fermentation in bottle.

D

Decanting

Pouring wine from its bottle into another container (a decanter). Done to separate older wines from their sediment or to give younger, structured wines more air so they open up.

Dosage

A small mixture of wine and sugar added to a traditional-method sparkling wine after the spent yeast is removed. It adjusts sweetness and helps balance acidity.

Dry / Off-Dry / Sweet (Still Wines)

Terms that describe how much sugar is left in the finished wine:

- **Dry** – little or no detectable sweetness.
- **Off-dry** – a gentle touch of sweetness.
- **Medium / Sweet** – clearly sweet, but usually balanced by acidity.

E

Elegance

A wine that feels refined and harmonious rather than big or heavy. Flavours are precise and balanced, not overwhelming.

Extraction

The process of pulling colour, tannin, and flavour out of grape skins, pips, and sometimes stems during maceration and fermentation. Too much extraction can make a wine harsh; too little can make it feel dilute.

F

Fermentation

The natural process in which yeast turns grape sugar into alcohol, carbon dioxide, and flavour compounds. This is how grape juice becomes wine.

Finish

The aftertaste of a wine, how long flavours linger on your palate after you swallow. Longer, more complex finishes usually signal higher quality.

Fining

A clarification step in winemaking. A substance (like egg white, bentonite clay, or plant-based fining agents) is added to bind with tiny particles, which then settle out, leaving the wine clearer.

Flor

Flor is a thick, protective layer of yeast that forms on the surface of wine, particularly in the production of certain styles of sherry like Fino and Manzanilla. This biofilm prevents the wine from oxidizing, which keeps it pale and contributes distinctive nutty, savoury, and slightly salty flavours to the wine.

Fortification / Fortified Wine

The process of adding grape spirit to a wine, either during fermentation (to leave residual sugar) or after fermentation (to increase strength). The resulting wines, such as Port, Madeira, Sherry, and Vins Doux Naturels, are more alcoholic and often more stable.

Fresh

A general term for wines with good acidity and bright, lively flavours.

G

Garrigue

A distinctive scent of wild Mediterranean herbs, thyme, rosemary, lavender, and scrub, often found in wines from southern France and similar warm, herbal landscapes.

Geosmin

A natural aromatic compound that smells like damp earth or beetroot. In small doses it can add earthiness; in large amounts it can dominate and be considered a fault.

GSM (Grenache–Syrah–Mourvèdre)

A classic Rhône-style red blend combining Grenache (ripe red fruit, warmth), Syrah (colour, spice, structure), and Mourvèdre (dark fruit, tannin, gamey notes). Typically full-bodied and complex.

Green

Flavours of unripe fruit or under-ripe stems (e.g., green bell pepper, grass). In some grapes (like cool-climate Cabernet Franc or Sauvignon Blanc) a little can be attractive; too much can taste hard or vegetal.

H

Heat Damage / "Cooked" Wine

Damage caused by storing or transporting wine at high temperatures. The wine can taste stewed, jammy, flat, or tired, with dull colour and baked fruit aromas. The damage is permanent.

Herbaceous

Aroma or flavour reminiscent of fresh or dried herbs (e.g., thyme, basil, cut grass). Common in some Sauvignon Blancs and cooler-climate reds.

Hot

A wine in which the alcohol level is so high that it causes a burning sensation in the mouth or throat. Considered unbalanced.

Hydrogen Sulphide (H_2S)

A sulphur compound that smells like rotten eggs or drains. Often a sign of **reduction** or stressed fermentations. A small amount may blow off with air; persistent H_2S is a fault.

I

Ice Wine / Eiswein

A very sweet wine made from grapes that have frozen naturally on the vine and are pressed while still frozen. The ice stays behind, concentrating the sugary juice. These wines are intensely fruity and high in acidity.

Intensity (Aroma / Flavour)

How strong or weak the aromas and flavours are. Wines can be light, medium, or pronounced in intensity.

J

Jammy

A description for wines with very ripe, almost cooked-fruit flavours (strawberry jam, blackberry compote). Common in warm-climate reds.

L

Lees

The layer of dead yeast cells and other solids that settle at the bottom of a tank or barrel after fermentation. Ageing a wine on its lees can add creaminess, richness, and savoury complexity.

Length

Another way of describing the finish, how long the flavours last after you swallow.

M

Maceration

Soaking grape skins (and sometimes stems) in juice or fermenting wine to draw out colour, flavour, and tannin. Essential for red wines and used to varying degrees in rosé and orange wines.

Malolactic Conversion / Malolactic Fermentation

A secondary process where lactic acid bacteria convert sharper malic acid (like green apple) into softer lactic acid (like milk). This softens acidity and can add creamy or buttery notes, especially in Chardonnay.

Mousse

The texture of the bubbles in sparkling wine. Fine mousse feels creamy and persistent; coarse mousse feels larger and more aggressive.

N

Natural Wine

Wine made with minimal intervention, typically from organically or biodynamically grown grapes, fermented with native yeasts, and bottled with little or no added sulphur. Can be vibrant and distinctive but also more variable and prone to faults if not carefully handled.

New World / Old World

Broad stylistic and geographic shorthand:

- **Old World** – European regions with long winemaking histories (e.g., France, Italy, Spain), often associated with tradition, moderate ripeness, structure, and an emphasis on terroir.

- **New World** – Regions such as the Americas, Australia, New Zealand, and South Africa, often associated with riper fruit, bolder flavours, and a more modern style. The lines are increasingly blurred.

Neutral Oak

Older barrels that no longer give strong oak flavours but still influence texture and oxygen exposure.

Noble Variety

A classic, historically important grape variety that produces high-quality wines in many regions (e.g., Cabernet Sauvignon, Merlot, Pinot Noir, Chardonnay, Riesling).

O

Oak Ageing / Oak Influence

Maturing wine in oak barrels (or using oak staves or chips) to add complexity. New oak can contribute flavours of vanilla, toast, coffee, coconut, baking spices, and can increase perception of body and structure. Older oak mainly influences texture and oxygen exposure rather than flavour.

Off-Dry (Still Wine)

A wine with a small but noticeable amount of sweetness. Often works well with spicy food or dishes with a touch of sweetness.

Oxidation / Oxidative Style

Contact with oxygen.

- **Controlled oxidation** in barrel can add complexity (nuts, honey, dried fruit).
- **Excessive oxidation** in wines that should be fresh leads to browning, flat flavours, and bruised-apple or sherry-like notes and is considered a fault. Some styles (certain Sherries, Madeiras, and traditional whites) are delib-

erately oxidative.

Old Vines

Vines that are several decades old. They often produce fewer grapes, but the fruit can be more concentrated, giving wines extra depth and character. There is no legal definition for *Old Vines*.

Orange / Amber / Skin-Contact White Wine

White wine made like a red: the juice is left in contact with the grape skins during fermentation. This adds colour (from deep gold to amber), tannin, and often savoury, tea-like, or herbal complexity.

P

Pétillant

French for "sparkling" or "fizzy." Often used for lightly sparkling wines.

Phenolics

A group of compounds in grape skins, seeds, and stems that contribute colour, tannin, bitterness, and some aromas. Key to the structure and ageing potential of red wines.

Pumping Over / Punching Down

Two main methods of **cap management** in red winemaking.

- **Pumping over**: drawing juice from the bottom of the tank and spraying it over the cap.
- **Punching down**: physically pushing the cap back into the juice.

R

Racking

Transferring wine from one container to another, leaving sediment behind. Helps clarify the wine and allows careful oxygen exposure.

Récoltant-Manipulant (RM)

Signifies that a Champagne is made by an independent grower who harvests and produces their own wine from their own vineyards. These are often called "grower Champagnes" and are known for being more artisanal and terroir-driven, reflecting the unique characteristics of a specific producer and their vineyards, rather than a large brand's consistent "house style."

Reduction / Reductive

A low-oxygen winemaking or storage environment. At best it can give flinty, smoky notes; at worst it can cause unpleasant smells (rubber, cabbage, struck match). Persistent off-odours from reduction are a fault.

Residual Sugar (RS)

The natural grape sugar left in a wine when fermentation stops. Higher RS means more sweetness, though good acidity can keep a wine tasting fresh.

Riesling

A high-acid, aromatic white grape that can produce everything from bone-dry to lusciously sweet wines. With age it often develops honeyed, toasty, or petrol-like notes.

Rosé

Wine made from red grapes with only brief skin contact, giving a pink colour. Styles range from very pale and crisp to deeper with more structure and fruit.

S

Saignée

A method of making rosé by "bleeding off" some juice from a red wine fermentation. The removed juice becomes rosé; the remaining must becomes a more concentrated red.

Screwcap

A metal cap closure with a threaded seal. Excellent at preventing cork taint and controlling oxygen. Widely used for both everyday and fine wines.

Secondary Aromas

Flavours that come from fermentation and ageing rather than the grapes themselves, such as bread dough, yoghurt, nuttiness, or creaminess.

Shape

The overall structural progression of a wine across the palate, including how it enters, expands and finishes.

Sherry

A fortified wine from the Jerez region of southern Spain.

- **Fino and Manzanilla** are pale, dry styles aged under a layer of flor yeast, giving salty, bready, almond-like notes.

- **Amontillado and Oloroso** are aged with more oxygen, giving deeper colour and nutty, savoury flavours.

- Sweet styles are often made by blending with very sweet wines such as Pedro Ximénez.

Sommelier

A trained wine professional, usually working in restaurants, who selects, serves, and recommends wines and helps guests choose bottles that suit their tastes and budget.

Sparkling Wine

Wine with dissolved carbon dioxide that creates bubbles. Made by several methods (traditional, tank/Charmat, ancestral, carbonation). Styles range from very dry and racy to richer, more creamy, autolytic wines.

Spritz / Slightly Sparkling

A gentle, light fizziness in a wine, especially in young or tank-fermented styles like some Vinho Verde or easy-drinking Italian whites.

Structure

The "skeleton" of a wine, mainly its acidity, tannin, alcohol, and (in some cases) sweetness. Structure shapes how a wine feels in your mouth and how it will age.

Sulphites / SO_2 (Sulfur Dioxide)

Compounds used in winemaking to protect wine from oxidation and spoilage. Also produced naturally in small amounts by fermentation. Usually present at low, safe levels; often (and somewhat unfairly) blamed for headaches that are more commonly caused by alcohol or histamines.

T

Tannin

A naturally occurring compound found in grape skins, seeds, and stems, and in oak. Tannins create dryness and grip on your gums. They help wines age and give structure, especially in red wines.

Terroir

A French term for the influence of place on a wine, including soil, climate, elevation, slope, local vegetation, and human traditions. Terroir explains why the same grape can taste very different from one region to another.

Texture

The tactile impression of a wine on the palate, such as smooth, crisp, creamy, or grippy.

Traditional Method (Méthode Traditionnelle / Champenoise)

The classic way of making sparkling wine used in Champagne and many top-quality fizz. The second fermentation happens inside the bottle, creating bubbles. The wine is aged on its lees, then clarified (riddled and disgorged) and given a small dosage. Produces fine, persistent bubbles and complex, bready flavours.

U

Ullage

The space between the top of the wine and the bottom of the cork. As wine ages, a small gap appears as some liquid evaporates. Very low ullage in older bottles can be a warning sign of possible oxidation.

V

VA (Volatile Acidity)

The part of a wine's acidity made up of compounds that evaporate easily, mainly acetic acid and ethyl acetate. In small amounts they can add lift; at high levels they smell of vinegar or nail polish remover and indicate a fault.

VDN (Vin Doux Naturel)

Sweet, fortified wines from southern France. Fermentation is stopped by adding grape spirit while sugar is still present, so the wines are both sweet and higher in alcohol. Classic examples include Banyuls, Maury, and Muscat de Beaumes-de-Venise.

Vintage

The year the grapes were harvested. Weather in that year affects ripeness, flavour, and balance. Some regions show big differences from year to year (high vintage variation); others are more consistent.

W

Weight

The sense of how heavy or light a wine feels in the mouth, influenced by alcohol, body and texture.

Whole-Cluster Fermentation

Fermenting entire bunches of grapes, stems included. This can add freshness, perfume, and a firmer, sometimes slightly herbal structure. Common in some styles of Pinot Noir and Syrah.

Wine Fault

An unwanted smell, taste, or texture caused by spoilage or a winemaking problem, for example, cork taint, oxidation, excessive volatile acidity, or strong reduction.

Y

Yeast (Native / Cultured)

Microscopic organisms that turn sugar into alcohol and create many of wine's aromas.

- **Native (or wild) yeasts** occur naturally in vineyards and wineries.

- **Cultured yeasts** are selected strains grown specifically for predictable, reliable fermentations. Both can produce excellent wines when managed well.

Chapter 23
Author's Note

Let's raise a glass to curiosity.

Wine doesn't ask for mastery. It asks for attention. It asks for curiosity. It asks for presence, the simple act of noticing how a wine moves across the palate or how it shifts a moment from ordinary to memorable. Writing this book has reminded me that the most meaningful knowledge isn't stored in facts, but in sensations: the lift of acidity, the warmth of body, the grip of tannin, the calm of earth, the spark of fruit.

If this book has done its job, you now know something far more valuable than a list of grapes or regions. You know how to follow your own pleasure. You know how to trust that you enjoy what you enjoy, and that your taste is neither right nor wrong, but *yours*.

Wine is a landscape translated into liquid. It's a conversation between nature and craft, between the world outside and the one inside you. Every bottle carries a story, but the most important part of the story is the moment you bring to it: the people you share it with, the mood you're in, the evening it becomes part of.

You don't need another wine book. You simply need a willingness to keep exploring, to taste something new, to follow similarity when you want comfort and difference when you want surprise, to let wine accompany life without overshadowing it.

If this book opened a door, however slightly, then step through it with ease. The rest is discovery. Wine is endlessly varied, and that's what makes exploring it so much fun.

Here's to your palate.

Here's to your curiosity.

Here's to all the wines still waiting for you.

Slainte!

-chris

Chapter 24

About the Author

Chris Sutherland is relatively new to the wine world and is passionate about translating the complexity of wine into clear, welcoming guidance for everyday drinkers. A former cyber security expert who built his career (legally) hacking and manageing complex and intricate systems, Chris brings the same instinct for clarity to the world of wine.

Now pursuing the WSET Level 4 Diploma, he focuses on lowering the barrier to entry for anyone curious about wine and showing readers how to trust their taste, explore confidently, and discover new wines through intuitive similarity rather than memorisation.

Chris is the author of *If You Like This Wine...* It is a modern, narrative-driven guide that helps readers find pleasure, not pressure, in every glass. He speaks about wine with warmth, accessibility, and a deep respect for its ability to connect people.

When he's not studying or writing, Chris is tasting, travelling, exploring wine regions, and building bridges between curious drinkers and the next bottles they'll love most.

https://decantingveritas.com/wine-101-blog

www.ingramcontent.com/pod-product-compliance
Lightning Source LLC
LaVergne TN
LVHW041616060526
838200LV00040B/1311